THE DECLINE OF
FRENCH PATRIOTISM
1870-1940

THE DECLINE OF FRENCH PATRIOTISM 1870–1940

Herbert Tint

WEIDENFELD AND NICOLSON

20 NEW BOND STREET LONDON WI

PRINTED IN GREAT BRITAIN
BY C. TINLING & CO. LTD., LIVERPOOL, LONDON & PRESCOT

To the memory of my parents

ACKNOWLEDGMENTS

During the preparation of this book I contracted an intellectual debt to many friends and colleagues. In particular I gratefully acknowledge the help given to me in the early stages by Professor Alfred Cobban, and by Mrs Dorothy and Mr William Pickles, Mrs Paule Scott-James, and Mr Donald Watt in reducing the number of factual mistakes. Professor Ernest Gellner's encouragement was a crucial factor throughout.

I am grateful to the Editor of the *Review of Politics* for allowing me to reprint unchanged an article of mine, which forms the main part of Chapter One.

CONTENTS

INTRODUCTION

'GOOD SENSE,' said Descartes, 'is of all things in the world the most evenly distributed amongst men, for each one thinks himself so well endowed with it that even those who are the most difficult to please in everything else are generally content with their share.' It is the same with patriotism. Like good sense, and virtue, it is a quality which is generally assumed to be so desirable that even those who apparently are defective in it insist on the excellence of their idiosyncratic interpretation, rather than admit to their lack of it. It follows that a history of patriotic attitudes will either have impartially to catalogue what different people said about their views on patriotism, and what they did about them, or it will have to presuppose a definition of patriotism and examine how far its requirements were met in the period under study. Fully mindful of the arbitrariness of such a procedure, I have chosen the second method. This was partly because it seemed the more interesting, and partly because I felt that many of the patriotic theories canvassed during the period 1870–1940 were too indecently hypocritical to be solemnly set beside rather more honest ones.

I have taken it for granted that a patriot will try to do the best for his country, if necessary by fighting for it. Given the loopholes that leaves for ingenious casuistry in determining the nature of this best, I have further assumed that it entails at least the inviolability of the national territory and national autonomy. On these assumptions one could not, like Maurras, call the defeat of France in 1940 a divine surprise, and yet deem oneself a patriot. Unsophisticated as this may be, I have gone so far as to make the desire for the recovery of Alsace-Lorraine after 1870 one of the main criteria of patriotism until the end of the First War. It

A*   ix

not only follows from my basic assumptions that so recent a territorial amputation should excite legitimate patriotic feeling, but I shall show that this was also at the time the expressed view of most articulate Frenchmen. From 1919 to 1940, Alsace-Lorraine having been restored to France, the minimum requirements of the patriot seem to me to turn again on territorial inviolability and autonomy. It is my case that, during the period with which this book is concerned, there was a decline in the number of people who cared about both these things.

I should like to thank the Government Research Division of the London School of Economics and Political Science, as well as the Central Research Fund of the University of London, for grants which enabled me to carry out a good deal of the work connected with this book.

London, March 1964   HERBERT TINT

CHAPTER ONE

THE PATRIOTISM OF GAMBETTA: FROM JACOBINISM TO COMBINAZIONE

WITH UNSUSPECTING frivolity, the imperial government of Napoleon III declared war on Prussia on 19th July 1870. No war had ever been more popular at the outset, at least among the politicians. Thiers and Gambetta might warn the country of its dangers, the insolence of the Prussians was held to demand punishment. Bismarck had been too clever for too long, not infrequently at the expense of France; lately, the Hohenzollern had had the incredible audacity to press their candidature for the Spanish throne; and now the French, according to their statesmen, had suffered a slight over the withdrawal of this candidature, because the Prussian king refused to make it explicitly irrevocable. These upstarts had to be shown who were the masters on the continent. Few doubted the outcome.

In any case, although of course it was not needed, France could surely count on the assistance of Austria and Italy; on that of Austria because of her undoubted desire to avenge Sadowa, and on that of Italy because of her gratitude for French help during the struggle for unification. When it came to help for Prussia, there would be none. It was confidently predicted that she would be isolated, that there was no real likelihood of assistance for her from the other German states. But even if all Germany banded together, how could she be a serious match for a nation that had fought and conquered the whole of Europe?

Spread out along the entire frontier, the French army, at its mobilization, appeared to suffer from growing pains: during the first fortnight of the war its supremacy was not clearly visible to Paris. Then, suddenly, everything became stunningly obvious: Wissembourg, Froeschwiller, Forbach had been decisive battles, and the French had not won them. Under strong pressure from three separate German armies, the French gradually withdrew to the strongholds of Metz and Sedan. But the retreat was neither properly planned nor, on the whole, orderly. The Emperor, with his army and Marshal Mac-Mahon, felt constrained to surrender at Sedan on 2nd September. When the news reached the capital there was turmoil; on the 4th, its deputies proclaimed the Republic. With the exception of Thiers, they combined to form the Government of National Defence. Gambetta secured for himself the Ministry of the Interior, after an undignified scramble to get to the building before the already designated Ernest Picard.

Despite the catastrophic turn of events, the air was full of hopeful rumours. It was true that Austria had held aloof and, after the first few weeks, had found little to persuade her to join the French side; and that Italy remained sulking over the Emperor's schizophrenic policy, which had helped to unify the kingdom while refusing to allow it to take over Rome as its capital.[1] It was also true that the Germans were hurrying towards Paris and that there was little to stop them. But, after all, Bismarck's quarrel had been with the Empire, and since the Empire no longer existed, it seemed that there was now nothing left to fight about. This was indeed the line taken by Jules Favre, the Foreign Minister in the new government. Bismarck's amusement at the naïvety of the argument cannot have been lessened by Bazaine's attempts to persuade him to leave his beleaguered army at Metz intact, so that he could recapture France for Napoleon's imperial crown. Such dreams could not last. France learned to her indignation that she could have peace, but that it would cost her Alsace and Lorraine, quite apart from a heavy cash indemnity. No Frenchman could at this stage have accepted such terms. Amid popular acclaim the republican government, recalling 1792, decided to raise new armies, and organized the defence and provisioning of the capital. On 19th September, Paris was invested.

It was soon realized that the delegation the Paris government had sent to Tours, to raise the new provincial armies, was too weak to carry out its complex task, and Gambetta left the capital on 9th October to stiffen its resolution and increase its enthusiasm. Their 'pacifism forgotten, parliamentary republicans of all shades were now united in demanding national measures to meet a national emergency.'[2] How well Gambetta, as virtual dictator, performed his task of raising new armies and popular morale, is much disputed. The implementation of the *levée en masse* decree of 4th November 1870, bringing in about 600,000 men, diversely armed and badly officered (most regular officers were in German hands), may perhaps be more the merit of Freycinet than of Gambetta himself.[3] What matters is the spirit that animated Gambetta and his republican friends. 'He conducted the war both well and badly, but more badly than well – but he certainly did conduct it, and as well as he could. And he had profoundly generous impulses – his philosophy was beautiful and noble. . . . He didn't know very well where he was going, but he went with ardour.'[4] Déroulède, reporting for duty to Gambetta at Tours after his escape from captivity at Breslau, finds in him all that a romantically patriotic soul could desire.[5] 'A girl from Metz cried out to me this morning, amid her sobs: "You have no right to take a corner of France and throw it as a sop to the foreigner, as a ransom for those who have badly waged a war".'[6] It was this sense of outrage which fanned the flames of patriotism in Gambetta and his entourage. Theirs was an obstinate, emotional, blind patriotism, against which practical arguments had no force.

And yet there were a great many practical arguments against the continuation of the war early in 1871. What had been left of the regular army when Gambetta assumed his powers at Tours, 180,000 men besieged in Metz, was surrendered by Bazaine on 27th October 1870. Paris had endured a siege of over three months, and relief seemed less possible than ever. The new armies, raised in the provinces by the Tours delegation, were not sufficiently well armed and officered to be a serious threat to the Germans. Among all the many attempts to snatch victory from *a priori* hopeless situations none had succeeded unequivocally. Even the ingeniously conceived threat to the German flank in eastern France had turned into a disaster.

Persuaded of the hopelessness of the situation, the Paris government, in the face of passionate, violent protests from Gambetta – Thiers now called him a *fou furieux* – decided to ask for an armistice. It was granted on 28th January 1871. Gambetta submitted, and resigned.

With the war lost, and German soldiers, now unopposed, occupying large tracts of French soil, Gambetta sought to serve the cause of the Republic against its many detractors. Not least because, for him, Republic and patriotism were allied concepts. Established by a bloodless revolution in Paris and a few provincial urban centres, imposed on a distraught population stunned into acquiescence and even acclamation by a succession of disasters leading up to the ignominy of Sedan, the future of the Republic was not by any means secure. It had not lived up to the reputation of the *mystique* of 1792. It had provided no Valmy. Instead of expelling an overweening enemy from the soil of France, the efforts of its amateur leaders had cost much blood, strangled many generous hopes, drawn hostile armies ever further into the very heart of the country. To no apparent purpose. Epitomized in the public eye by Gambetta, the Republic seemed to stand for a continuation of the struggle, indubitably destined to put what was still unoccupied by the enemy at the latter's mercy. The elections demanded by Bismarck, to show whether the French accepted the policy of the armistice – with the resultant loss of Alsace and Lorraine – exhibited the war-weariness of the population. The occupied territories voted largely for republicans, the others against. About four hundred anti-republicans, most of them legitimist supporters of the heir of Charles X or Orleanist supporters of the heir of Louis Philippe, were sent to the National Assembly; and even thirty Bonapartists, in spite of the discredit thrown on Napoleon III and his followers; but only about two hundred republicans. Gambetta's Jacobinism, that mixture of quixotically romantic patriotism and republicanism, seemed to be at a discount. The Assembly elected Thiers, its most prominent moderate member, to be Chief of the Executive Power of the Republic, without prejudice to the continuation of the republican régime.

But the republicans were to receive an even ruder blow. Gambetta's moderation at Tours, in internal affairs,[7] and the timorous middle-of-the-road policies of the Paris government, had at first allayed the fears of those to whom a Republic meant guillotines and the June days of 1848. Much was indeed heard about *la république démocratique*, but little about *la république sociale*. Could it be that the republicans had really changed their spots? Were they now merely patriotically bellicose, and genteel advocates of the long-established principle of universal suffrage and its political counterpart, parliamentary government? Could the traditionally Orleanist middle-class now have so much in

common with the heirs of 1789 and 1848? Such musings came
to an abrupt end with the outbreak of the civil war.

Given the fact that someone as astute as Thiers was at the head
of the government when the Commune broke out, it is difficult
at first not to assume that it was deliberately provoked. The
majority of the Parisian population had been tried so hard during
the siege, that the measures adopted by Thiers' government,
causing even greater – in the eyes of many, unnecessary – hardships, were likely to inflame the political and social situation to a
dangerous degree. There was first the psychological point, that
although the lower middle-class and the workers of Paris had
suffered as much as anybody else during the siege, Trochu, the
officer commanding the Paris armies, had treated them as second-
class citizen soldiers. They formed most of the 343,000 *gardes
nationaux* who had turned out to defend the capital, but Trochu
distrusted them politically, and with some ostentation relied on
his 75,000 regulars. Faced by only about 235,000 Germans, the
gardes – not unnaturally – felt that Trochu's prejudices against
them had prevented him from waging his war more effectively.
No sooner had Thiers formed his government than he took three
measures hardly calculated to conciliate them. He lifted the
moratorium on business debts, proclaimed during the siege, and
thus added considerably to the already great distress of the many
small shopkeepers of the city. He stopped the pay of 1·50 francs
a day for the *gardes*, except for those who could prove hardship.
And he announced that the National Assembly would henceforth
sit at Versailles, not in Paris, thus adding insult to injury to the
city that had come to look upon itself as the nerve centre of
French political life. Whatever it was that had led the government
to take these decisions, whether it was a deliberate provocation
designed to offer an opportunity to put the Parisians in their
place, or simply crass stupidity, or a mixture of both, it was an
affront demanding either meek submission or violent reaction.
Thiers could hardly have counted on meekness, and when, on
17th March 1871, he sent regular troops to remove the guns from
the heights of Montmartre – a further sign of distrust – riots
broke out and the civil war had begun.

Under the sneering gaze of the Germans garrisoned in the
northern and eastern outskirts of the capital, the French weighed
into each other with their customary ardour. Bismarck allowed

Thiers an army of 100,000 men to conquer his countrymen, and the Chief of the Executive Power of the Republic put it under the command of Mac-Mahon, the imperial Marshal, who had surrendered with the Emperor at Sedan and had thereby hastened the capture of Paris and final defeat. Perhaps Thiers' only display of tact at this time was that he had preferred Mac-Mahon to Bazaine.

The rest of this story holds few surprises. The mayors of Paris tried to mediate and failed. The rebels proclaimed elections for a *Conseil Général des Communes de Paris* and obtained sixty-five seats, against nineteen for the 'moderates'. The most enthusiastic rebel support came from traditional revolutionaries, socialists of the Socialist International, Bakunin's anarchists. From a broadly-based popular revolt against quite unnecessary and humiliating provocation, the Commune became the preserve of fanatical extremists. Similar movements in Lyon and Marseille were quickly overcome by government forces, made up of provincials not too unhappy at having a crack at the urban troublemakers. In the capital it took a little longer; but after reaching its height between 20th and 27th May 1871, the battle there too was won by the government. In the savage fighting of those last few days neither side was inclined to take prisoners and, even after Paris had been completely captured by Mac-Mahon, the butchery among suspected *communards* went on until a total of over twenty thousand Parisians had died. 7,500 more were deported to New Caledonia. Many went into exile.

Whatever verdict may be passed on these events, it must be admitted that they were unlikely to have persuaded the workers and lower middle-class that the Republic existed also for their benefit. Their patriotic fervour first slighted, and then pronounced dangerous by an admittedly democratically elected bourgeois government, they were driven into a position where class differences became of greater significance than the concept of *patrie*. It was the beginning of the end of left-wing patriotism. But from the point of view of the principle of constitutional government, there is no doubt that the rebels had acted misguidedly. They had no legal justification for taking up arms against their constitutionally elected representatives, however distasteful they might have found some of their enactments. Even from the point of view of political expediency their revolt was unfortunate. It had alienated many Frenchmen who had almost come to believe that the republicans had broken with their tradition of violence. It is for both these reasons that Gambetta, resting at San Sebastian after his exertions at Tours, deplored the Commune.

With Thiers in charge of the government, perpetuating by his cautious policies the prosperity France had begun to enjoy during the Second Empire, Gambetta was for a time in the political wilderness. He witnessed the payment of the war indemnity of five milliard francs within only two years of the end of the war, which was one welcome result of the continuing sound economy under Thiers; he saw the consequent, if reluctant, departure of all German occupation troops, except, of course, from the 'lost' provinces; the fortification of the new frontiers in accordance with the plans of Séré de Rivière; the abolition of the *garde nationale*; the introduction of obligatory universal military service. So that, by May 1873, France was well on the road to recovery, sufficiently at least for her representatives to feel able to play at internal politics again; and they turned Thiers out of office.

Nor did they replace him with another republican. The majority of the Chamber was royalist, and when it now proceeded to divide the powers previously exercised by Thiers, it elected Mac-Mahon President (of the Republic), and the Duc de Broglie Prime Minister. The days of the republican régime seemed numbered.

Gambetta, the acknowledged leader of the majority of the republicans, realized that despite republican successes in the many by-elections, the country was wary of republican designs, especially after the Commune. He felt that the most certain way of ensuring a royalist restoration was to frighten the electors with radical republican programmes. 'What,' he wrote to the impatient Juliette Adam, 'what, I ask you, would be the value in these formidable elections of an exclusively republican policy, excessively ardent, incisive in its programme, alarming in its doctrines, compromising in its representatives? It would be swept away like straw before the wind, and all we should have left to console us for the blindness of the multitudes would be sterile oratory.'[8] Accordingly, the *fou furieux* gradually transformed himself into a moderate statesman. But it was moderation dictated solely by an acute sense of political possibilities and, as such, came to be called, derisively, 'opportunism'. It paid however. By-election after by-election returned republicans to the Assembly, until it began to appear that the right had misunderstood the voters of 1871 if it had seen in their verdict a desire for a monarchic restoration. The country, it seemed, had wanted peace, not Henry V; and a moderate democracy, not absolutism.

It is true that Gambetta was slow to practise the prudence he preached. There is, for example, the notorious Grenoble speech, of which he delivered himself, still in the days of Thiers, on 26th September 1872, and in which he sent a shudder down the spine of every French bourgeois, the very voter he could not do without. 'Yes,' he exclaimed in rhetoric rapture, 'I foresee . . . I announce the arrival and the presence on the political scene of a new social class which has been active in the affairs of the country for nearly eighteen months, and which is certainly far from inferior to its predecessors.'[9] The republicans had, however, been much provoked. The royalists were noisily persuading each other of the imminence of the restoration. They ostentatiously organized religious pilgrimages to atone for the alleged evils of the revolution that had brought France so low. They championed the 'moral order' with which Thiers and his supporters hoped to replace the spirit of 4th September. Worst of all, their traditional alliance with the Catholic Church was threatening to embroil France in war with Italy, through their demand for the restoration of the Pope's temporal power, at least over Rome. Gambetta felt that some stand had to be made. The good of the country demanded a break with the traditions of the right, with the ludicrous gearing of French politics to church needs that had first resulted in Italy's refusal to come to the aid of France in 1870, and now brought the two countries to the verge of war. Times, Gambetta wanted to think, had changed:

'What do you expect? There are in France some social classes which have found it difficult for forty-five years to face up not only to the French revolution, but also to its consequences . . . And it is in this lack of decision and courage of a notable part of the French bourgeoisie that I find the origin and explanation of all our misfortunes, our shortcomings, of all that is still uncertain, vague and unhealthy in today's politics. One asks

18

oneself, in all conscience, how these men can close their eyes to a spectacle that ought to be obvious to them. Have they not since the fall of the Empire witnessed the arrival of a new generation, intelligent, fit to take part in government, anxious for all its right? . . . Is this not a typical warning that the country, after having tried many forms of government, wants at last to call on another social class, to try the republican way?'[10]

None of this may be in tune with the pragmatic opportunism that Gambetta recommended to his fellow republicans, but it was the heartfelt reply of the grocer's son to those who wanted to put the clock back. It was also the reply of the patriot. The right, with their anachronistic clerical vision, distorted the international picture. What quarrel had France with Italy? France had but one national enemy, and that was Germany. Moreover, there was persistent talk of Bismarck's desire for a preventive war as an answer to France's impressive recovery, and Gambetta did not want French attention to be diverted to medieval objectives.

But the patriot now also had enemies on the left; the internationalists were gaining ground. Gambetta castigated their, to him, crazy idealism as much as the cynically interested policies of the right. If the right showed its obliviousness to the national interest in such episodes as the capitulation of Bazaine – reminiscent of the behaviour of the royalist armies of the first revolution – or involvement in clerical intrigues in Rome, the extreme left showed it in its participation in the Lausanne Peace Congress of 1871. To the organizers of the Congress, he wrote:

'I have never been a very keen supporter of the ideas and principles of cosmopolitanism. There is about them something that is too vague, too idealistic, despite the appearance of a certain brilliance and speciousness. I believe that their most assured result is to efface, or reduce too greatly, the love of one's country and one's sense of civic responsibility. In the present situation of our country, what matters, on the contrary, is that our hearts attach themselves more than ever to the principles dictated by a devotion to the national cause, and that they find their inspiration in the French idea. I love my country too much to sacrifice any part whatever of its prosperity or strength to a system, however generous it may be, or appear to be.'[11]

He himself suffered from few inhibitions when it came to rousing his countrymen to face up to the need for *revanche* in the early 1870s. Thus, on 16th November 1871 at Saint-Quentin, on the anniversary of the battle for the town, he exclaimed:

> 'What we have lacked is what people who have allowed themselves to be enslaved for too long always lack: faith in themselves and a proper hatred of the foreigner. Let us never speak of the foreigner, but let it be clear that we always think of him. Thus you will be on the road to revenge.'[12]

In a circular letter sent to Alsace and Lorraine to advertise the *République Française*, that daily newspaper he had first conceived in 1868 as a popular propaganda medium for republican ideas, Gambetta is more outspoken still:

> 'I want to make it a platform from which we shall demand each day before Europe our rights and our ravished provinces. France is at the mercy of Germany. We are in a state of *latent* war; neither peace nor freedom nor progress is any longer possible in Europe.'[13]

And it was not with Italy in mind that he paid tribute to the army, by inaugurating the henceforth annual celebration of the birthdate of Hoche; or when he preached patriotism to the workers of the Loire:

> 'Wherever there is a French mother, she must bring up her children . . . in the religious love of France . . . If there is anything that is consoling . . . in the midst of the sadness and the mourning of our mutilated land, it is . . . the thought that the mothers, French and patriotic, will ensure that France will have her defenders and avengers.'[14]

And more specifically:

> 'France . . . has witnessed the theft of part of her possessions, which she must retake . . . Let us always think of what we have to do, but let us never talk about it.'[15]

Gambetta soon realized, however, that just as there were excellent reasons for a more moderate approach to internal political matters, there were still more pressing reasons for a more moderate approach to foreign affairs.

There are two main reasons for Gambetta's increasing prudence. First, there was the realization, reinforced by impressions gained in his own travels in Germany, that France was as yet no match for her enemy. And this not only on purely military grounds, but also because her moral position in the world was being further impaired by that instability of government which was already becoming a feature of her political life after the fall of Thiers in 1873. Secondly, moderation seemed desirable on internal political grounds. For, as it gradually dawned on the country that the possibility of a monarchic restoration was becoming more remote, in the face of the legitimist pretender's intransigence over his white flag, moderate Orleanists and Gambetta's republicans began to nurse hopes of a successful united bid for power. The close relation in Gambetta's mind between a republican régime and *revanche* has already been established.

It is obvious that the introduction of conscription for a period of five years is not in itself enough to produce a strong army. An overhaul of a military machine of the size of the French requires much thought and time; it was not, in fact, until 1876 that the War Office was reorganized along more modern lines. It was further clear that, for purely demographic reasons, France was at a disadvantage in relation to Germany. The French birth-rate, ever since the Napoleonic period, was declining, that of Germany rising. Granted the prevalent view that the German High Command was expert at its job, it could therefore not be held that the mere improvement of training methods and organizational expertise would suffice to provide France with a military weapon of a size sufficient to avenge her defeat. What France needed was allies.

But what a potential ally needed, as was demonstrated in 1870, was proof of French ability to be a sound ally in her turn. And soundness in an ally means at least two things: he has to impress militarily, and the reliability of his military promise has to be unambiguously established by the stature of his government. Since it has been seen that France, at this stage, possessed neither an impressive army nor an impressive government, the basic requirements of a worthwhile alliance were lacking, and with them the possibility of a successful show-down with the Germans.

'And yet,' Gambetta wrote to Juliette Adam, 'I shall shout

myself hoarse repeating it again and again, if only France had the will, she could quickly make up for lost time, regain friends and allies, form armies and once again fire Europe with confidence and hope. A few years of governmental discipline, of financial sacrifices, of unfailing and unostentatious liberal policies, of subdued diplomatic activity (which need not entail the absence of either effort or prudence) and we should promptly regain the sympathy of neutrals, the respect of nations now indifferent to us, and – who knows – more circumspect handling, more esteem (precursors of intimidation) from our enemies.'[16]

In a letter to Jules Claretie he reaffirmed his patriotism, which present prudence had in no way impaired:

'Yes, everything for the country, we must love it absolutely and be ready to sacrifice everything for it, down to our most private preferences. And this is a little more difficult than offering one's carcass or fortune. I prize nothing more than that beautiful title: *Patriot before all else*.'[17]

Nevertheless his public references to foreign affairs were becoming more cautious.

The erstwhile hero of French resistance to German domination was painfully surprised at the lack of understanding his increasingly circumspect patriotism encountered among even his closest friends. From the moment he was elected chairman of the budget commission of the Chamber of Deputies, after the 1876 elections had assured a republican majority in that House (though not, as yet, in the Senate), Gambetta's activities assumed a significance which his previously private endeavours had not possessed. When, therefore, it was rumoured that he was planning a secret meeting with Bismarck, of all people, this seemed to even many of those who were well-disposed towards him nothing short of scandalous. Thus Juliette Adam, for so long Gambetta's admiring friend and political idolatress, was moved to write:

'Gambetta seeks to give me a thousand proofs of his most fraternal friendship, but his *combinazione*, the influences which act on his mind and feelings, pull him more and more in a direction which is in opposition to the ideas that we have held so passionately in common.[18] – I remain overwhelmed! My love for the Republic is conditioned by my love for France. I have seen my Republic in terms of the Republic of '92, causing heroic and victorious armies to spring fully armed from the earth; but if this Republic becomes the ally of the Prussians, if the defender of our cause comes to an understanding with the man whose claws have torn from us the heart of the nation, Alsace-Lorraine, in that event I no longer have a place among my friends, I shall go to my Bruyères and shut myself up with my dead.'[19]

On a less emotional level, one may indeed wonder whether Gambetta was not beginning to lose his grip. The might of Germany seems progressively to have become such an obsession with him that he was prepared to grasp at any straw, however illusory, if it appeared to hold a promise, however dubious, of some kind of peaceful accommodation with Bismarck. It is true that his assessment of the situation in 1876 is perfectly reasonable:

'Our enemies neglect nothing to prepare for it (i.e. victory over us in the event of war), their progress in that respect is really formidable, and after having followed and even seen in actual operation their troops of all arms, I continue more than ever to implore my country to disinterest herself more radically than ever in the quarrels of Europe; for we possess unfortunately no force that would be a match for the troops I have just seen.'[20]

But what of his answers?

As early as 1875 he is said to have written to the exiled Ranc in Brussels that, given their wanderlust, colonies might be a suitable bait for the Germans in future negotiations. It is not entirely clear what this means, indeed doubt is cast on whether this letter has ever existed in that form at all.[21] Deschanel[22] gives the following quotation from its supposed content:

'If, by an act of diplomacy, we could avoid the conflict that is in the making, or at least postpone it, or, better, stop the bloodshed that you and I foresee, ought we not to try? How? – our colonies! With you I can be frank: is it better to preserve for France her far-away lands or her future generations? Let us face this frightening dilemma squarely: either the lives of young Frenchmen, or parts of our colonial territory. Ought one not to profit from this tendency to go to far-away places, from this

German taste for colonies? They have none; they want some. And we have what they want . . . Is this not our chance?[23]

In another letter to Ranc he is alleged to have said:

'An unexpected opportunity comes to me. The Chancellor is coming to Paris; he insists on this trip and expresses the desire to talk with one or two French personalities. Must I remain aloof? Is that really my duty as a Frenchman? And yet! You know that he dreams of a colonial future for his country, that his country is strong, perhaps invincible. Must we not avoid making the noble but useless sacrifice of our young generations, whose disappearance would weaken France for ever?'[24]

At least two interpretations are possible of these supposed letters. First, they can be taken as evidence of growing hysteria about the German menace, about the constant threat of a preventive war while France was still weak, where colonies would be used as a bargaining factor to keep the Germans momentarily happy; in other words, abject appeasement. Secondly, there is Deschanel's statement that these letters show Gambetta's readiness to trade colonies for Alsace-Lorraine, thus achieving *revanche* by peaceful means. The second interpretation is attractive in as much as it could be proof of level-headed statesmanship. Its only defect is that it is difficult to establish it persuasively. There is nothing in the texts printed by Deschanel to suggest unequivocally that Gambetta had Alsace-Lorraine in mind at all. The full text, if it ever existed, is not at present available, but one would imagine that Deschanel would quote the part best calculated to bring out his view. On the other hand, everything points to Gambetta's pathological – if not unfounded – fear of renewed German aggression, and, though appeasement might have been alien to the Gambetta of 1870, it cannot be ruled out in 1875. This is borne out by his other reactions to Bismarckian policy.

There is, for example, that tragi-comical reaction to a brief and heavily veiled reference to France made by Bismarck in a Reichstag speech in 1878. 'The friendship which happily links us with most European states, I can even say, at the moment, with all . . .', the German Chancellor is reported to have said.[25] And on this slender evidence Gambetta based a most remarkably fantastic set of theories, crediting Bismarck with a complete change of heart, entailing *inter alia* the abandonment of power politics, and the inauguration of the rule of moral law in international affairs. More specifically, Gambetta saw in it the possibility of friendly collaboration with his powerful neighbour in the creation of a new Europe, and an atmosphere in which the lost provinces would be returned to France as a matter of moral course. Here is what he wrote to Léonie Léon:

'You may have read . . . the speech of the *Monster*, which I too managed to read before going to sleep. I am delighted, fascinated; this is just what I had desired, awaited, without having dared to count on it. We occupy in it, in a veiled allusion, an important and distinguished place. The balance and distri-bution of forces on the continent are there admirably indicated. Things have to be settled, and in a way that best conforms to the old-established law of nations; this is, in truth, more than we could expect from the fantastic and violent mind of that adventurer of genius who had fashioned the new Germany by means of iron and fire and in accordance with the terrible formula: might is right. In that man there now breaks the radiant dawn of law: it is up to us at present to profit from the circumstances, dispositions, and rival ambitions, to put forward our most legitimate claims and to found with him the new order. I am thus full of hope: peace assured for several years, the World Exhibition[26] out of danger, the powers summoned to draw nearer to France if they want to act, and even if they simply want to deliberate and maintain the *status quo*.'[27]

To an evidently distraught mind, capable of such extravagant conclusions, a policy of appeasement in the international climate of 1875 need not have been alien. That this mood did not last is beside the point. What is significant is that he could allow himself to be led into the most outrageously illogical positions by what must have been a morbid fear of German might. It led him into thoughts of appeasement that came perilously close to treason, not only in the eyes of political enemies, but as we have seen, in Juliette Adam and her friends, also in the opinion of those who had learned to admire him in 1870 and 1871. No one, least of all a politician in the public eye, can afford to allow himself to be judged by his motives alone. And Gambetta's actions, particularly the open reference to founding the new order in Europe together with Bismarck, could legitimately arouse suspicion about his claim to deserve the title 'Patriot before all else'.[28] Perhaps it is because Gambetta realized this that his meeting with Bismarck never finally came about.[29] Yet a disturbing precedent in appeasement had been created. A prominent republican had thought of bargaining with the nation's enemy.

We have said that Gambetta found opportunism desirable for two reasons, and one of these – the need for prudence in dealing with Bismarck – has now been analysed. From the point of view of internal affairs, opportunism was expected to have more immediately positive results. It was calculated to lead Gambetta to political power, and thus to give him the chance of putting the Republic firmly on her feet by providing her with the strong governmental institutions he had advocated as long as a decade earlier. Once that work was accomplished, France would have every hope of regaining her leading role in world affairs. Then, with complete confidence, she could openly raise the question of Alsace-Lorraine, before a Europe that would have to listen.

When the right had manifestly failed to bring about the royalist restoration, and when the country at various by-elections – and finally in the general election for the Chamber of Deputies in 1876 – had shown its republican inclinations, the road to political success seemed to lie mid-way between a return to autocracy and the projected socialist adventures of the radical republicans. Here the Orleanist and republican middle-classes could meet, to give France the strong centre majority Gambetta considered necessary for her future salvation. Both parties essentially wanted the same two things: a stable society, in which they held the reins of government. They also wanted to avoid the same two dangers: a return to autocratic government, and a social revolution. The doctrine they had in common could be called liberalism, were it not for the violent anti-clericalism of the republicans.

It was, therefore, political expediency which dictated the evolution of these two, at first disparate, groups. The Orleanists jettisoned their royalism, and the republicans sought to rid themselves of what masqueraded as the social heritage of 1792. But while, for the Orleanists, royalism had never been more than a convenience, and could thus be shed without doing serious damage to the morale of their members, the alleged social heritage of

1792 was to many republicans a fundamental tenet of their political creed. Indeed, its abandonment became one of the chief causes of republican disunity. At all events, when President Mac-Mahon played at *coups d'état* in 1877, Thiers' Orleanists and Gambetta's republicans decided to join forces. Thus, a conservative republicanism made its first appearance as a serious challenger for political power.

But at what cost to the republicans? Apparently, the immediate result was almost all gain. Not so much in terms of votes (the republicans lost about fifty seats, but tremendous pressure had been exerted on the electorate by government agencies), as in the fact that all republican groups were sufficiently impressed by the spectacle of collaboration between Thiers and Gambetta to sink their differences during the election. Republican discipline ensured that no two of their number should oppose each other in the same constituency, and it was observed by politicians as diverse as Thiers and Clemenceau, Gambetta and Grévy, Dufaure and Ferry. Although Thiers died before polling day, those whom he had helped to bring together recognized the need to stay that way at least until the Senate election of 1879, where they had to get a majority if they were constitutionally to rule the country alone for the first time.

It can, however, be cogently argued that the ultimate cost to the Republic of Gambetta's deal with Thiers was disastrously high. It is true that this *minimum de république* allayed the fears of foreign capitals as well as those of the majority of articulate Frenchmen. But it seems no less true that it shut the door in the face of that rising working-class, whose coming to power Gambetta had so vibrantly welcomed in the Grenoble speech of 1872.[90] In bartering their social heritage, Gambetta's republicans betrayed the dreams of many of the most ardent supporters of the republican ideal. And it did not take long for the Republic to become the preserve of bourgeois cronies, at the very moment when the working-class was rapidly becoming conscious of its position and power.

Hence the progressive alienation from the affairs of the country of at least a third of its population. After all, what comfort was the working-class, or any advocate of social reform, to find in Gambetta's famous declaration of political faith, made to a workers' delegation at the Exhibition of 1878:

27

'Those who imagine that it is incumbent upon, or possible for, a government to bring about the happiness of everyone, those people are labouring under an illusion. There is only one thing that the government owes everyone: justice. Since everyone is his own master, it is proper that everyone should make himself happy or unhappy by the good or bad use of his liberty. The State limits itself to the guaranteeing of equal rights to all, rich and poor, great and little. What we want is not an aristocratic, or bourgeois or plebeian Republic, but a national one.'[31]

It is doubtful whether Benjamin Constant, or any other post-1815 liberal, would have disagreed with these aims. It is also doubtful whether, in such a society, the worker could have protected himself any better in the 1870s than during the July Monarchy. The democratic Republic does not legalize trade unions until 1884. It is true that employers' associations are not legal until then either.

Despite its victories, conservative republicanism was thus a social and political anachronism from the moment of its appearance. No doubt that is why it managed to make the Republic palatable to the apprehensive bourgeois electorate. After 1879 however, when the Senate too gained its republican majority, and the country Grévy as its first republican President, the alliance that had assured its triumph began to disintegrate. The common enemy, royalism, had been defeated; a more unbuttoned approach to politics had become possible. And republican politicians indulged in it so enthusiastically that it required the dangerous set-backs of the 1885 elections before differences could again be composed for a while, for opportunistic reasons.

It was during these six years, from 1879 to 1885, that Gambetta's dream of strong republican government, destined to regenerate the land, was found to be hopelessly chimerical. After all the emasculation and renunciations to which the republicans had to submit before the Orleanist marriage, the only thing that Gambetta's conservative Republic could show the world was internal dissension on every important subject, not excluding *revanche*. Thus, Clemenceau's radical demand for a graduated income tax elicited catcalls from his conservative colleagues; Ferry's school reforms offended liberal republicans like Jules Simon, since they were designed to discriminate against catholic schools; the request for an amnesty on behalf of the exiled *communards* was met for a long time by frightened refusals from the conservatives; the emergence of Jules Guesde, as a Marxist politician of some persuasive power, added to the centrifugal force of the republican extreme left which, like the extreme right, saw the new régime as nothing more than a shabby conspiracy of self-seeking bourgeois politicians. Gambetta himself gives an accurate enough impression of the political scene:

'We are here in an indescribable chaos. Power resides in the streets, it is being offered to any passer-by; but it seems that the merchandize is too soiled, everyone runs away from it and makes his excuses. The President is giving up; the Chamber, with its thousand groups, goes round in circles like a herd of cattle, hysterical with fear. And, during that wonderfully edifying flight from responsibility, the East goes up in flames, Europe laughs at France and the Republic, we go down, we crumble. It is impossible to discover a way out of this cesspool. The system of voting by constituencies[32] and those it has elected is getting bogged down under our very eyes. It makes one cry with rage.'[33]

Nor was there unity when it came to foreign affairs. There were those who hoped and worked for an alliance with Russia, and there were those who preferred an alliance with England. Each country had its appeal for different people. Russia appealed to the extreme right because it was reactionary; yet despite its reactionary character it was also preferred by the radical left, because it was the alternative to England; for England was seen by both as fickle and insincere, ready to do France down at any time. On the other hand, Gambetta and some of his collaborators preferred an alliance with liberal England, in spite of the fact that many of their political friends had felt let down when England failed to intervene in 1870. Thus Juliette Adam wrote: 'England, having allowed us to be reduced to powerlessness, believes that she and Germany will share out Europe between them.'[34] But when another of Gambetta's dreams failed, i.e. the possibility of luring Austria away from Germany, he was prepared to work for a triangular alliance between England, Russia and France.[35] 'Before long I expect to see Russia and England with us, provided we have an acceptable internal policy.'[36] The trouble, however, was that what was acceptable to England and Russia, that is a stable and conservative Republic, was not necessarily now acceptable to the French. And, at the very least, it has to be admitted that the cautious middle-of-the-road conservatism of Gambetta had failed to bring about internal political stability, that basic requirement for any serious foreign ties. That is why over a decade had to elapse before Russia agreed to an alliance, and why England took more than twenty years over it. And even then it was fear of Germany, rather than respect for France, that brought these alliances about.

But, if Gambetta lamented the fractionism of his fellow republicans, their attitude to the colonial question that arose in the 1880s moved him to a veritable jeremiad. Since the Berlin meetings of 1878, France had been given to understand that neither Germany nor England saw any objection to her occupation of Tunisia. On the principle that any gift from such donors must be suspect, the French at first refused to be enticed. Indeed, at the very least one may say that Bismarck would have viewed with equanimity the movement overseas of considerable French forces, as well as Italian anger at French action in a zone Italy considered to be within her rightful sphere of influence. On the other hand, it is also true that there was in any case no great enthusiasm in France for colonial expansion. Apart from the cost of such adventures, without any apparently adequate return, the actual hostility to colonial expansion can be accounted for in the words of Clemenceau. Asked at the end of his life if he would oppose the colonial policy of the 1880s now as he had done then, he replied:

'In the same way . . ., and with the same energy if we still had the German menace always before us, a declining birth-rate, an army and navy barely sufficient to defend the homeland, and if, finally, France persisted in wanting colonies without providing colonists. The French don't want to leave Paris, Bordeaux, Marseille. The French don't want to have children. What's all this fuss about colonies then?'[37]

It is interesting that the man who led France in the crucial years of the First World War should still retain these views at the end of it, when to many observers it was precisely the lowness of the birthrate which had made colonial troops so welcome an addition to French strength.[38]

Now, in March 1881, Tunisian tribes penetrated into Algeria and killed some French soldiers. The Bey refused to help re-establish order along the frontier, though given the ineffectualness of his authority, it is doubtful if his words would have been heeded in any case. Ferry, as Prime Minister, after a rousing speech about national honour, obtained additional military credits in April, sent 38,000 men to Tunisia and a naval squadron into Bizerta in May, and within three weeks a treaty was signed, making Tunisia a French protectorate. The very speed of the operation gave voice to the suspicions of the anti-colonialists, whom Ferry had temporarily silenced in the April debates by means of highly coloured reports about the border situation. Their newspapers began to poke fun at the apparently inordinate size of the French force and, not least, to question Ferry's motives. He had said that France did not want conquests, but here she was with a new colonial territory on her hands, even if it was called a protectorate. The din became so great that Ferry decided to reduce the size of the Tunisian force to fifteen thousand men. But the south of the protectorate was by no means pacified, and the reduction of the French forces at the bidding of his political opponents was consequently a foolish act. After a hasty general election in August 1881, Ferry had to increase French strength in Tunisia to fifty thousand, but this time progress was slower and, as a consequence, criticism more clamant than before. Gambetta was outraged by the attitude of Ferry's opponents. To him, the appearance of irresolution given by the government in the face of pressure from left and right, with the whole of Europe looking on, was little short of treason. 'I found myself unable to tolerate such a lowering of republican France before Europe and I intervened. In a few minutes I made them ratify a firm policy, one of national pride.'[39] Earlier he had said, more clearly: 'I am only saddened by the help foreigners obtain from my electoral opponents at home. It is very sad to see the extreme (radical) republican party losing even the notion of patriotism.'[40]

But who are the patriots in this case? If it is taken for granted that Germany is the real enemy, then the fact that France is as yet no match for Germany does not in itself provide sufficient grounds for pronouncing patriotic the dissipation of slender

31

resources overseas. And if it is argued that the prestige value of a swift victory is here greater than the loss of resources, the same cannot be said about Italian reaction to it. Seduced into the ranks of the colonialists by members of the catholic hierarchy[41] – who had their own reasons for disliking the Italian government – Gambetta could hardly have taken a more decisive step to encourage the Italo-German alliance. Juliette Adam might have exaggerated the desire for collaboration with France which she noted in frequent conversations with prominent Italians,[42] but it cannot be doubted that the Tunisian affair made sure of prolonging French isolation in Europe, and thus her inability to face up to Germany. There is not even any evidence that the relative merits of an Italian alliance on the one hand, and the control of Tunisia on the other, were ever seriously thought about.

It was not long before another occasion for a clash of ideas about patriotism was provided: Egypt. For half a century the Upper Nile had been under French influence. After England had acquired her financial interests in the Suez Canal in 1875, a condominium of the two powers was established in 1879. In 1881, a revolt of Egyptian army officers threatened the political and economic arrangements the two powers had made with the Khedive, and each country sent a cruiser to Alexandria to watch over its interests. The governments of Germany, Austria, Russia and Italy then intervened. The Freycinet government, following upon that headed by Gambetta, took fright at these complications and refused to commit itself to action with England if the Egyptians should attempt to obstruct the restoration of the Anglo-French position. To Gambetta's great wrath, the timidity of the government was no more than a true reflection of what he considered to be the spinelessness of the Chamber.

'At the moment when that honest and correct Casimir Périer ended his questions about the state of affairs in Egypt, he forgot himself so far as to give that pack of lackeys to understand that circumstances may arise such that the government of the Republic might perhaps be forced to appeal to the patriotism of the country and of the Chamber! Formidable booing answered him, and we had to witness this explosion of public cowardice without hearing a single protest from anyone. Finis Galliae: we are ripe for servitude. The Uhlan can come, what is the province that tempts Bismarck? He can take it without effort. Oh, what an ending. I have not recovered from that dark hour. I have had enough of this revolting life; I am looking for a way out.'[43]

England was left to act alone. The French position in Egypt was lost by default.

No doubt Gambetta's outlook had been soured by the failure of his seventy-three-day ministry (November 1881–January 1882). But it is not altogether realistic to accuse all the opponents of the Tunisian and Egyptian adventures of lack of patriotism. What has already been said in the case of Tunisia applies equally to Egypt: it was certainly arguable whether France could afford the military luxury of oversea intervention when, by common consent, two of her provinces were crying out for rescue at home. And this still fails to take into consideration the periodic crises which arose from rumours about Bismarck's intentions of waging a preventive war. If it was true that France was not ready for a show-down with Germany, her readiness can hardly have been increased by sending valuable troops and materials to North Africa. On the other hand, it is no less true that, once embarked on these wars, tame submission to a Tunisian or Egyptian challenge must have damaged French prestige, postponing the day when allies would come to her and, with them, the possibility of *revanche*. And it is difficult to resist the view that, in both Tunisia and Egypt, France had been provoked. Nevertheless, since many of those, including Clemenceau, who opposed Ferry and Gambetta on their North African policies did so because they felt that the nice calculations about prestige overseas and un-readiness at home came out in favour of manning the new fortifications in the Vosges mountains, they can hardly be said to have lacked patriotism. As for those of the extreme left who opposed these wars in the interests of internationalism, whom could Gambetta blame for their lack of patriotism but himself and his friends?

It would however be disingenuous to pretend that the frequent coalitions of the extreme left with the extreme right were to be accounted for solely in terms of their preoccupation with the Vosges border. If it was true of Clemenceau's radicals some of

B   33

the time, it was scarcely so with the collectivist left of Guesde,
and no more convincingly true of the royalist right. Each group
had its own special reasons for wishing to upset the centre coalitions that had formed most of the governments since 1876. But
two reasons they had in common; first they found the centre
ideologically repulsive; second, they hoped to benefit, politically,
from its discomfiture. When it is recognized that there were
numerous self-interested dissolving forces at work within the
centre itself, it becomes clear that, among the politicians at any
rate, pious references to a strong France were becoming so much
cant. The dubious habit of keeping one envious eye on a ministry
and the other on Alsace-Lorraine progressively produced such a
confusion of impressions and reactions in the majority of deputies,
that Gambetta was led gloomily to forecast the end of it all:

> 'As time goes on, the Republic, with its tendency to decentral-
> ization, and its democratic prejudices pushed to extremes, will
> see its strength and its resources in soldiers melt away. Equality,
> for the army, means indiscipline and lack of cohesion; liberty
> means criticism pushed to the point of denigration and calumny
> against leaders . . .; fraternity is cosmopolitanism, humanitar-
> ianism, international stupidity; all these will doom us and, after
> a few years, they will throw us, an easy prey, under the feet of
> the Teutons, united with the Latins from across the Alps.[44]
> We are slipping on to the slope of the South American Re-
> publics . . . And what becomes of France in all this? That is
> the least concern of this degenerate race.'[45]

While the politicians thus seemed to betray the ideal of *revanche*,
which in the 1880s was still the acid test of patriotism for the
man-in-the-street, Déroulède published his clarion calls to arms.
In 1881, the year of Gambetta's ministry, he cried out:

> *'France, veux-tu mon sang? Il est à toi, ma France!*
> *S'il te faut ma souffrance,*
> *Souffrir sera ma loi.*
> *S'il te faut ma mort, mort à moi.*
> *Et vive toi*
> *Ma France.'*

As for *revanche*, he had written:

'Je la demande à Dieu terrible et sans recours
Prochaine et sans merci, je la demande aux hommes.
Les chemins les plus sûrs sont parfois les plus courts.'

Despite misgivings about the campaign, prompted by the German threat, Déroulède wanted to volunteer for service in the Tunisian war. But Gambetta is said to have dissuaded him; he was needed nearer home. Indeed, Gambetta seems to have found the *revanchard* attitude of Déroulède as admirable as he had found the indifference of his colleagues repugnant. When, in November 1881, he formed his government, Déroulède was made a member of the Commission for Military and National Education, whose task it was to advise the Ministry of Education on patriotic and physical instruction in the schools. The government, as is known, was short-lived, and Déroulède refused to work for long with its successor, which was just one more version of a well-worn and uninspiring theme. Never less than contemptuous of politicians, he launched the non-political *Ligue des Patriotes*. This was to be a rallying point for all those Frenchmen who could never forget that two French provinces were awaiting liberation. Gambetta joined it within twenty-four hours of its formation.

With Gambetta having to look for patriotic support more and more outside the Chamber, his relations with the army are of some significance. His regard for it was tinged with an 'Army of the Loire' nostalgia, and he always treated it with a consideration that bordered on the religious. Thus, when it was rumoured during the crisis of 16th May 1877 that some dark conspiracy existed between Mac-Mahon and the army, he protested: 'Who are they, then, those people who dare associate the name of the army and the sacred interests it represents with some infamous conspiracy!'[46] The army was the conscript instrument of universal suffrage that stood between a dangerous enemy and a vulnerable nation; it was the *sine qua non* of France. Scenes like that of 14th July 1880 were not unusual, when old Marshal Canrobert, with tears in his eyes, embraced Gambetta who had just finished his speech at a military ceremony: 'I have never despaired of the future; envisage it as I do, with confidence,' he had said. 'Can high hopes be denied one by the side of men who will know how to defend our soil against all attacks? I shall only add one word: Let us remember!'[47] His enemies alleged that he was plotting a *coup d'état*, that his popularity with the army would lead France to war. But, in spite of his disillusion with democratic republicanism, there is nothing whatever to suggest that he was prepared to indulge in unconstitutional activities in 1881, any more than he had succumbed to a far greater temptation to do so ten years earlier at Bordeaux.

Within eight months of the formation of the *Ligue des Patriotes*, Gambetta was dead. The Republic, frequently kind to its dead politicians, gave him a national funeral. In the *Drapeau*, Déroulède recalled France's debt to the organizer of resistance in 1870-1, as did most newspapers; but he added that Gambetta was not only one of the greatest Frenchmen who had ever lived, but also, approvingly, that he would have done the impossible to achieve *revanche*. No doubt. But by 1882, and partly through Gambetta's own misjudgments, great hopes were not permitted. The country was too disunited. By his *combinazione* he had alienated the extreme left and its working-class supporters, and, at the same time, had given his own entourage an example of idealistic forgetfulness which few of them could decently forbear to follow. He had preached union, but his actions had divided those whom he had wished to see together. If, by 1882, patriotic feeling had to find a home in Déroulède's unofficial *Ligue*, that is because Gambetta's policies, or at any rate those to which he too subscribed, had alienated the petty bourgeois and worker who had personified it since Valmy. And the right, in the Chamber and outside, had not yet discovered it.

CHAPTER TWO

DÉROULÈDE AND THE
'LIGUE DES PATRIOTES': 1882–7

ONCE GRÉVY had taken over the Presidency of the Republic from Mac-Mahon in 1879, the opportunist republicans' accession to power had received its symbolic consecration. It mattered little that Gambetta, who had after all created and popularized this emasculated version of republicanism, now disavowed and fought it, thinking it no longer necessary to turn the other cheek whenever Bismarck felt like slapping the French. Solidly bourgeois with a healthy regard for bourgeois interests, the opportunists intended that nothing should be allowed to endanger their prospect of a long and prosperous reign. Grévy, with unwonted lucidity, had as early as 1871 expressed their attitude of a decade later. 'France,' he had said, 'must forget about Alsace-Lorraine',[1] and the opportunists, ably led by Ferry, tried hard to do just that. They bullied the Catholic Church and embarked on the laicization of education, they purged the judiciary and the civil service, they sent armies to dubious victories in Indo-China and Africa, they even provided topics for heated popular debate by getting themselves involved in shady financial transactions. Thus the country was quickly introduced to a system of government under which foreign affairs needed to occupy little time of public political discussion. As for home affairs, the opportunists enjoyed an adequate majority in both Senate and Chamber, so that debates on such topics, though often bitterly vituperative, were never a serious threat to the continuation of their rule. Nor did they show any inclination to face the social problems arising from ever increasing industrialization. The republicans now had their own captains of industry, and the voices of the Schneiders of Le Creusot succeeded in drowning those of Jules Guesde and other socialists for many years to come.

Thus, in the early eighties, the Orleano-republicans (children

37

of the marriage of Thiers and Gambetta) had firmly established their régime – to the great delight of the German Chancellor. For Bismarck had never hidden his belief that a republican government in France would serve German interests better than a monarchy, since it was more likely to keep the country divided.[2]

But a republican government bent on peace with Germany at all costs was almost more than the Chancellor could have hoped for: 'We must tell our country the truth, we must dispel the illusions which would lead us into new catastrophes. In the presence of a Germany of forty-five millions, which will have sixty in twenty years, and eighty in fifty years, the hope of revenge is chimerical.'[3] No doubt public sentiment had not caught up with public prudence, so that such pronouncements were unlikely to elicit displays of nation-wide enthusiasm. But the bourgeoisie, at any rate, was pusillanimous – its attitude to joint Anglo-French action in Egypt in 1882 was typical – and the moderate *Journal des Débats* put not too fine a point on it when it said:

> 'What we bitterly deplore is not so much France's weakened position as its spontaneous and satisfied acceptance by public opinion . . . The head of our Government may have been imprudent in declaring openly that France would land no troops in Egypt . . . but we must confess . . . our humiliation and agree that it conforms exactly with the spirit of the Chamber and of the country.'[4]

But Ferry and his opportunists were able to purge themselves of *revanchard* feeling to a far greater extent than has so far been suggested. Piqued by Britain's readiness to deal with Egypt even without French help, and by her having done so perfectly successfully, the opportunists actually contemplated a Franco-German alliance. To be sure their serenades were played behind the diplomatic scenes, and were perhaps no more outrageous than Gambetta's momentary flirtation in the seventies with the idea of Franco-German collaboration to found the New Order in Europe. And, of course, there was no reason why France should pretend to love the British who had seldom gone out of their way to further French interests anywhere. But if the criterion of patriotism is what one does for the survival and prosperity of one's country, then the absence of illusions even among the opportunists about German intentions should have stamped these

French approaches as unwise at best, if not treasonable. Economically, the Treaty of Frankfurt was probably bearable although article 11, which gave the Germans most-favoured-nation status, seemed to many Frenchmen oppressive. And the emotional shock of the loss of Alsace-Lorraine could have been, after more than a decade, quite properly absorbed, to the point where its implications could be rationally considered. But especially on a rational level the loss of the Rhine frontier was serious. For it was clear that Bismarck considered France as the main source of possible trouble for the Reich, and that the Vosges border – opening up northern France and Paris – was for him the guarantee of French good behaviour. Beside the constant threat that Germany might suddenly end France's probation, of what significance were Franco-British clashes about their respective interests in the scramble for faraway colonies?

In these circumstances, right-wing attacks on the German policy of the opportunists might seem to signify their conversion to patriotism, their desire at least to keep alive the memories of 1870-1. 'Ferry has been caught in Prussia's trap,' was among their more moderate comments.[5] But these were histrionics, indicating no more a genuine will to face up to German designs on France than did their stentorian strictures in the seventies. Since the defeat it had become good popular politics to accuse one's opponents of pro-Germanism, and the right was loud in its charges of betrayal against the republicans whenever, as in the crisis of 1875, an opportunity presented itself. That their sole aim was the political discomfiture of the defenders of the republican régime will become obvious when we come to deal with the Boulangist crisis. It would certainly have been the first time since 1789 that the right was more concerned with external than internal events, except perhaps for its interest in the Pope's temporal power in Italy. Bazaine's conduct at Metz was more characteristic of its priorities, and the attitude of the *Figaro*[6] more so than that of the *Gazette de France*.

That the radicals were sincere in many of their reactions cannot be doubted. Juliette Adam's single-minded dedication to *revanche*, that had led her to break with Gambetta, now expressed itself in bitter onslaughts against 'the great advantage of renouncing the lost provinces in an alliance with the bombarders of Strasbourg'.[7] Rochefort in his *Intransigeant* and Clemenceau in *Justice* both belaboured Ferry's 'surrender' to Germany and the abandonment of Alsace-Lorraine it must in their view imply. As an article in *Justice* put it, France's colonial adventures, which the Germans encouraged, left Bismarck the 'absolute master of Europe; he commands, and the French government obeys . . . everyone knows the price of M. de Bismarck's friendship . . . no tyranny is heavier than his alliance'.[8]

If, in the end, nothing came of the Franco-German pipedreams, it is largely because popular feeling had been whipped up against them by the more or less genuine wrath of the extremist press of the left and right. But these rather negative manifestations of patriotism did not last long. If much of the press managed to preserve some dignity in the face of Bismarck's disappointed hectoring, the monarchist *Français* was a model of meekness. 'Assuredly, we furnish no pretext whatsoever for an aggression and we do not believe that any party is mad enough to make *revanche* a part of its platform in the approaching elections.'[9] And Clemenceau, that fire-eating radical, was soon sure that he could win the October elections (1885) on a programme of social reform and the maintenance of peace. 'In foreign affairs, [the spirit of the Revolution] asks for influence only as a consequence of the Republic's peaceful progress and of the spread of ideas. It approves war only in defence of the *patrie*.'[10]

It is against this background of patriotic forgetfulness and empty bluster that the formation and growth of the *Ligue des Patriotes* must be seen. For, once the opportunists had succeeded in wrecking Gambetta's ministry, it had become clear that over-seas adventures would continue at the expense of military strength in the Vosges, and that the unity of the nation would be further jeopardized by anti-catholic legislation in the educational field. Déroulède, and many of those who had already deplored Gambetta's coolness towards *revanche*, decided that something had to be done to uphold what they took to be the honour of France. As a first step, Déroulède resigned from the committee that advised the Minister of Education on patriotic and military training. 'Your hopes', he wrote to Ferry, 'are not the same as mine, Minister. You would like to fashion a nation without military spirit, as you have already tried to fashion a nation without God. These are two things too many.'[11] Then, on 18th May 1882, at a big rally at which Thiers' widow was to hand over a standard to the

Association of Societies for Physical Training of the Seine, Déroulède made a speech in which he laid the foundations of the *Ligue*;[12]

> 'It is because force has triumphed over justice that you want justice to have force,'[13] he declared. To achieve this, his audience was invited to 'develop everywhere and in everyone the spirit of patriotism, which makes for the passionate love of one's country; the military spirit, which makes one serve it with patience and valour; the national spirit which is the exact and reasoned knowledge of the interests and needs of the whole nation, and which must be allowed neither to crumble away, at home, into a particularistic spirit, nor to dissipate itself, abroad, in a humanitarian spirit . . .'

He concluded:

> 'Let us be Frenchmen, good Frenchmen, nothing but Frenchmen. So far as the brotherhood of peoples is concerned, we shall talk about that the day Cain hands back what he has taken away from us.'[14]

And so, in the presence of many prominent Frenchmen, among whom the celebrated historian Henri Martin was promptly made President, the *Ligue des Patriotes* was formed. The names of Gambetta, Hugo, Carnot and thousands of others soon appeared on its growing list of supporters. Where the politicians had been too timorous or self-interested to give a lead, the citizens were taking over. 'Alsace and Lorraine! That is the only thing worth living for!' These words of Gambetta, forever on Déroulède's lips,[15] summed up their aim.

The *Ligue's* first concern was the unity of the nation. It felt that Bismarck's mischievous hopes for a divided Republic had been too generously fulfilled. Déroulède appealed to every Frenchman to forget his political squabbles for the sake of the nation as a whole. 'Republican, Bonapartist, Legitimist, Orleanist, these are with us only Christian names: *Patriot*, that is the surname.'[16] Even the anarchists got a share of the warmth of brotherly feeling: 'these miserable Frenchmen are still French', Deloncle wrote indulgently.[17] In the same spirit, much was made of Hugo's emotional letter in which he expressed his desire to join the *Ligue*, affirming that 'we belong to the same family, we belong to the same *patrie*'.[18] Even anti-semitism was eschewed, though it was beginning to make considerable headway since the collapse of the *Union Générale*.[19] All this was in accordance with the third article of the *Ligue*'s constitution, which said that 'it shall concern itself with neither internal political nor religious questions'.[20] Only thus did it succeed in gathering the eclectic following that included Juliette Adam, the *revanchard* founder of the *Nouvelle Revue*, and Buisson, whose opportunism was thought reliable enough in government circles to make him Director of Primary Education for fifteen years; Paul Bert, whose opportunism was hardly more suspect, and Hugo, who was by now too old and uncritically revered for his left-wing sentimentalities to count against him.

The *Ligue* saw to it that its views were given the widest publicity. Apart from using the meetings of every available rifle club and physical training society for propaganda purposes, it organized three hundred meetings of its own in sixty towns between 1882 and 1885. In the same period, it set up fifty-two regional committees which helped to distribute its 200,000 pamphlets and 250,000 other publications. It ran its own newspaper, the *Drapeau*. It sponsored local inquiries into economic, commercial and industrial conditions, largely to determine how far the Treaty of Frankfurt was responsible for the increasing depression. It organized national shooting championships. It succeeded in collecting 250,000 francs for distribution to rifle clubs and societies for physical training.[21] Few Frenchmen were able to ignore the existence of such an active movement.

But in spite of the noise the *Ligue* made about patriotism and the forgetfulness of French politicians, it soon became apparent that its leaders too were prepared to sacrifice principle to popularity. It is true that there was a good deal of public bluster, not least from Déroulède, and that from time to time the Germans felt moved to protest against it. But Déroulède's outbursts were the result of his native impetuosity and stage sense, and they were usually counterbalanced, in those early years, by some show of moderation. There was for example the occasion on which he tried to draw a distinction between *revanche* and *revendication* (here, a just claim), and ended up, it seemed, by inciting his countrymen to a holy war against Germany:

'*Revanche* is war caused by hurt pride and envious hatred that a conquered people wants to wage against its conquerors; it is the war that a recovered and, since 1815, even enlarged Prussia, has prepared against us since Jena. *Revendication* is a right which asserts itself, justice arming herself, equity become militant: it is the holy war that a conquered people must wage against its conquerors.'[22]

It has to be admitted that these ingenious inanities reflect very fairly the intellectual level at which Déroulède managed to operate. But once it was obvious that such inflammatory talk cut no ice except with the already converted, that in fact it frightened quite a lot of people, and that acts of violence against Germans in Paris perpetrated by members of the *Ligue* actually caused much revulsion, Déroulède blew cold again, substituting an appeal to national self-defence for his rousing call to holy war: 'Yes, France, defend yourself! Defend yourself in your property and your work; do not attack, do not provoke, but defend yourself.'[23] It will be seen that the history of the *Ligue*, until Déroulède resigned from it in 1887, evolved between these two extremes.

One of the favourite and least controversial activities of the *Ligue* was the encouragement and organization of rifle-shooting competitions and physical training societies. It was felt that such an investment in lithe bodies and keen eyes would stand France in good stead when the moment of reckoning came. Indeed, every successive government approved of these aims and at length actually helped financially in the organization of national championships. Chief support came, as one would expect, from the War Ministry, where Gambetta's Campenon was in charge.[24] General Saussier, the governor of Paris, also showed the *Ligue* great benevolence. War Ministry support continued under Boulanger, who took over after the 1885 elections. Déroulède had not, however, waited till then to meet this rather flamboyant republican general 'We did not wait until he came to power before giving him proof of our feelings for him . . . we even remember the friendly welcome he gave in the past to us and our ideas.'[25]

More controversial, if predictable, was the *Ligue*'s attitude to colonial expansion. 'When condemning faraway wars, the *Ligue* has had no motive other than its ardent desire to maintain in Europe the sole endeavour of French diplomacy and arms.'[26] 'It is not with great new supplies of African sand and Asiatic silt that we shall ever fill the gap in the Vosges.'[27] In fact, the *Ligue* saw with unaccustomed clarity what few, if any, ministers seemed to be aware of: that the frittering away of French military resources in China and Africa made, first, for English hostility that might prove dangerous in the event of war with Germany and, secondly, for Russian hesitation over the periodically, and most unofficially, mooted Franco-Russian alliance, since it was difficult for the Russians to see of what use this might be to them when the French army was dispersed beyond the oceans.[28] The *Ligue* was most keen on the Russian alliance, ever since General Skobeleff had travelled around France in 1882 preaching the virtues of a common war against Germany. The War Ministry, at least, knew its priorities, and in January 1885 General Campenon resigned in despair over the waste of forces in Tonkin.

Indeed, it soon became clear that the *Ligue*'s basic anti-German programme had other controversial political implications that made it increasingly difficult for it to keep up its non-partisan façade in home affairs. The progressive weakening of the country owing to the economic depression, the growing disrepute of Parliament, the hamfisted approach by Ferry and his friends to religious and educational problems which embittered already acute national divisions, these were among the many reasons that led Déroulède and the *Ligue* to abandon their early political neutrality. Perhaps it was still true for them that in a national movement political affiliations provided no more than the Christian names before the national family name, but they were now convinced that such a family would chatter itself out of organized existence if it were not firmly guided by those who had its collective well-being at heart. In this the *Ligue* echoed the despairing strains of Gambetta.

The decisive moment came in 1885, and was symbolized by the resignation in March of the second President of the *Ligue*, Anatole de la Forge. 'You', he wrote to Déroulède, 'are an authoritarian patriot, I am a liberal one.'[29] He had already found it difficult to accept the more violent demonstrations of the *Ligue*'s rowdies which, in September 1882, had led to a raid on a Germany restaurant in Paris. But it was not until 1885 that the *Ligue* openly approved of demonstrations that were at once violent and politically one-sided. In February took place the funeral of the socialist author and journalist, Jules Vallès, who had been an ardent *communard*, and among those who wanted to pay their last respects were a number of German socialists. It is not clear whether the *Ligue* was directly responsible for the students' demonstrations that followed this outrageous violation of French sovereignty, but it drew from Déroulède the lunatic approval: 'Yes, let France be French!'[30] At first sight, this may look like a display of petty nationalism and nothing more, except perhaps of stupidity, since the German socialists were convinced that the Reich should not keep Alsace-Lorraine and said so in the Reichstag the moment some of them were elected in 1886. But the *Ligue*'s quarrel was as much with the socialists in general as with the Germans in particular, as is proved by their extraordinary conduct at Buzenval in January 1886. There they objected to the red flag that flew together with the tricolour and, when it was not taken down, boycotted the official celebrations and held their own, separately. 'The unity of the flag is no less essential to our nation than the unity of its law, of which it is the symbol,'[31] thus Déroulède in the *Drapeau*. The *Ligue* was in this case ostensibly objecting to the internationalism of the socialists, but Déroulède had fought the Commune in the Versailles army, and his sympathies were never subsequently on the left. After Anatole de la Forge it fell to Déroulède himself to become the *Ligue*'s President, and his anti-left prejudices became its policy.

In the face of what he took to be the continuing decline of the country – and what to the opportunists was no more than an agreeable period of irresponsible power – Déroulède was now prepared to go beyond the simple demand for political discrimination against the socialists. He insisted that to fulfil the role he had assigned to it, the nation had to reorganize its government and administration. It had to have a government that would govern and an administration that would administer, without fear or favour, strongly, and in the national interest:

'What do you think of a country whose Parliament is reduced to proposing and to voting the following agenda: (26th May 1885) *The Chamber, having confidence in the government's resolution to have the national flag respected, proceeds with the business of the day* . . . That is why, patriots, the immediate task of the *Ligue* is to fight above all against this internal disintegration. Before coming to the help of the threatened *patrie*, let us come to the aid of the State in its decline.'[32]

'The day may come,' the *Drapeau* said, 'when France can afford to be liberal; for the moment strength and liberalism are mutually exclusive.'[33] At the time of the elections in 1885 Déroulède still called himself a 'resolute supporter of an open but authoritarian Republic'[34]; but while he certainly wanted an authoritarian state it was a patent lie that he now still wanted it to be open. And, to emphasize just how far the *Ligue* had departed from its original aims, when he ultimately decided to withdraw his candidature he did not justify this decision by his wish to keep the *Ligue* out of internal politics, but solely, and disdainfully, by his refusal to get mixed up in the party system.[35] This disdain is no doubt connected with his growing unpopularity in government circles. At Le Mans, in August 1885, he was officially asked to remain silent at the unveiling of a statue to Chanzy. He was becoming a diplomatic embarrassment to the prudent Grévy's prudent ministers.

When Déroulède says that after the election of 1885 he hoped for great things from Boulanger, whom Clemenceau (it is said) had installed at the rue Saint Dominique, one can believe him. With the naïve impetuosity which was his chief characteristic, Déroulède actually went to the War Ministry to offer Boulanger the *Ligue*'s support in a *coup d'état*. He was rather too early. But while Boulanger was in office Déroulède continued to hope, as did many better men thereafter. Indeed, there seemed some reason for his optimism, for Boulanger made a point of showing that he took the army seriously, and the Germans less so. As a result, Déroulède asked the *Ligue* to be patient, and not to press the demand at its General Meeting in November 1886 that he tour the provinces to spread the *revanchard* gospel. 'I thank you,' he said, 'but I insist that we have faith in the present government . . . Those who govern us seem to be going ahead; it is not up to us to precede them but to follow them respectfully . . . [now] we must remain silent, since we have at last a standard bearer in General Boulanger.'[36] And, more specifically: '[Boulanger] is the first of our ministers for six years who has publicly spoken of our right to the respect of Europe and to the independence of our country.'[37] The implied reference to Gambetta jolts one into the realization that the meaning of patriotism had undergone some drastic changes since 1870. Full-hearted and, no doubt of necessity, national in its appeal during the heroic period of the Army of the Loire, a petty conspiratorial poetaster seemed to be succeeding in dragging it down in the public eye to his own level. He was making it narrow, choleric, crude, and upon these foundations Boulanger built his even more garish edifice. Part-time patriots like Clemenceau, if a little more sophisticated, failed to arrest this lamentable decline in generosity, taste and dignity.

Thus, while Boulanger was in office, the agitation of the *Ligue* took on a more moderate form. But this was not only because of the General's quixotic gestures, for these became much less frequent after Grévy had managed to communicate his alarm at the resultant worsening of Franco-German relations to the War Minister's colleagues. It was as much the result of the realization that, while few Frenchmen would be prepared to renounce Alsace-Lorraine for ever, even fewer would be prepared to make war for the recovery of these provinces. The provocative tone of the *Ligue* had lost it much sympathy, and had indeed created a certain amount of hostility to it. The fact that ministers could, in 1885, openly ostracize Déroulède without causing any kind of public outcry is the measure of his decline. He was painfully aware of this. He spoke more and more of defence and less of holy wars. At Vincennes, during the second national shooting championships for which he had managed to get a government subsidy, he stated plaintively: 'We are neither *provocateurs* nor are we impatient or imprudent; I would say that we are prudent, that we are only that, and that we have never been anything else.'[31]

But with typical disdain for the facts, he confused his desire to reassure with the fulfilment of the desire. On the occasion of Hugo's funeral he appropriated the acclamations of the public largely for himself and his group, declaring that 'no one any longer confuses our independent attitude in the face of foreign countries with the provocative attitude we used to have attributed to us. Not one of the sturdy workers, whose acclamations went straight to our hearts, is any longer in doubt about what we serve and what we want.'[39] Déroulède's capacity for self-deception is pricelessly illustrated in the *Figaro*'s report of the funeral.[40] According to Marot, the generous salutes from the leader of the *Ligue* in the procession bore no relation whatever to the acclamations of the public, which were not intended for him at all.

But an organization like the *Ligue* has its own logic, no matter what its leader might say from time to time. It was summed up first by Louis de Peyramont, who split the *Ligue* and rallied some extremists around his paper, the *Revanche*. The moment the *Ligue* ceased being militant, he said,[41] it lost its *raison d'être*. The mere injunction to keep alive the memory of the lost provinces was after all unnecessary, because they were never really in danger of being forgotten. The *Ligue*'s agitation against overseas military commitments made sense only if it thought in terms of either the danger of German aggression in Europe, or the recovery of the provinces by force. Although there were occasions when it looked as if Germany might attack, the *Ligue* saw its function in terms of the recovery of Alsace-Lorraine, and its desire to keep the army at home was popularly associated with the need to use it for the recovery of these provinces. It is of course possible to separate these two issues, to say that it is one thing to want the army at home in a purely defensive capacity, and another to agitate peacefully for the eventual restoration of Alsace-Lorraine to France. And this is what the *Ligue* did say, from time to time. But the extremists thought this too craven.

Not that Peyramont and the other dissidents went much beyond Déroulède at his most euphoric. They never appear to have said openly that they wanted war at a particular time to gain their chief purpose. But they certainly did not exclude it when they continued Déroulède's agitation against article 11 of the Treaty of Frankfurt which, according to them, bore harshly on the French economy. They exhorted the workers 'to put their blood at the disposal of the *patrie*' to achieve their aim.[42] Peyramont collected much of what was left of the *Ligue* after moderate, honest, and respectable citizens had turned their backs on it. He openly called for a military Republic[43] and excommunicated the socialists.[44] But he was much more immoderate than Déroulède, and called even Boulanger a German slave.[45] The *Revanche* organized demonstrations against German art, science, and music, and successfully prevented a projected run of *Lohengrin* at the Eden-Théâtre by threatening a brawl.[46] If Peyramont is entitled to any glory it is solely because Bismarck at times felt moved to protest at the actions of his gangs.

It was left to a German judge to sum up the basic dilemma of the *Ligue*. On 13th June 1887, there opened in Leipzig the trial of eight Alsace-Lorrainers. They were charged with having belonged to the *Ligue*, and that this entailed their readiness to use force to disrupt the Reich. Four were found guilty and condemned to imprisonment in a fortress for terms of between one and two years. The court reasoned as follows:

'The court . . . declares further that the argument must be rejected according to which the *Ligue des Patriotes* only had one aim, namely a defensive one: for in that case it would be difficult to see how the recovery of Alsace-Lorraine could be effected through a defensive war.'[47]

The *Ligue* failed to win lasting popular support precisely because no-one except a few hotheads dared face the risk of an offensive war, and because if it could not preach that, it had little to offer that could stir the public imagination. It also failed as a rallying point for those who treasured the dignity of France, largely because of the ineptitude and pettiness of its founder. It was therefore left to peter out in ignominious street brawls.

Déroulède himself resigned from the movement in 1887, two years before it was finally outlawed. His bet was now on Boulanger.

CHAPTER THREE

BOULANGER

THE ELECTION of 1885 put an end to the complacent rule of the opportunists. The right[1], having received only one and three-quarter million votes in 1881, managed to poll over three and a half million in 1885. Despite the uneasy alliance of Ferry's opportunists with Clemenceau's radicals in the interests of parliamentary republicanism, the total seats of the right rose to 201 (from ninety), compared with an overall republican drop from 457 to 383, split about evenly between radicals and opportunists. Given the underlying differences between these two major republican groups, an elementary aptitude for arithmetic was sufficient to suggest that the political importance of the right in the new Chamber was going to be considerably increased. This, in turn, entailed that the right could no longer afford to sit on the fence on most of the important issues, as it had done after its demoralizing defeat in 1881, contenting itself with taking pot-shots at anything that happened to be comparatively unpopular with the public at any given time.

The future of Alsace-Lorraine was one of these problems. It was in connection with this that the new prominence of the right helped to clear up a confusion which it had itself encouraged, and that appeared increasingly to link patriotism with right-wing ideologies. In and out of Parliament, these anti-democrats were composed of two distinct groups. There were, first, those to whom government by élite was a basic credo, and to whom the Parliamentary Republic was consequently basically abhorrent. Most of these were royalists (e.g. the Baron de Mackau) and had as aristocratic a disdain for the mean little men who wielded power under the Republic as for the people who had put them there. Secondly, there were those who, like Déroulède, blamed the parliamentary system for the internal divisions of the country and its consequent weakness in relation to Germany. For them the desire for strong government and hostility to the régime came at the conclusion of the argument.[2] The aristocratic right, in decline at least since 1876, knew as well as everyone else that hints about the heinousness of the Treaty of Frankfurt would always please the voters. Even those enjoying material prosperity had had their pride hurt in 1870-1. Particularly if no specific action was demanded from them, the mere thought that some day their conquerors would themselves be defeated gave them a kind of reassurance. Most politicians, whether of the left or the right, in fact accused each other of pro-Germanism when Bismarck was quiescent, and of warmongering when he was threatening to erupt, attempting to capitalize on this aspect of French susceptibilities. But, in the early eighties, both right-wing groups, lacking the responsibilities of government, could adopt a more belligerent tone than their opponents. The result was that the clamour for *revanche* and strong government became confused, until it seemed that the demand for the one always went with the demand for the other. It was this confusion that the results of the 1885 elections helped to clear up. They created the conditions that enabled General Boulanger to play his special part in the development of the Third Republic. When he had done, it was no longer possible to believe that the demands of patriotism preoccupied Mackau, Clemenceau, and Déroulède to the same extent.

Boulanger made his ministerial debut in January 1886 at the age of 48, and he owed it largely to the new balance of power in the Chamber. Generals whose republicanism was thought to be genuine did not flourish in great numbers in the 1880s, and after 1885 the republicans thought it more important than ever that someone reliable should be at the War Ministry. There are at least two accounts of how Boulanger was picked. The first, that he had been suggested by General Campenon (himself reputedly a protégé of Gambetta) is given by Freycinet,[3] his first chief. The other has it that Clemenceau admired his fights with Cambon, who was Resident-General in Tunisia while Boulanger was commander of the army of occupation, and that he had insisted that the General was the right man for the rue Saint Dominique. Clemenceau appeared to see in him a late nineteenth-century version of a Jacobin General:

'Boulanger was radicalism in jack-boots. At home, democratic reforms in the army and soon, abroad, a policy of *revanche* towards Germany; in brief, the Jacobinism of Boulboul (as Clemenceau called him) satisfied the radicals.[4]

Whether this last account is correct or not, the fact that it has been given credence is enough to show the increased importance of the radicals in the new Chamber. 'Today,' said the *Figaro*, 'it is to the friendship of M Clemenceau that General Boulanger owes his portfolio. The radicals have seized the War Ministry. That is perhaps the gravest symptom of the situation.[5] The *Journal des Débats*, with nasty premonitions, only just retained control:

'After the purge of the administration, after the purge of the magistrature, let us hope that we are not going to suffer the most dangerous, the most odious, the most intolerable of all purges, that of the army.'[6]

At first the highest hopes of the radicals and the greatest fears of the aristocratic right appeared justified. One of Boulanger's first actions was to remind the army of the existence of the new republican régime. Although the occasion of the resignation of Mac-Mahon in 1879 was the refusal of the latter to sanction a minor purge among higher army officers, which then proceeded without him, the average brass-hat was still a royalist, and likely to exhibit this fact in derisive chitchat about republican personalities and institutions. In a circular to the army its new chief stated bluntly that 'there will be no politics in the army by anyone.'[7] The Chamber seemed delighted and immediately gave him a vote of confidence of 374 to 163. His handling of the delicate situation during a strike at Decazeville in March further enhanced his standing with the republicans. What, it had been asked awkwardly, were army units doing in the strike area, two years after trade unions had their existence and activities legalized? Were bourgeois politicians and businessmen up to their old tricks again? It was remembered that Thiers, the father of the Third Republic, had assured the Prefect of the Nord at the time of the Anzin strike in 1872 that 'the means of repression will not be found lacking'. But with the mellifluous grandiloquence of the republican tradition that is in such circumstances sometimes mistaken for the expression of a social conscience, Boulanger assured his audience that the army was not there as a threat. It now represented the nation, he said, and even the workers were old soldiers. In case the logic of this argument was not entirely clear to the deputies, he conjured up an imaginative picture of solidarity between the strikers and the armed representatives of the middle-class republican majority: 'Perhaps', he exclaimed, 'at this very moment, each one of the soldiers is sharing with a miner his soup and his bread ration.'[8] Perhaps. Clemenceau, who still had some twenty years to go before gaining first-hand experience in strike breaking, led the applause on the republican side. The workers and the army were being flattered and united; all was well with the Jacobin dream.

But the opportunists too were to have their hearts gladdened by their new War Minister. Old hands at the art of petty persecution, devoid even of the appearance of generosity presented by the declared social programme of the radicals, Ferry and his friends had decided to exile certain members of the royal family. Although it had been obvious for some time that the Elysée under Grévy was no centre of scintillating society, and that the careful bourgeois who occupied it was full of resentment at the brilliance of the Comte de Paris's soirées, a royal marriage on 14th May 1886 was an occasion of such lavishness that the President's opportunists could contain themselves no longer. The expulsion law of 23rd June was the result. It was Boulanger, however, whose contribution to this orgy of republican pettiness seemed to catch the popular imagination. On the eve of France's national day, he acquainted the Chamber with his own decision to dismiss the Duc d'Aumale and some other members of the royal family from the army. His speech aroused such enthusiasm that its *affichage*[9] was voted by an overwhelming majority. Had any member of the government still doubted it, it would have become clear on the following day that the General was rapidly becoming a popular hero. Whatever grouses they had against the government forgotten, the people of Paris turned out in their thousands to acclaim Boulanger, the friend of the people, the reformer of the army. The government decided that the ovation given to its War Minister must also in a sense have been for it, and was grateful. It was a long time since the republicans had been so happy.

It was not to last. Although two days after his triumphant return from the review at Longchamp Boulanger was again flattered by crowds at the Opéra, there was distinctly less pleasure to be derived from the *Figaro* of a day later, 17th July. The Duc d'Aumale allowed the conservative daily to publish letters he had received from Boulanger, in which he had expressed gratitude for help the Duke had given him in obtaining promotion in 1880. Aumale's charge of course was one of ingratitude. Interviewed by the *Temps* and *Voltaire*, Boulanger denied the authenticity of the letters. Thereupon the *Figaro* published two more. In the first, Boulanger expressed his faith in the leadership of the Duke; in the second, he requested Aumale's help to obtain promotion. No longer able to deny that he had in fact written these letters, the War Minister sought to wipe out his previous lie with a pious republican defence of his actions, saying that, 'when the conspiracy of princes obliged me to choose between my former chief and the Republic, I remained faithful to the Republic'.[10] Grévy and Freycinet thought for a moment of asking for his resignation[11] but decided that his popularity amply atoned for his mendaciousness.

The country was certainly still rallying to Boulanger, and when the Freycinet cabinet fell after the summer recess, in December 1886, Goblet retained him. It would have been difficult to persuade the electors that the man who had vastly improved the food and hygiene of the conscripts, had allowed them to wear beards and given them more leisure, who was proposing to reduce conscription from five to three years and to generalize the use of the new magazine rifles, that such a man's services should be dispensed with after so short a time.

Meanwhile the German government had become apprehensive about Boulanger's popularity, and even more about his intentions. It is not clear how far they were serious about this, and how far they merely used him as an excuse to push through the Reichstag Bismarck's military law, designed to increase the size of the army. But Boulanger certainly gave them cause for alertness. He made mysterious frontier inspections, built new barracks in the Belfort area, rehearsed mobilization procedures, stopped the export of horses, drafted a law about allowances in case of war. By the end of January 1887 the German Secretary of State for Alsace-Lorraine talked openly about the likelihood of war, putting much of the blame on the mischief created by the *Ligue des Patriotes*, and expressly denied – for what that was worth – that he was exaggerating the seriousness of the situation for the sake of the military law. Bismarck himself had said earlier in the Reichstag, with some plausibility:

'Why then should General Boulanger, if he came to power, not attempt war? If we consider that a military dictatorship is possible in France – and that kind of dictatorship has existed there several times – who is to guarantee that that hypothesis will not come true?'[12]

The Chancellor anticipated events a little, but even the French press was beginning to wonder whether the situation was not running away with the government. Thus the *Figaro* which, admittedly, one would expect to waste little sympathy on Boulanger:

'It is from the external point of view that the General consti- tutes, let us not say a danger, the word would be improper, but a source of wonder [*étonnement*], which can become dangerous . . . a provocation, or at least a threat.'[13]

Some papers already referred to him as General Revanche.

Although both the German and the French press and politicians continued for some weeks to alternate between threats and protestations of peaceful intentions, April provided a test case for the real aims of the two contestants. It was then that the French frontier police official Schnaebelé, born in Alsace, was arrested by German police for having been implicated in secret service activities. Two allegations were made against the Germans (apart from the obvious one that Schnaebelé had been seized to provide Bismarck with a new opportunity to humiliate the French). First, that the man had been abducted from French soil, which was difficult to prove. Secondly, that he had made arrangements to meet a German official, and that the official's invitation to see him on German soil constituted a safe conduct. Here was a perfect pretext for war. The French government could make it impossible for the Germans to withdraw from this situation with dignity, or the Germans could outrage French feelings by refusing to examine the incident. Thus France could have tried to regain the lost provinces, and Germany to keep France weak. If nothing much came to pass between the two countries, except a lot of invective, it was surely a clear sign that neither really wanted to risk a war. In fact, nothing did come to pass; even Boulanger succumbed to the soothing effect of the many Elysée meetings at which Grévy was forever counselling prudent inactivity. Not a single prominent patriot went on record as saying that France ought to go to war, while Mackau (leader of the aristocratic right) actually asked Grévy to ensure a peaceful solution. On the German side, Bismarck climbed down, albeit with little grace. He agreed that the invitation Schnaebelé had received from the German official was tantamount to a safe conduct, and had him released. That Bismarck did not expressly acknowledge that the Germans had acted wrongly did not stop Flourens, the French Foreign Minister, from heaving a sigh of relief and rushing to congratulate the Chancellor in exaggerated terms for having resolved the crisis in a manner 'as much in keeping with the principles of international law as with the relations of *bon voisinage* which should exist between two great nations', and to add that the conduct of France would always be guided by the same principles.[14] On reflection, the cabinet did not allow the message to be sent.

In keeping with a now well-established tradition, the moment the crisis was over the *revanchards* blew hot again. Having demonstrated that their patriotism was limited to a choice vocabulary, they now resumed their campaign against the opportunists. Boulanger, they maintained, had caused the enemy to capitulate; but if a cowardly government had not tied his hands he would have taught the Germans a far severer lesson. Far-removed though this was from the facts – even if he had been given his head the German General Staff would have had little cause to tremble in its boots – the public assumed as a matter of course that the Schnaebelé 'victory' was Boulanger's, and his apotheosis was complete.

Thoroughly sickened, and not a little worried, by the results of the General's irresponsibility, the opportunists at last decided that he had to disappear from the political scene, no matter what the cost. Already before the Schnaebelé affair Ferry, Freycinet, and Grévy had talked about the desirability of ousting him. It was not simply that their vanity had been hurt by his. The popularity of the War Minister had become a double danger. Abroad, it had been largely responsible for the difficulties with Germany. At home, the consequences of his ambitions were incalculable. Accordingly, the opportunist President of the Budget Commission, Rouvier, forced the Goblet ministry to resign, and kept Boulanger out of his next government. Naturally, the *revanchards* were beside themselves with anger. Rochefort, editor of the *Intransigeant*, and already for some time a vociferous radical *revanchard*, fulminated:

'We cannot tolerate that the keys of our frontiers are handed over to the enemy [by the exclusion of Boulanger], none of us wanting to be condemned to speaking German in our old age. The deputies who associate themselves with the *plot* that is being woven around the present defender of the patrie . . .'[15] etc., etc.

Some radicals and, according to Zévaès, most of the public, demanded that Boulanger should immediately return to the War Ministry.[16] Even more radicals, however, and most of the opportunists, had had enough of the General, and the Senate informed Grévy that no government that included Boulanger could count on its support. The opportunists thus remained adamant.

The electoral results of 1885 now exhibited some of their more fascinating implications. However much obstinacy the opportunists managed to display in their resolution to keep Boulanger out, the facts of parliamentary arithmetic remained largely what they had been a year earlier. Since the opportunists were not strong enough to govern alone and were now deprived of support from some of the left, they began to look to the right. For the first time since 1875, republicans were openly prepared to rely on the support of the enemies of the régime. And the reason why they were prepared to accept this support, and why the right was prepared to offer it, is to be found in their joint desire for a quiet life in foreign affairs. How else would the *rente* remain stable? Clemenceau's *Justice*, however, made it clear that the radical leader had not changed his mind about the merits of his protégé, and thus continued to have some odd bedfellows: Louis de Peyramont's *Revanche*, Michelin's *Action*, Séverine's *Cri du Peuple*, Eugène Mayer's *Lanterne*, Rochefort's *Intransigeant*.

And it was no time at all before the supporters of Boulanger had made him into a popular martyr. If not all the politicians and editors who rallied round him were animated by patriotic fervour, the masses probably were. It is difficult always to disentangle those who use patriotism as a means to attack a government they dislike from those who dislike the government because it attacks patriotism. But the popular image of the General had become so over-simplified that there seemed at any rate no problem about where patriotic duty lay. No complex calculations were required to determine whether France could afford to send armies overseas without weakening her position in Europe; no agonizing appraisal whether war with Germany was opportune. The question was simply whether the already discredited opportunists had meekly sacked their idolized War Minister at the behest of the Germans. Rochefort and the other Boulangists taught the crowds to answer this with an indignant 'yes'. Their irresponsibility was to cost France dear.

Within a week of Boulanger's fall, Rochefort found an occasion for a popular demonstration. There was a by-election in the Seine department, and although the radical-socialist Mesureur actually had Rochefort's support, and was the only candidate, the *Intransigeant* asked electors to add Boulanger's name to the ballot papers. The result was a little obscure, since the papers containing the names of both Boulanger and Mesureur were not counted, and nearly 13,000 papers were classed as miscellaneous. But ballot papers which contained only Boulanger's name amounted to 38,457, and that was an impressive enough show in such circumstances.

Five days later, 28th May 1887, and two days before the ministerial crisis was at last resolved with the formation of the Rouvier government, there was the first violent demonstration. To the cries of *C'est Boulange, lange, lange, c'est Boulanger qu'il nous faut*, crowds gathered at the Opéra, and were finally dispersed by the police. Three days later, in the area of the Cercle Militaire, Boulanger was again acclaimed by large crowds. It is said that in the rue d'Antin alone the police had to cope with two thousand demonstrators. With a nervousness that was soon to become a well-grounded habit, cavalry was ordered to take up positions near the Palais-Bourbon and the Elysée. Since the demonstrations were continuing, the government decided that the idol had somehow to be separated from the idolators; and before 14th July, unless even more serious trouble was to be risked. Accordingly, on the 4th, Boulanger was given a new command, an army corps, at Clermont Ferrand, 250 miles from Paris. The lyrical drawings and writings depicting his departure on the 8th are known well enough. Fifteen to twenty thousand Parisians escorted him from the Hôtel du Louvre to the Gare de Lyon, clung to the engine of his train, lay on the track to prevent his departure, in a fantastic paroxysm of hysterical adulation.

On the 11th, 357 to 111 votes endorsed the government's policy, 111 radicals being outvoted by 210 opportunists, aided by 147 of the right. The atmosphere now grew calmer as the summer recess approached, though the Longchamp review on 14th July gave Déroulède and the *Ligue* a chance to demonstrate that they resumed full freedom of action after the dismissal of Boulanger. Ten days later occurred the last significant event before Parliament dispersed. Ferry surprised himself and his friends with a humourous remark, calling Boulanger a 'Saint-Arnaud de café-concert', as a result of which he was challenged by the General to a duel. But the archetypal opportunist had lost none of his prudence; he declined the challenge, on the grounds that it was too dangerous.

The anticipated political lull during the parliamentary vacation was of short duration. Indiscretions, rumours, and then full confessions, brought before the public a first-class scandal that involved several personalities associated with the régime and, in the end, the President of the Republic himself. It was the Wilson affair. From small beginnings – the President's son-in-law having used his position at the Elysée to obtain decorations for friends and for those who might show him consideration in return, and having had his private letters officially stamped at the State's expense – it was largely because of Grévy's parental obstinacy in refusing to disavow Wilson that the Republic had a rare row on its hands. The enemies of the opportunists smelt blood. Soon Clemenceau's radicals were to make common cause with Déroulède and Rochefort, and it began to look so black for the government that Mackau could nurse hopes of a royalist restoration, which made him abandon his friends in the republican government without a qualm. It was Clemenceau who struck the first decisive blow. When the government understandably tried to hedge, in an attempt to delay the day of reckoning, he insisted on a vote. Thus, on 19th November 1887, Rouvier was defeated by 317 votes to 228.

The government crisis which followed was prolonged by Grévy's refusal to vacate the Elysée, where even the opportunists now saw him as a liability. So bleak was the outlook for the régime as a whole at this stage that the initiative passed to conspirators of all kinds. If these had anything in common, it was that – with the exception of the opportunists who squabbled among themselves

– they were all variations on the same Boulangist theme. For the General was suddenly propelled back into the centre of the political arena. In great secrecy he took part in talks with such connoisseurs of dark intrigue as Rochefort and Déroulède, Eugène Mayer and Clemenceau. During the two nights which their more impressionable chroniclers have qualified as 'historic' (28th and 29th November 1887), these gentlemen plotted against the opportunists. Meanwhile tension was mounting in the country, as it seemed that the discredited bourgeois who pretended that he was leaving the Elysée without regret, if sadly,[17] might be succeeded by Ferry, the unpopular colonialist who had increased the price of bread. By now 'the opportunists are literally scared and stupefied; the radicals are faltering, anxious, feeling overwhelmed'.[18] But these historic nights produced nothing in particular. What, after all, could the basically democratic Clemenceau have found to agree with in the authoritarian incoherencies of his fellow conspirators, while the proposed military saviour sat among them in expectant silence?

It was in fact a sign of the growing irrelevance of Boulanger's person, as distinct from the popular myth, that he could be called away from this historic meeting without apparently disconcerting his colleagues. And it was a sign of the growing ambiguity of the myth that the persecutor of princes was called away from his republican extremists to have Mackau offer him the moon, if only he consented to the restoration of the monarchy. He had become the symbol of all the discontents.

On 3rd December 1887, the day after Grévy's resignation, the Versailles Assembly elected Sadi Carnot as the new President. He had obtained 616 votes against 188 for General Saussier, the candidate of the right. If little was publicly known about Carnot, he had at least a reassuring name. But although Ferry had been kept out of the Elysée, the popularity of Boulanger continued to grow, and it was now Tirard's first government that had to cope with the problems raised by the General's use of by-elections for cheap publicity and arrogant demonstrations. On 26th February 1888, although ineligible since he held a military command, Boulanger presented himself at no less than seven by-elections, in which he polled the admittedly not impressive total of about 55,000 votes. The haze which shrouded the General's intentions was a source of much worry for Clemenceau and some of the other more extreme radicals, as it had been earlier after the scenes at the Gare de Lyon. It soon caused them to break with him for good. The importance of the defection of Clemenceau's radicals lies in the fact that it left the General in the hands of an ill-assorted collection of adventurers, who had only one thing in common: they all hated the democratic régime. The ludicrous fact is that if one man among them could be said not to have shared this hatred it was Boulanger himself.

For the first time since the opportunists' break with Boulanger it therefore appeared – though probably not to the majority of the crowds that acclaimed him – that a clear challenge was being made to the democratic institutions of the country. That it was made on behalf of several, and some mutually exclusive, interests was beside the point. Extremists of all kinds saw in the popularity of the fluid Boulanger a means to the abolition of democracy. Only authoritarian governments could bring about the socialist Republic, the restoration of the monarchy, the war of revenge against Germany, or whatever it was they demanded. Only authoritarian governments would act, where so far there had never been more than talk.

'The *Figaro* is asking me why my friends and I are Boulangists. The answer is that the General is the only person in France capable of expelling from the Palais-Bourbon the chatterers who deafen us and are unpleasant people.'[19]

Thus Barrès. But few others with intellectual pretensions were seduced by the Boulangists. The tone of the *Cocarde*, founded expressly to support the Boulangist cause, was hardly likely to appeal to them either.

In the face of these threats the government seemed to do little. Relieving Boulanger of his command at Clermont Ferrand, because of his constant (and now overt) absenteeism, did no more than relieve him of the illegality of engaging in political activity. On the very day on which his dismissal was confirmed by a court of inquiry (27th March 1888), he obtained 40,000 votes in the first ballot of a by-election, fought against a member of the right (25,000) and the radical Doumer (17,000), though the latter was returned at the second ballot. What was more important, his motley followers now attempted to found a coherent movement, with a clear-cut fighting programme, the *Comité républicain de la protestation nationale*, or *Comité national* as it became known later. All the usual names were connected with it: Rochefort, Déroulède, Le Hérissé, Eugène Mayer, Laisant, Laguerre, etc., including even a senator, Naquet, whose radicalism was so extreme that he had successfully sponsored the bill for the return of divorce (1882-4); and a royalist, Thiébaud. The aims of the *Comité* were summed up in the slogan *Révision, Dissolution, Constituante*, meaning that it wanted the revision of the constitution (promised since 1875), entailing the dissolution of Parliament and the convening of a Constituent Assembly. Its emblem was the red carnation, according to the *Cocarde* the General's favourite flower.

On the 30th March, Laguerre proposed *révision* in the Chamber and, with the very first push, the *Comité* brought down the government with 368 votes to 237. It is true that the ground had been cunningly chosen. When the Republic was ushered in with a majority of one, Broglie and his friends had burdened it with a Senate that was to ensure the *minimum de république*. The republicans had promised themselves that they would, as soon as possible, do without the upper House altogether. But as it too became gradually republican, the opportunists in power found it useful as a curb on radical enthusiasm, and were reluctant to abolish it. Naturally the radicals failed to be moved by such arguments and continued to press for the promised revision. Laguerre, therefore, with his motion couched in general terms, managed to unite the extreme left with the extreme right, though the latter did not mean by revision what the radicals meant. It can consequently not be said that the vote signified any endorsement of Boulangism, though it certainly gave it a tactical victory.

President Carnot, throughout the Boulangist crisis, gave evidence of political astuteness that was at least the equal of Grévy's, thus belying the dimness that Clemenceau allegedly attributed to him at his election.[20] Within four days (3rd April 1888) he managed to present the country with its first radical government. Floquet, who led it, occupied a political position halfway between the opportunists and Clemenceau, and was able to unite a moderately pink majority against the right. More important, he appeared unimpressed by the General. As the latter's supporters were beginning to organize themselves, Floquet's unruffable disdain helped to put heart into those who sought to counter the Boulangist threat. Already in March socialists like

Brousse, Faillet, Joffrin and Allemane, usually ostentatious in their aloofness from bourgeois politics, had issued a manifesto warning workers of the authoritarian danger of Boulangism, and expressing their readiness to collaborate with the government in the defence of the Republic. Allemane had helped to found a newspaper, *Le parti ouvrier*, to put the socialist position to the proletariat. Similarly, the Paris Municipal Council, if not quite as red as it used to be, now openly denounced 'the plebiscitary and Boulangist campaign', having been in a state of increasingly effervescent alertness since 1887, when it seemed that Ferry might be elected President of the Republic. The attraction that Boulangism had for the proletariat, especially in those days of depression,[21] with its sweeping (if largely unspecified) reforms, made these socialist pronouncements very timely, if the mistakes of 1848 were to be avoided. They certainly did not like the bourgeois Republic, but the prospect of a military dictatorship made a socialist future even less likely.

But it is the changing attitude of the majority of the radicals which most affected the evolution and ultimate fate of Boulangism. Between February and April the General's new organization, the *Comité*, could still rally many radicals at by-elections by contrasting the image of General *Revanche* with a government allegedly lacking in patriotic spirit. But the lucidity that had enabled Carnot and Floquet to recognize that the continual appeal to patriotism was merely being used for political ends, of whose authoritarianism they disapproved, that lucidity gradually also came to the majority of radicals. And the moment they turned against him Boulanger had lost the possibility, if not the hope, of gaining power constitutionally. At the end of May, Clemenceau and the socialists Ranc and Joffrin founded the *Société des droits de l'homme et du citoyen*, in which they sought to unite 'all who have remained faithful to the Republic . . . (against) the Boulangist adventure which is so humiliating for our country'.[22]

But, knowing the General's vanity and the public's taste for acid rhetoric, it is likely that Floquet's treatment of Boulanger was at least as effective as the creation of the *Société des droits de l'homme*. Boulanger had been sent to Parliament in the middle of April by the department of the Nord and, at the beginning of June, took what he thought was a suitable opportunity to reopen the question of the revision of the constitution. Floquet, with immense relish, delighted his majority with an ironical indictment of Boulanger's supposed ambitions, ending:

'But we must take heart. At your age, General Boulanger, Napoleon was dead, and you will never be more than the Siéyès of a still-born constitution.'[23]

At the *chansonniers*, where the reputedly pro-Boulangist Paulus now had most vocal rivals, Victor Meusy embroidered on Floquet's reflection:

'That France may forever acclaim you,
That we may put our fate in your hands,
For a start please give up the ghost, sir,
Napoleon at your age was dead.'[24]

A month later, on 12th July 1888, Floquet again brought his powers of invective to bear on the General, who had this time demanded a dissolution. Boulanger could not cope with this kind of treatment. He resigned his seat and challenged the Prime Minister to a duel. Floquet, with a feeling for panache that Ferry had certainly lacked, accepted. To the merriment not only of the Prime Minister's supporters, the General who was to have led the avenging armies against the ravishers of Alsace-Lorraine was ingloriously wounded by their unmilitary chief, and Boulangists throughout the country feared for his life until it was announced that he had managed to consume an orangeade. On 22nd July, Boulanger lost the Ardèche by-election.

Less and less was now heard of *revanche* in the Boulangist camp, except in the *Comité*'s popular propaganda, and more and more of the General's desire for resolute and honest government. Of course, the one did not exclude the other, and it was because many of his supporters – notably Déroulède – thought that the latter was neccessary for the successful completion of the former that they continued to further the General's cause. If one has to recognize that Gambetta also had held these views, one has still to admit that neither the retired President of the *Ligue des Patriotes* nor the retired commanding officer of the army corps at Clermont Ferrand was a Gambetta. When Parliament returned from its summer vacation the stress was all on probity, and it was in the ordinary run of Boulangist business that it could be carried on by a socialist deputy from Nîmes, Gilly, who accused the budget commission of having a dozen Wilsons on it. But soon no mere invective was required. In November 1888 the news began to trickle through that the many investors in the Panama Canal were likely to lose their money, and that a number of prominent republican politicians had shady connections with the failure of the project. It was all still very vague, but very welcome to the Boulangists. Having already made good his failure in the Ardèche department by the successes on 19th August (Nord, Charente-Inférieure, Somme), Boulanger now felt that he could accept Clemenceau's challenge to present himself in a genuinely republican constituency.

On 27th January 1889, he stood in the Seine department. It must be recognized that this was certainly an act of courage, for the Paris region (which is what the constituency amounts to) still had a reputation for left-wing republicanism, and most politicians of that colour had by now disavowed him. The question was whether the electors would dissociate themselves from that verdict. Rochefort's *Intransigeant*, *La Presse* (Laguerre), *La Jeune République* (Labruyère) and the *Cocarde*, the publication of prints and songs, the many Boulangist speeches and banquets, all these combined to create a propaganda effort of a magnitude that Zévaès likens to that which led Louis Napoleon to the Presidency in 1848.[25]

The Seine election was to be the climax of the Boulangist period. It developed into the most exacting trial of strength between the supporters and the adversaries of the General. His opponents decided to put up a single candidate, Jacques. On his own side, the monarchist *Soleil* wrote demurely that it was possible that many monarchists would vote for Boulanger, and the Orleanists swallowed the fact that the General was supported by Rochefort and at length decided to vote for him too. If the monarchists lacked enthusiasm in supporting him, it was Boulanger's own ambiguous attitude towards them that was largely responsible. Although he had talked to most of their important representatives – he had seen Jerome Napoleon in Switzerland as early as January 1888 – he seems to have expressed no clear views on the question of the restoration. Still, they did support him. Only the Guesdists and Blanquists put up their own candidate, despite all this concentration, wishing a plague on both bourgeois houses. 'Workers of Paris,' declared Guesde, 'the brass hat Boulanger and

65

the boss Jacques both belong to the same hostile class which has, for over half a century, made the lot of ours, of proletarian France, one of hunger and bullets.'[26] The General summed up adequately enough what the election was really about in his first poster:

> 'I was overthrown as a minister under the pretext that I meant war, and I am being assailed now as a candidate under the pretext that I mean dictatorship.'[27]

While the votes were being counted, Boulanger and his chief supporters, including Déroulède, awaited the results at the restaurant Durand. But thousands of ordinary people were gathering all around it, most of them to acclaim Boulanger, presumably whether he won or not. The police, whose job it was to control the crowds, the army, and the *garde républicaine* were a serious worry to the government, for their loyalty was uncertain. And the restaurant Durand was in the Place de la Madeleine, only just across the river from the Palais-Bourbon; not far from the Elysée. When the results became known the crowds became delirious; indeed, they must have exceeded even the most optimistic hopes of Boulanger himself. Of all the Paris arrondissements, only one (the Third) voted against the General, giving him altogether 244,070 votes against Jacques' 162,520 and Boulé's 16,766. Both inside and outside the restaurant the demand that Boulanger march on the Elysée rapidly gathered volume. The crowds were with him, the police was with him, the army was with him. Now was the moment to banish the chatterers from both the Elysée and the Palais-Bourbon, to give France honesty and forcefulness at the top.

But the General was not to be moved. His supporters inside and outside grew glummer and glummer as he piled objection upon objection. By midnight the enthusiasm of the crowds was spent, the disorder of his lieutenants unmistakable, the political fate of the General sealed. The ministers who had been on, and over, the verge of hysteria went home to sleep in peace. Their Republic was safe. Freycinet, then at the War Ministry, thought that 'legal scruples' had been responsible for Boulanger's refusal to act, for one can probably ignore the alternative, which was cowardice:

'If he had made his way to the Elysée at the head of the *Ligue des Patriotes*, followed by the mass of his supporters, who can say that he would not have swept away all obstacles?'[28]

The rest of the Boulangist story is, dramatically, an anti-climax. Although the movement continued, and the royalists showed an increasing interest in it, the momentum it had lost that night at the restaurant Durand was never regained. It even lost the initiative. When Floquet resigned (14th February 1889[29]), the second Tirard ministry included at the Interior Constans, whose cunning was to write the epitaph of Boulangism. He set to work within a few days of taking office. First, he dissolved and fined the *Ligue des Patriotes* on the pretext, which any government could have found any day, that the *Ligue* had issued a statement criticizing government action overseas. It is an indication of the *Ligue*'s level in 1889 that the offending statement deplored the shedding of Russian blood by the French at Sagalo (East Africa), where they apparently stopped a Russian gentleman (Atchinoff) from proceeding to Abyssinia to propagate the doctrines of the Russian Orthodox Church. At the time of its dissolution (6th April 1889) the movement claimed a membership of 240,000.

Constans then proceeded against the General himself. On 4th April, Parliament was asked to lift Boulanger's immunity and, on the 8th, the Senate heard of the decree asking him to appear before the *Haute Cour de Justice* four days later. But both these steps were unnecessary, as Constans probably knew. He had taken good care that Boulanger should not be in the dark about his intentions and, on 1st April, the putative saboteur of the bourgeois régime had duly crossed the border into Belgium. In August, Boulanger, Rochefort, and Dillon who had provided much of the money for the *Comité*, were sentenced to deportation to a fortress. By then all three were in Belgium.

The General Election of 22nd September 1889 hastened the end. While the opportunists and radicals again agreed not to split the republican vote, Boulanger's continued refusal to commit himself to a monarchist restoration lost the *Comité* much active right-wing support.[30] In fact, only forty-five overt Boulangists were returned, beside 165 other opponents of the régime. If one allows for the diversity of the social and economic views among the Boulangists, it is doubtful if the net result of the 1889 election was materially different from that of 1885, when the right obtained 201 seats. The right thus had every reason to be depressed. That the popular appeal of Boulanger, combined with the now notorious shortcomings of the opportunists, was unable to gain it even a modest increase in votes indicated to its most ardent supporters that its future must be bleak. The country had shown that it disliked the prospect of reactionary government, whether royalist or not, even more than the continuation of an opportunism that at last promised to reform itself in a radical alliance. The fact that the right in the Chamber now had Déroulède and Barrès sitting among it did little more than foreshadow the shape of things to come. There was going to be an attempt to give it a coherent doctrine, but no immediate promise of greater public support.

The Paris municipal elections in April 1890 confirmed the Boulangist débâcle. Its completeness will be seen in the difference between the results of the January 1889 by-election, in which Boulanger was elected in all but one of the arrondissements, and the municipal results not much more than a year later, when only two Boulangists were elected. The right saw the situation with some lucidity and decided that wisdom enjoined it to drop the reluctant dictator. 'General Boulanger will gradually disappear from the scene, and even the trace of his influence will be effaced,'[31] wrote the *Soleil*; and the *Gaulois* sneered: 'We hope he will find another glorious part to play in life, but we must admit that his mission has ended.'[32] The *Figaro* was more concise: 'The Boulangist comedy is over,'[33] it stated, and its conclusion was shared by the *Comité National* itself, which 'maintained intact its programme of French reconciliation and social reforms', but saw no point in 'troubling the country with temporarily sterile activities'.[34] But it was the *Autorité* of Cassagnac which put the aristocratic right's case against Boulanger with conclusive frankness: 'It is the fault of General Boulanger that we have not succeeded . . . And why? Because he meant only to act legally.'[35]

The two years that remained of his life were spent in continued exile. He still schemed and hoped, for a while, and now hated the ungrateful right so much that he turned to the extreme left for a love that was to be equally unrequited. Even his patriotism had gone sour. When Déroulède suggested that there would be a great resurgence of patriotic feeling if only he were to return to France to stand his trial, General Revanche threw him out of the house.

On 30th September 1891, he committed suicide on the grave of his mistress.

There is clearly a rich comic opera element in the Boulanger story. But if it is seen in proper perspective, the vain but hopelessly confused soldier who gave it its name may elicit some compassion. For over five years the most diverse but experienced politicians used the popularity which his rodomontades had won him, without any scruples, for their own ends. They courted him when they thought he might be of use, and dropped him when he could be of service no longer. If one is looking for the real villains in the anti-republican conspiracies, one will have to look beyond poor Boulboul.

But if one is looking for the real patriots – and it was after all as General Revanche that Boulanger first made a hit – one will have to look beyond the anti-republican conspirators. Clemenceau had stopped seeing Germans under every ministerial bed by 1885, and his early delight at the General's sabre-rattling was purely atavistic. Thereafter he was no more patriotic than a good many opportunists. The patriotism of the right is best characterized by its plea to Grévy to save peace at any price during the Schnaebelé affair, despite the electoral use it made of the usual patriotic slogans. During the 1889 election campaign there was barely a mention of the existence of Germany, still less of *revanche*. If a left-wing Boulangist like Castelin, at Laon, was prepared to rehash the story that Boulanger and the *Ligue* had been sacrificed to the wrath of Bismarck,[36] the future prophet of nationalism, Barrès did not care to trouble his electors at Nancy with any reference to Germany whatever.[37] In this he showed the same discretion as the majority of his allies on the right. Only a professional patriot like Déroulède kept the anti-German pot boiling between elections, but the quality of that brew has already been sampled.

CHAPTER FOUR

PATRIOTISM MOVES RIGHT

THERE WERE two main forms of patriotism after 1870; a strong form, demanding *revanche* at the earliest possible moment, and a weak form, enjoining dignified resistance to further German bully-ing, without however excluding the eventual recovery of Alsace-Lorraine by some means, usually unspecified. It has been seen that both forms ceased being of major political importance by 1889. As it became clear that German power had increased rather than decreased since Sedan, and that France had made no correspond-ing advances herself, realistic 'strong' patriots like Gambetta, and even more emotional ones like Déroulède, lost much of their conviction, if not their fervour. On the other hand, as Bismarck's attitude became less menacing in the eighties, those who repre-sented the weaker form of patriotism needed to give ever less evidence of it; the political difficulties at home could, therefore, claim all their attention. Thus national prudence and political self-interest jointly encouraged patriotic discretion.

At this point a new generation appears on the political scene. It had witnessed the collapse of republican dreams in the social and political miasma of the eighties, and the diminution of France that was its consequence. It opposed youth, energy, and idealism to the decrepitude, complacency, and cynicism of those in power. It blamed the materialistic democracy for the decline, and ad-vocated government by an élite, animated by spiritual ideals, so that the decline could be reversed. It owed much of its inspiration to Taine and Renan.

I Taine

Born in 1828, Taine devoted his adult years, until 1870, to scholarly, literary, historical and philosophical criticism, his liberal views having cut short his career as a school-teacher under the Second Empire. He was anti-romantic and, though a positivist, was sufficiently critical to recognize and condemn the *a priori* elements in Comte's doctrines. In fact, Taine thought of himself as a detached observer of mankind; there was little else that an intelligent and honest liberal could be under Napoleon III, if he wanted to remain unmolested.

In 1871, however, he was astonished at the depth of feeling the reverses of his country aroused in him: 'Grief and anxiety give me a fever . . . My heart has stopped beating in my breast . . . My soul is like an open wound.'[1] Lest this kind of reaction be taken too much for granted in a French intellectual at this time, it should be recalled that Renouvier, for example, saw fit during these same fateful months to affirm that he would rather be ruled by a Prussian general than by a committee of the National Assembly. Taine, now forty-two, felt that he must volunteer for the army, but was rejected on medical grounds. In common with other liberals, notably Renan, Taine had for a while accepted Madame de Staël's glowing account of German civilization. But in his case, the enthusiasm did not last long. Jules Simon, Taine's philosophy tutor in his last year at the *École Normale*, noted with satisfaction that the Hegelian influence on his pupil was waning. If, before 1870, he retained a rather awesome admiration for the elemental character of the Germans, it is also true that he recognized its dangers earlier than most of his countrymen. He observed that, 'there is no younger race. This implies both good and evil.'[2]

Unable to serve militarily, Taine put his pen to the service of his country. In two letters to *The Times* he warned that Prussian-led armies would soon constitute a danger also to the British. Shortly the Germans were to read his leaflets, the *Temps* published his articles on universal suffrage and methods of voting, the *Journal des Débats* carried a letter from him suggesting ways of raising money more quickly to pay the indemnity that would send the Germans back home. It was in this spirit of patriotic devotion that he assisted in the creation of the *École des Sciences Politiques*, with the conviction that what France needed was a scientific study of political institutions and political ideas. It was in the same spirit that he himself set to work on his *Origines de la France contemporaine*, to find out how 1870 could have happened to a country like his, and to see what lessons French history held for France's future regeneration.

'If the government which the future holds in store for us is not too anti-liberal, I think that the duty of all of us is to write articles, make speeches, etc., instructive and disagreeable, to expose and confess publicly our errors, to show how our faults caused our reverses, to propagate the knowledge of foreign languages, tactics, of other nations and of history, to persuade people that they have to work, obey, live properly, and not be too demanding when it comes to happiness.'[3]

Taine's diagnosis of the reasons for the decline of France is that, since the eighteenth century, the French had worshipped false gods. Since the enlightenment, he asserts, the basic credo of intelligent Frenchmen had been the ultimate sanctity of the individual and the ultimate wisdom of the individual. Like Descartes, the aspiring proletarian, the ambitious bourgeois, the dilettante aristocrat, all felt entitled – as a birthright – to reject all they had ever learned from society and, putting their faith in the findings of their own reason, to live in accordance with its precepts alone. And, as the scientists believed in the uniformity of nature, so these men and women believed in the ultimate uniformity of the precepts of all individual reasons. That this uniformity proved somewhat elusive dismayed no one, since with education and scientific progress the perfect life of human concord was, in their view, inevitable. They competed with each other in the elaboration of ambitious plans for the reorganization of society, in speeding up the liquidation of past errors, which had made life a burden when it ought to have been beautiful and entirely satisfying. With holy fervour, a multitude of reforming zealots, animated by vastly diverse ambitions, threw themselves into the Revolution of 1789. The convulsions of those days, according to Taine, continued to be felt throughout the nineteenth century, and their latest consequence was the defeat of 1870. Taine is quite certain that the political and social results of this faith in human reason are as wholly deplorable as its premises are tragically false. Reason, unaided by empirical reference, can indeed tell us about the logically possible, but not about the empirically feasible; it can tell us about contradictions in our reasoning, not which part of the contradictions it might be wise to shed. Man neither lives nor reasons in a vacuum, he exists in a context, and the context helps to fashion him to such a degree that if he tries to alter it too drastically his life finds itself deprived of meaning, he is left without roots, and he dies.

But when a whole nation seeks to guide its destiny in accordance with such precepts, when it disavows its past and foolishly hopes to build on the foundations of abstract reasoning alone, then the whole nation is doomed. And this was the danger France was running in the 1870s:

> 'A people, on being consulted, may, indeed, tell the form of government it likes, but not the form it needs; this is possible only through experience; time is required to ascertain if the political dwelling is convenient, durable, proof against inclemencies, suited to the occupant's habits, pursuits, character, peculiarities and caprices. Now, as proof of this, we have never been content with our own; within eighty years we have pulled it down thirteen times in order to rebuild it, and this we have done in vain, not having yet found one that suits us.'[4]

Without the sardonic bitterness of de Maistre, moved, in fact, more by sorrow than by anger, Taine nevertheless tries to point the same moral. Nations that attempt to give themselves constitutions present, in his view, the same silly spectacle as do adolescents who petulantly clamour for total liberty: the operation may be successful, but the patient will surely come to a sticky end:

> 'The point is to *discover* it, if it exists, and not to put it to the vote ... The social and political mould into which a nation may enter and *remain* is not subject to its will, but determined by its character and its past. It is essential that, even in its least traits, it should be shaped on the living traits to which it is applied; otherwise it will burst and fall to pieces.'[5]

A second major cause of the weakening of France is to be found in the rigorous centralization of her government and administration. The feeling of being an integral part of a community began to be lost, Taine argues, at the moment when the local leaders one knew, and whom one had been brought up to respect, were supplanted by emissaries of the centralized Paris government whom one did not know, and was often taught by erstwhile local leaders not to respect. And with this loss of feeling of belonging to a small intelligible community was lost the basis of real patriotism:

C*

'Under Henri IV courtiers remained at home; they had not entered into ruinous expenditure to belong to the court; favours were not then *due* to them as at the present day. . . . The court is the sepulchre of the nation.'[6]

This process began in earnest with the centralizing policies of Richelieu, was continued by Louis XIV, carried to absurd lengths by the Revolution and Napoleon, and adapted, without major change, by the Republic. Those who followed Taine will see in the apparent omnipotence of the state far more sinister threats, the least controversial of which is the danger to the nation as a whole of corruption or ineptitude among those in power.

But the full magnitude of the difficulties that Taine tried to face eludes one if one thinks of him merely as someone who opposed abstract constitutions, individualism, and the dissolving effects of centralized government. If these were the positive enemies of the future he hoped for, there was a more negative one of no smaller importance: cynicism. Nearly a century had, after all, elapsed since the Revolution, and in that century various social and political remedies had been tried and abandoned for lack of general acceptance; many more had been suggested and found hearers. After 1870, these diverse remedies continued to have their diverse advocates, and thus added to the difficulties of finding a real solution, not only because they provided *a priori* dissidents, but also because they had left behind them thousands of disillusioned men and women who had given up all hope or wish for social answers to social problems. The Church, discredited through its association with the Second Empire, failed as a rallying point, so that the religion of the majority of the French, for centuries the most important galvanizing social and political force, looked as dead as the monarchy. There remained the myth, inherent in cartesianism and loudly proclaimed in the century before and after the Revolution, that, through the inevitable progress of mankind in all spheres by means of the sciences, societies and the individuals composing them would reach perfection. We have seen in previous chapters what happened to these optimistic hopes at the hands of their self-appointed guardians. But the bourgeois politicians who gambled away the generous hopes of their constituents might have thought twice if the sciences, in which they and their predecessors had put their hopes, had managed to provide the answers promised by some of the headier optimists of the century. As it was, Boutroux was demonstrating what many had for long suspected: the contingency of scientific laws, the logical impossibility that from the scientific procedure of induction any universal proposition could ever follow and be shown to be true.[7] Thus, with science and religion both apparently unable to deliver the certainties demanded of them, with all the old political and social creeds impatiently discarded, with the Prussians menacingly poised on the doorstep, what was the bright republican now in power to do? He made what money he could how he could, and had a good time while he could. *Revanche* would wait, and was suicidal anyway, while the social problem, in Gambetta's often misquoted words, did not exist.

Admittedly, when Taine first conceived the *Origines*, the new politicians who were bent on ushering in the republican era did not present quite that spectacle. But the impact of Taine's influence was felt most strongly in the 1880s, when entrenched power had made the republicans cynically complacent always, and corrupt sometimes. It was then that, particularly among the intellectuals, the abstract character of the concepts that allegedly animated republican politicians was seriously challenged, and a return was demanded to the old, well-tried traditions. That this counter-revolutionary doctrine was often vague is beside the point; what matters is that, in many cases, it was put forward by people who were not simply disgruntled with the régime on personal grounds, but who genuinely believed – and who can blame them? – that French public life had reached the low water mark, and that drastic changes were needed to make it morally respectable and politically adult. While it will not be forgotten that an honest, militant republican like Gambetta had observed with ever growing gloom the deterioration of republican cohesion, morale and political morals, and had insistently advocated firm republican solutions to halt it, the young intellectuals of the 1880s, coming with a fresh mind to the problems of their time, were understandably less enthusiastic about a return to the pure milk of revolutionary doctrine, which had started with the guillotine, led to Waterloo, to almost a century of political trial and error, the Commune and, according to their new mentors, had brought about the ultimate catastrophe of 1870-1, and the fetid political atmosphere of a decade of republican government since then.

75

Taine's desire to find a solution to these problems was entirely disinterested. His contribution was that of an earnest scholar. And as a scholar he was above all an historical determinist. His writings on art, philosophy, history and politics are all attempts to account for what is being examined in deterministic terms – 'that everything, physiology, psychology, history can and must be considered from a deterministic point of view is certain.'[8] One consequence of this is his agreement with Tocqueville that 1789 did not mark a complete break with the past, a view so facilely held by many.

But just what positive solutions to the political problems of France this historical determinism entails is not very clear. There are moments when Taine writes like a radical determinist seeking to eliminate the concept of free will from sensible discourse. His often quoted *le vice et la vertu sont des produits comme le sucre et le vitriol* surely is an example of this. In that case, however, injunctions to the French to return to their old traditions would be as pointless as any others for, in a deterministic world, everything happens because it necessarily must. There would be no merit in what some call virtue, and no demerit in what some call vice. This, indeed, is the line taken by some of Taine's successors. But the fact that he reproached them for such conclusions suggests that his views were logically less rigorous than one might have thought. Bourget, for example, is taken to task for the rigid determinism of *Le Disciple* which, according to Taine, had done a disservice to both morality and science:

'Personally, in the *Origines de la France contemporaine*, I have always put the moral estimate next to the psychological explanation. In the description of the Jacobins, of Robespierre and Bonaparte, my preliminary analysis is always deterministic and my final conclusion rigorously justiciary.'[9]

And in a letter to Jules Lemaître, who had given his portrait of Napoleon[10] a somewhat tepid review, Taine explains the criterion by which he judges the moral worth of those whose determining psychological factors he had previously assessed:

'I have a criterion for the history of society, and I had and have now others for the history of art and science. There is one scale for evaluating philosophers and scientists, another for evaluating politicians and men of action; has the man one is analysing wanted, and known how, to diminish or at least not to increase the present and future sum of human suffering? In my view that is, so far as he is concerned, the basic question.'[11]

It seems, therefore, that the determinism of Taine is restricted to the non-moral sphere, in such a way that while matter cannot help being determined by will, will can help being determined by matter. Individual responsibility for actions can thus not be disavowed:

> 'Determinism and responsibility are not mutually exclusive; on the contrary. The most rigid and convinced moralists have been necessitarian determinists; not only Spinoza, Leibniz and other isolated great minds, but practising sects, the stoics for five hundred years, the calvinists and puritans since the Reformation.'[12]

From a logical point of view, this dualistic division of the universe is entirely arbitrary, since it is hardly possible to provide proofs for determinism or its converse, in any sphere. However, it reveals much about the character of its author. Taine had learnt to appreciate the value of scientific thinking, but had, at the same time, retained a great respect for the individual human being to whom he attributed an inalienable dignity. If the Commune left him a liberal rather than a democrat, his humanism sets him apart from many of those who claimed to have been inspired by his positivism. Maurras and Barrès are cases in point.

Taine's solution to the political problems of his country rests on the grand *a priori* assumption that there are three forces which shape the destiny of nations:

> 'We can affirm with certainty that the unknown acts towards which the current of the centuries leads us will be brought about and regulated entirely by the three primordial forces; that if these forces could be measured and calculated one could deduce from them, as from a formula, the properties of future civilization, and if, despite the obvious roughness of our notation and the fundamental inexactitude of our measurements, we want today to form some idea of our destinies, it is upon an examination of these forces that our forecasts must be founded. For, once we have enumerated them, we shall have given a complete account of all actively conditioning forces, and,

once we have considered race, environment and momentum, i.e. the internal spring, external pressure and the already present momentum, we shall have exhausted not only all actual causes but also all possible causes of change.'[13]

From the unproved, not to say unprovable, *race-milieu-moment* assumption about how nations are fashioned, Taine then draws the logically illegitimate conclusion that a nation's past ought to govern its future. The conclusion is illegitimate because, as Hume had shown a century earlier, from empirical facts no 'ought' follows logically if an enclave of free will is postulated, as it is in Taine. It may be thought expedient or sensible to consider past events in planning the future, but if there is free will – as Taine himself supposes – a decision about the future need not be rendered senseless merely because it failed to consider the past. Nevertheless, Taine insists that history must guide politics. Politics, he says, ought to be an application of history in the way medicine is an application of the natural sciences. In politics, however, remedies can only be partially successful, since one can influence the social constitution of a state no more easily than one can influence the physiological constitution of an individual.[14] Now, according to Taine, history shows that from the point of view of race, the French are naturally frivolous, fickle, excitable, quick-witted, argumentative. Moreover, their social and political environment has been conditioned by centuries of strong centralized government, and this has killed all sense of social and political responsibility. The result of this combination of racial and environmentally conditioned characteristics is that 'one street fight is sufficient to establish the Republic or to change the dynasty, one audacious raid to bring about a plebiscite that will proclaim the Empire. Through our revolutions the system remains the same: bureaucracy, universal and mechanical. Whatever the name of the new régime, everybody accepts or acclaims it as quickly as the preceding one, and it is just as fragile.'[15]

Taine makes no attempt to show how anything other than strong government could have made a nation out of the racial ingredients he enumerates. Indeed, had Taine not been a liberal, he might well have felt that the need for strong centralized government necessarily followed from such racial characteristics. But, as others were prepared to put up with only a *minimum de république*, so Taine was prepared to put up with only a *minimum de gouvernement*. 'Protection against brigands from within and without', that is the sole function of government according to Taine. In no case can it be true that a government's function is to promote a particular religion, or to acquire 'glory', or even to secure the happiness of the governed.[16]

> 'Hence the notion of the state: the aim that those associated in it have in mind is to have each member's will respected, insofar as it does not put restraint on that of someone else. The formula is: inviolability of each member's will, except when it violates another's.'[17]

Having eliminated as silly those who hoped to shape the destiny of France in the belief *qu'il suffisait de décréter pour faire*, and as unwise – if not immoral – those who tried to give France a strong centralized government, *produit de l'esprit classique*, Taine proposes government by an élite. The burden of his argument rests on the belief that 'the real starting point is that, in the true interest of the community, power ought to be in the hands of the most able and most honest'.[18]

> 'The present system of universal suffrage prevents many of these men from participating in political life from a sense of delicacy; they abhor the charlatanism of rabble democracy. If universal suffrage must stay, at least let it be as indirect as possible.'[19] Only in that way can good government be achieved.

It is difficult to see what the relationship between the alleged racial traits of the French, as revealed by Taine's reading of history, and the doctrine of liberal government by an élite might be. No doubt, a people which is 'frivolous, fickle, excitable, quick-witted, argumentative' requires the best politicians for its government. But so does any other people. The frequency with which the French have had recourse to 'strong' government, before and since Taine, might suggest to those as mindful of historical lessons as Taine wants us to be that such government is the only one capable of governing France effectively. It is, indeed, hard to resist the conclusion that Taine advocates liberal government by an élite simply from personal preference, in which case one would find it no easier to decide why such a conclusion should be honoured with being accounted scientific, as being any less *a priori* than those Taine dismisses as absurd precisely because they are *a priori*.

In fact, although Taine had begun the *Origines* with high hopes for the regeneration of France, his despair grew *pari passu* with the progress of the work. He seemed to recognize that liberalism did not, after all, provide the answer, yet strong government he continued to abhor. As he prepared the last volume, he wrote:

> 'There only remains for me to expound and explain the social aspects of the family in France, the family as the product of the Civil Code and the other institutions of the Consulate and Empire. This final study, if I can write it, will have an even sadder effect than the earlier ones . . . I was probably wrong, twenty years ago, to undertake this series of researches; they darken my old age and I feel more and more that, from a practical point of view, they are useless. A fast and powerful current carries us away. What is the use of writing a thesis about the depth and speed of the current.'[20]

He did not live to complete the work. His notes suggest that he intended to stress particularly the dispersal of the population of France, that twenty-six million lived in the country and only ten million in urban areas, and the encouragement this gave to individualistic tendencies.[21] France, he concluded, was destined to become a second-rate power, unable, through her lack of unity, to withstand any serious internal or external challenge. For a man who had devoted the last twenty years of his life to the search for a means to restore France to her former greatness, this was indeed a lamentable end. He died in 1893.

II *Renan*

Renan remains an enigma to his reader, as long as he assumes that a man of Renan's renown cannot really have been guilty of the basic contradictions apparently contained in his writings. But he was. The limpidity of his style is every bit as limpid as it seems. The contradictions it so elegantly exhibits are of the very essence of their author. The reader who wants to understand Renan must have the courage to believe his eyes. Rationalist expectations of logical coherence have to give way to the realization that the author is of interest for psychological, not logical, reasons. He represents a state of mind, rather more subtle than that of Taine, which was lucid enough to recognize the logical vanity of all but the most tentative affirmations about anything, and yet was too weak to prevent itself from suffering from this lack of certainty; so much so, that it often passionately canvassed the merits of some particular doctrine, only to relapse again, exhausted, into a resentful scepticism, once the logical lunacy of the escapade had become clear.

Ernest Renan was born at Tréguier, in Brittany, in 1823. While still at the church school in his native village he felt an urge to enter the ministry, and when his sister, Henriette, moved to Paris, she succeeded in interesting the abbé Dupanloup in her brother's career. At fifteen Renan obtained a bursary at Dupanloup's seminary in Paris. His ability was obvious to all who met him, and his entry to the renowned seminary of Saint-Sulpice in 1841 gave him all the chances he might have needed for a life of distinguished service in the church. But by 1845 he was convinced that he could not sincerely enter the catholic priesthood. After a period of spiritual turmoil, he left Saint-Sulpice to earn his living as a schoolmaster. He wanted above all to satisfy his considerable intellectual curiosity, and he felt that the influence of the church would have too inhibiting an effect. The origins of Christianity were his most important interest and, after obtaining his doctorate in 1852, he worked on the *Histoire des Origines du Christianisme*, which became his chief title to fame. *La vie de Jésus* is the most popular part of the long history. But the unwontedly natural treatment of the subject cost him his Chair of Semitic Languages at the Collège de France in 1864, after he had held it for only two years.

By now, Renan was sufficiently well known to be able to earn his living by his pen. Several of his articles had been collected in the *Essais de Morale et de Critique* (1859), others appeared in *Questions contemporaines* (1868). When the Empire collapsed in 1870 the republicans gave him back his Chair. Although the political upheavals of the seventies and eighties made him more conscious of public affairs than he had been before, it is difficult to attribute to him the same depth of patriotic feeling that one finds in Taine. Indeed, where Taine spent the last two decades of his life probing France's history for an answer to her political plight and was driven to deep despair over what he found, Renan continued his *Origines du Christianisme* and, on its completion, began a three-volume work on *L'Histoire d'Israël* (1887-91). It is true that he does concern himself with political questions, for example in his *Drames Philosophiques* (1888) and in the *Réforme intellectuelle et morale de la France* (1871). But politics never seem to have been of paramount importance to him, even if one recalls that he presented himself as a parliamentary candidate on two occasions, once in 1869 and again in 1878.

Renan's doubts about the efficacy of reason in the search for true statements about the world began early:

> 'Some doubts have occurred to me about the use of reason . . . You start from a point of view . . . and base on it a series of logical propositions. Rousseau, for example. The result is absurd . . .'[22]

This was in 1846. Although he is here concerned with the use of reason in politics, he adopted the same attitude towards the rationalist approach in all realms. In the late eighties, towards the end of his life, the scepticism remained:

> 'What is the end of mankind[?] Is it the well-being of the individuals who compose it? Is it the achievement of certain abstract, objective ends? . . . Everyone replies according to his moral temperament, and that is enough.[23] – Who knows whether real intelligence does not demand the refusal to come to conclusions?'[24]

Dialogue, he felt, was the most appropriate literary form for the expression of abstract ideas:
> '[Ideas] of that kind must not be directly denied, nor directly affirmed; [their truth] cannot be demonstrated. What one can do is to present their various aspects, showing their strength, weakness, necessity and equivalents.'[25]

Even where he appears at his most affirmative, he alleges that he is merely contemplating possibilities. When Mazzini reproached him for the reactionary character of the *Réforme Intellectuelle et Morale de la France*, Renan objected that the work did not contain his actual opinions.[26] What tends to make Renan tiresome is the appearance of intellectual dishonesty he thus creates: the pungent, often persuasive, view, disavowed as soon as it is challenged. But this seeming fluidity is the result of the interaction of the two, mutually hostile, sides of his temperament; the cautious sceptic seeking to redeem the rash heresiarch. It is the proof that, in the final analysis, Renan remains a sceptic.

Like Hume, however, Renan recognized that if reason leads to scepticism, then – for practical purposes – we shall have to entrust ourselves to some other faculty. Living entails making decisions, and decisions cannot be based on a refusal to come to conclusions.

'Not seeing too much is the necessary condition for the forceful use of the human faculties.'[27]

'The wise man is he who sees that all is imagery, prejudice, symbol, and that imagery, prejudice, and symbol are necessary, useful and true.'[28]

'The dead planets are perhaps those where criticism has killed the tricks of nature, and I sometimes think that if everyone came to our [sceptical] philosophical conclusions, the world would come to a stop.'[29]

This belief leads Renan to admire displays of enthusiasm, to postulate value in any act, provided only that it was an energetic affirmation, no matter of what. In this extreme reaction from scepticism, we recognize the ancestor of Gide's Lafcadio. Indeed, like many a desk-bound intellectual, Renan finds the thought of action so attractive that he is prepared to make the intensity of energy displayed in action the criterion of the value of the action as well as of whatever idea it was meant to serve. He thus echoes writers as disparate as de Maistre, Stendhal and Nietzsche:

'When one risks one's head for one's ideas, only those who are God-intoxicated, men carried away by a powerful conviction, are prepared to come forward. In the past, nine out of ten innovators were violently silenced but the tenth was well and truly original . . . the bill-hook which cuts out the weak branches merely gives the others greater strength.'[30]

The bourgeois, 'all shrivelled up at the back of his shop',[31] is for Renan an even sorrier sight than the sceptic who suspends judgment. The prudent refusal of the former to glory in disinterested displays of enthusiasm is much meaner than the intellectual's aversion to being duped:

'Ah, how pale and profane is life in France! People think they are in the world for business, to build houses; and the houses have square windows, are themselves square. I want houses to be like churches, life considered as something holy, and that damned profane attitude abandoned which makes people laugh, play cards, smoke; that everything be considered holy. How beautiful life would be then!'[32]

In these idealistic, irrational *Schwärmereien*, Renan sees himself as the true son of a Breton ancestry:

'The characteristic trait of the Breton race, at all levels, is its idealism, the pursuit of a moral or intellectual aim, often mistaken, always disinterested . . . Any career involving self-interest would have found me a nonentity, clumsy, less than mediocre.'[33]

Renan, Alphonse Daudet sums up admirably, is a deconsecrated cathedral.[34] A sceptical but fervent aesthete, he enthuses from the limits of reason to the limits of unreason. But however elegantly he moves between these two extremes, his scepticism always claims him in the end.

Renan's writings on history and politics are shot through with the basic contradictions that have been noticed in his intellectual make-up. His scepticism accounts for his distrust of change, and his idealism for his utopian dreams. Either, but not both, could be developed with some semblance of logical consistency; but neither, alone, represents the whole psychological complex that was Renan.

In politics, if he bothers with it at all, the consistent sceptic is an apologist for the *status quo*. That the world is what it is is undeniable, but he would consider it logically improper and politically unwise to try to change it in accordance with doctrines whose validity must be dubious. He knows all about the inadequacies of induction, and the results of deductions from *a priori* ideas he takes as no more than amusing diversions, like crossword puzzles; after all, that is why he is a sceptic.

Renan admits:

'I am essentially a legitimist. I was born to serve faithfully, and with all the devotion of which I am capable, a dynasty or constitution derived from uncontested authority.'[35]

Although these sentiments are equally explicable in terms of his

Breton ideal of disinterested service, they are clearly prompted by the desire to perpetuate the *status quo*; 'The revolutions,' he adds, 'have made my task very difficult.' He makes the same point when he shows the revolutionaries the implications of their acts:

> 'Whoever lives by the sword will perish by the sword. If the guns which were aimed at M Sauzet and the Duchess of Orléans on 24th February 1848 were innocent, then the bayonets which invaded the Chamber on 2nd December 1851 were not guilty.'[36]

Only the *status quo* is certain, tampering with it is likely to be self-defeating.

But in a dynamic society, like the French in the post-revolutionary period, the defence of the *status quo* had to become either the defence of lost causes, or the defence of the fait accompli. For the sceptic, the propagation of lost causes occupies the same logical position as the propagation of revolutionary ideals. Both seek to promote a state of affairs different from that which actually prevails, and therefore seek to supplant the certain with the necessarily uncertain. In these circumstances, Renan logically became the apologist of the fait accompli, rather than of a (non-existent) persisting *status quo*. Thus, in 1852, he swore allegiance to Napoleon III simply because the Emperor had been successful. His acceptance of the Third Republic is to be accounted for in the same way, for he had even less admiration for bourgeois democracy then for the fumbling dictatorship of Napoleon III. Finally, his warning against Boulangism, because 'it would be the most horrible adventure experienced for centuries',[37] is as typical of the sceptical position as the acceptance of Boulangism would have been, had it been successful.

But the defence of the fait accompli does not prevent the sceptic from interesting himself in the causes that have brought it about. Indeed, while Renan considers abstract conjecture about future bliss a waste of time, and actual attempts to promote it logically and politically inept, the study of history, which allows us to understand the present, is for him the only worthwhile scientific pursuit. 'History is the necessary form of the science of all that is Becoming.'[38] This view of history is on all fours with the vogue of philology in Germany and France in the nineteenth century, during which the study of the history of languages was equated

85

with the science of language, and is not necessarily connected with the optimistic Hegelian twist that makes the past a guide to the future.

Renan's account of the origins of historical events bears out his belief that he owes such positive views as he has largely to Germany:

> 'I . . . owe to Germany all that I prize most: my philosophy, I could almost say my religion. I was at the seminary at Saint-Sulpice around 1843, when I became acquainted with the Germany of Goethe and Herder.'[39]

Like many French liberals, Renan, prior to 1870, had seen Germany as the leader of European enlightenment, as the country that had given birth to the Reformation and had courageously perpetuated its ideas in the face of universal reaction:

> 'Germany has made the most important revolution in modern times: the Reformation. Moreover, during the last century, Germany has produced the most beautiful intellectual developments there have ever been.'[49]

It was this admiration for the intellectual achievements on the other side of the Rhine that had moved successive generations of French liberals to support the cause of German unification, particularly when they found their own country so manifestly a prey to counter-revolutionary tendencies of all kinds.

It was an admiration that died hard. Even in 1879 Renan had not abandoned his desire for Franco-German intellectual collaboration.[41] There is no reason to doubt the accuracy of the Goncourts, when they record Renan's anti-French outburst even on the morrow of Sedan:

> 'Tuesday, 6th September 1870 . . . Berthelot continues his distressing revelations, at the end of which I cry out: – so, everything is finished; the only thing left for us is to bring up a generation dedicated to revenge. – "No, no!" shouts Renan, who had got up, redfaced, "not revenge; let France perish, let the *patrie* perish. There is the kingdom of duty, of reason, which is above these things".'

One can see why Renan should want to contest the authenticity of this report; it must have been rather embarrassing in

1890 when the Journals appeared. But similar sentiments were already expressed in the *Cahiers de Jeunesse*:

> 'I should sell France for the sake of obtaining a truth that would advance philosophy . . . Let the cossacks come, so long as they leave me the libraries, thinkers, academies . . . I shall increase my worth from within; what does it matter to me what pride attaches to the *name* of France or cossack.'[42]

What Herder, in particular, had taught Renan was to look on historical events as expressions of rational man in the process of self-realization. Man is conceived as developing in accordance with principles inherent in him, and is therefore not to be thought of as indebted for his development to any outside source. Inasmuch as these principles are rational they are intelligible, and it is the job of the scholar to discover the nature of these principles. The egocentric aspect of the Reformation, as well as of liberalism, is obvious in this doctrine. Hegel, on the other hand, 'the founder of the philosophy of history',[43] helped to provide Renan with a quasi-moral apologia for any given event, or fait accompli, since the rational principles said to preside over human development must equate each actual stage of this development with the rational. Thus, what is must be rational, and what is rational is assumed to be right.

The shortcomings of this doctrine are not difficult to find. A fait accompli is not necessarily unambiguous. 1871, for example. Alsace-Lorraine had been severed from France by a victorious Germany, but the majority of the inhabitants of these provinces did not want to be part of the Reich. Were the French to reconcile themselves to the loss, or heed the sentiments of their erstwhile countrymen? What did the cult of the fait accompli enjoin them to do? For Hegel, indeed, there would be no problem, since he identified the real with the physically triumphant. But it is one thing to subscribe to the view that what is happening now was latent in the past, and quite another thing to say that the only thing of significance that happens is physical. Renan, in contrast to Hegelian doctrine, considered that the wishes of the inhabitants of Alsace-Lorraine were the important aspect of 1871, and thereby exhibited the fundamental inadequacy of the concept of the fait accompli as an historical and political datum.

The events of 1870-1 led Renan to examine the question 'What is a Nation' in a famous lecture at the Sorbonne (1882):

'I have weighed each word with the greatest care. It is my profession of faith in human affairs, and when modern civilization has collapsed as a result of the fatal ambiguity of words like *nation, nationality, race*, I should like those twenty pages to be remembered.'[44]

His argument is simple, and logically consistent with his endorsement of the liberal ideals immanent, according to him, in the Reformation and the 'best' German thought since. A nation, he argues, is a sum of individuals who freely choose to live together. In the preface of 1887, he adds that 'Switzerland is perhaps the most legitimately composed European nation.'[45] But he recognizes that, on the whole, a 'nation, like an individual, is the culminating point of a long history of endeavour, sacrifices and devoted service . . . The Spartan song – "We are what you were, we shall be what you are" is in its simplicity the essence of the anthem of all *patries*.'[46] Yet the relation between tradition and nationality is, in the last resort, only a contingent one:

'Alsace is now a land Germanic in language and race, but, before being invaded by the Germanic race, Alsace was a Celtic land, like a part of Southern Germany. We do not deduce from that that Southern Germany must be French; but let no one come and argue that, as of ancient right, Metz and Luxembourg must be German. None can tell where this archaeology would stop . . . With that philosophy of history, the only rights in the world would be those of the orang-outang.'[47]

A common history or a common language or a common race therefore fail to be necessary determinants for a nation legitimately constituted. The free consent of individuals alone satisfies that condition. The implication is, of course, that the inhabitants of Alsace-Lorraine did not freely consent to belong to the Reich.

Renan, in fact, seldom exhibited the fatalistic detachment that could put up with the fait accompli as such, however it was understood. From the forties onward, his interest in historical determinants was motivated less by a desire to account for a fait accompli than by an endeavour to discover pointers to the future in the past. It is in the kind of future he postulates that the sceptic is seen to give way to the Celtic idealist.

There is an engaging eighteenth-century optimism about Renan's idealism, at least about its early forms. He held that the putative rationality of the universe not only accounted for the necessity of a present fait accompli, but also that its proper understanding would allow one to determine the shape of things to come. Reason, he thought, impatient of the material restraints put on its full unfolding, would finally shake itself free and reign supreme. Saint-Simon and Comte had made this view respectable in the nineteenth century, despite the events of the French Revolution, and Renan adapted it to meet his own requirements. For it was not reason as understood by Saint-Simon and Comte that he found attractive; theirs was largely at the service of materialistic ends. As he conceived it, reason was a kind of universal self-developing substance, like that of Spinoza or Hegel, whose goal was spiritual excellence. 'The end of mankind is not repose: it is intellectual and moral perfection.'[48] In this rational pantheistic machine, the individual is a mere cog:

> 'Something is in the process of organizing itself at our expense, we are the plaything of a superior egoism that pursues an end through us.'[49]

Thus, as in Taine, a rigorous determinism seems to be postulated. But, like most determinists, Renan is not content with determinism alone; he wants to be able to assure us that we are heading for a particular goal, and also encourage us to will its speedy attainment. To convince us of the accuracy of his teleological prediction, nothing could be more efficacious than a persuasive doctrine showing that the end is inevitable on deterministic grounds. To convince us of the excellence of certain moral views, nothing could be more persuasive than the doctrine that they accord with the inevitable ends of the universe. But what has to be shown, first, is that in a system in which the ends are thus determined, the means are open to free choice. They clearly cannot be, since the ends are said to be deducible from past and present data. Free will – in the strict sense – could not be compatible with such a degree of predictability. Consequently, statements asserting that 'the end of mankind, and therefore the aim the politician must pursue, is the realization of the highest possible human culture'[50] are an unhappy combination of the logically acceptable and the logically unacceptable. Like everyone else, the politician will be compelled to act in terms of the deductive logic of the system. Exhortations are pointless; except as further manifestations of the system.

Renan's ideal of moral and intellectual perfection leads him, after 1848 – and decidedly after the Commune – to denigrate democracy. In the early forties he still hoped that the hitherto neglected masses could be won over to reason, as he understood it. But this hope soon left him:

'The contemptible democratic system seems even destined to bring about the extinction of all complex culture and discipline.'[51]

'All consciences are sacred, but they are not equal ... Animals, too, have their rights. Has the Australian savage the rights of man or those of the animal?'[52]

And he concludes: 'All civilization is the work of aristocrats.'[53] Materialism, whether proletarian or bourgeois, he abhors as the enemy of all he wants to promote,

'for the end of humanity is not that the individual should live in comfort, but that . . . perfection should become real . . . Our petty system of bourgeois government, aspiring mainly to guarantee the rights and procure the well-being of all, is conceived from the point of view of the individual and has produced nothing great. Would Louis XIV have built Versailles, if he had had to contend with crabbed deputies wanting to cut down his budgets?'[54]

The pursuit of perfection must be ruthless, the weaker necessarily ministering to the needs of the more advanced, 'to the glory of God'.[55] The result would be most poetic: 'a form of slavery, experienced and suffered with delicacy and resignation.'[56]

The cultural élite are therefore the legitimate rulers. This reign of an oligarchy would not be odious, for its power would not serve either private or class interests 'but those of reason . . . Whoever is sacrificed to ideal ends has no right to complain, and his fate, in the eyes of the infinite, is worthy of envy.'[57] Indeed, Renan, in a Nietzschean dream, looks forward to the time when his élite can be improved by artificial means:

'A widespread application of physiological discoveries and of the principle of selection could bring about the creation of a superior race, whose rights to govern will not merely derive from its science, but from the very superiority of its blood, its brain, its sensibility. It would consist of a kind of Gods . . . It is up to science to continue the job where nature has left it.'[58]

Once these superlative creatures have succeeded in translating the rationalist dream into actual fact, the universe will be an harmonious, perfect organism. Then 'the whole of living nature would produce one central life, a great anthem emanating from milliards of voices, as an animal results from milliards of cells . . . That will be science, that will be spirit.'[59]

From the super-heights of Renan's consummated pantheism, the French political scene did not look impressive. Moral and intellectual perfection was not the most conspicuous ideal of the nineteenth century. Instead, democratic materialism was in the ascendant, and its rapid progress must precipitate the decline of all that was not selfish. For Renan, this was the result of many centuries of struggle between the two influences that shaped the history of France, the Germanic and the Roman. Culminating, in recent times, in 1789, this struggle was between the *a priorist* centralizing tradition of Rome, and the empirical individualistic tradition of the Germans. What had so lamentably affected French life since 1789 was that the Revolution marked the triumph of the Roman element.

Renan could admire the sheer audacity and energy of the revolutionaries:

'The French Revolution is the first attempt by mankind to take up its own reins and the direction of its own affairs. What has to be noted is the incomparable audacity, the marvellous and bold attempt to reform the world according to reason, to attack all prejudice, blind custom, apparently irrational behaviour, and to put in its place a system worked out like a formula, put together like an artificial machine.'[60]

But the appreciation is very much tempered by his disdain for the ideas of the revolutionaries, as well as for those who benefited from them. 'Jealousy is the sum of the moral theory of these supposed founders of our laws. But jealousy is the basis of equality, not of liberty.'[61]

One must not make too much of Renan's defence of liberty. The liberty he wanted to safeguard was that of the intellectual, not that of universal suffrage. It was this, and the prestige of the ideals in favour of which Renan proposed to exercise it, that 1789 and its aftermath had sought to destroy. The nineteenth century, to the great misfortune of France, had produced no one capable of reversing her spiritual decline. The ineptitude of kings and the nobility after 1815, the shameless materialism of the July monarchy[62] and the Second Empire,[63] had failed to give France a chance to recover from the prosy hideousness of the Revolution:

'The surest sign of a decline of a society is in its indifference to noble causes, as a result of which the great political questions appear secondary to industrial and administrative questions.[64]

The war of 1870 was the direct result of the cult of self-interest, of 'a deplorable political régime which made the existence of a nation dependent on the presumptuous bragging of narrow-minded soldiers, on the spite and injured vanity of light-weight diplomats.[65] – A nation that has fulfilled its programme and achieved equality cannot fight a young people that is full of illusions.'[66] It was therefore the Roman revolution of 1789 which led to the Germanic victory of 1870.

Nevertheless, Renan's patriotism was aroused by the defeat. 'Everyone now feels anxious and lost. Our friend Renan is among the most despairing.'[67] This explains his letter to Berthelot, in which he exhorts him not to go to England: 'The more unhappy our country, the more loth we must be to leave her.'[68] It may also explain his plaintive defence of France in his maiden speech to the Académie Française:

'When a nation, as a result of what it takes to be its earnestness and its application, has produced what we have produced with our frivolity: writers superior to Pascal and Voltaire, scientific brains better than d'Alembert and Lavoisier, a nobility better brought up than ours in the seventeenth and eighteenth centuries, women more charming than those who smiled on our philosophy, an impetus more exceptional than our Revolution, a greater readiness to embrace noble fancies, more courage, more refined knowledge of the world, greater equanimity before death, in short, a more attractive and witty society than that of our fathers, only then shall we be conquered. That day has not yet arrived.'[69]

He even went so far as to suggest that France could one day avenge her defeat, as Prussia had now avenged Jena. 'Above all, let us be humble. It took Prussia sixty-three years to avenge Jena; let us take at least twenty to avenge Sedan.'[70]

But the remedies Renan prescribed for the regeneration of France took as little account of the political faits accomplis of the post-revolutionary period as his general political theory has been seen to do, and no more than those of Taine. The behaviour of the Germans in 1870-1, and the subsequent excesses of the Commune, had strengthened Renan's conviction that only intelligent and firm government by an élite could save France. The Germans were not the liberal crusaders he had imagined, nor were the French petty bourgeois and the workers the repositories of rational virtue he had hoped for in the forties; 1870 and 1871 had provided final evidence for both sad conclusions. On the one hand, 'see how naïve we were. The German nation we wished to welcome as a new personality in the concert of peoples was conceived by us in the image of what we had read, according to the principles laid down by Fichte and Kant . . . the enemy of old superstitions, having justice and the ideal for its symbol. What dreams we had.'[71] On the other hand, even before the Commune, he was confirmed in his distrust of the lower classes. Writing in the *Journal des Débats* in November, 1870, he noted that, 'at this moment, Lyon, Marseille, Bordeaux, are revolutionary communes, barely admitting to a federal link with Paris.'[72] The only answer was an immediate appeal to the few genuine aristocrats France had left:

'Now, let us save ourselves. A country can only save itself by acts of faith and confidence in the intelligence and virtue of a few citizens. Let the small number of real aristocrats which is still among you pull you out of the difficulties in which you find yourselves. Afterwards you can take your revenge on them by excluding them from your Chambers and your elective councils. At the present moment we must have men belonging to the élite of the spirit and of courage.'[73]

A little later, still nursing the hope that the naturally superior will triumph over the inferior he even exhorted the French to acquire colonies:

'A nation that does not colonize will irrevocably be a prey to socialism, to the war between rich and poor. The conquest of a country of an inferior race by a superior race, which sets itself up within it in order to govern it, is not in the least shocking . . . Nature has made a race of workers; that is the Chinese race . . . a race of farm-labourers, i.e. the Negro . . . a race of masters and soldiers, i.e. the European race.'[74]

Thus, an aristocratic imperialism is Renan's solution to the pro
lems raised by the 1870 defeat. Only someone as impervious to political realities as he could have advanced such a doctrine at such a time.

These views were, however, supplemented by others which endeared him more to the future masters of his country. The moral and intellectual weakness of France, he declared, was as much the fault of catholicism as of materialism:

'France has wished to remain catholic; she shows the results of this. Catholicism is too hieratic to give a people moral and intellectual nourishment; it encourages transcendental mysticism as well as ignorance. A pupil of the Jesuits will never make an officer that can be put against a Prussian officer.'[75]

Education has for too long been in the hands of the Church; 'in the struggle that has just ended . . . what we lacked was not courage but brains.'[76] – The time has come when Christianity must cease to be a dogma and become poetry.'[77] The Italian occupation of Rome and the excesses of ultramontanism had robbed catholicism of its prestige. The only hope for the catholics, as well as for France, lay in the separation of Church and State. This separation Renan had already advocated when he stood for Parliament in 1869, and was the one part of his programme that distinguished him from the rest of the liberals. He expected that separation would lead to the final dissolution of the Church.

Education must henceforth be scientific. It must be free but not obligatory. It must concentrate on depth rather than spread. Although Renan thought primary education vital as a weapon against fanaticism, he considers the discovery of general truths more important. 'A fanatical people is always a danger to science,'[78] but 'the important thing is not to glean here and there a few particular ideas', which is presumably all the elementary pupil is able to do, 'but to grasp the spirit which embraces everything'.[79]

Like Taine, he hoped for great things from intuition, though at least for the former it was not meant to supplant patient research. Renan was a member of two committees, in 1877 and 1893, that advised on the reorganization of education in France.

In his last years, political realities gradually made some impact on his views. The recognition that even the few aristocrats he had talked of in 1870 were difficult to find is enshrined in his dismal picture of French prospects under Henri V:

'It is beyond doubt that the reign of Henri V would be the reign of fanaticism and ineptitude. It is impossible to have any truck with it, directly or indirectly, whatever the dangers inherent in the Republic might be, and whatever risk there is that the Republic will bring back the Prince Imperial in a few years' time.'[80]

France was clearly saddled with a quasi-democratic régime; one could only make the best of it. Indeed, even if it looked very much like making a virtue of necessity, he professed that in some respects the Republic was better than a monarchy: 'The concessions one had to make to the Court, to Society, to the clergy, were worse than the little annoyances that democracy can cause.'[81] If such a system cannot now be much of a match for the Germans militarily, there was a good chance that its moral and intellectual sickness would in time infect the Germans too. 'France is surer to have her revenge through her faults than as a result of qualities she has never had.'[82] This is the reverse of Bismarck's argument that a divided Republic is better for Germany than a united monarchy, and was a view that Kaiser William II was later reluctantly to share with Renan.

Disappointing though these conclusions were for him, that he wanted to accept them with fairly good grace is shown in his Prayer to Athena, quoted by Poincaré.

'You whose basic dogma is that all goodness comes from the people . . . putting my faith in you, I shall resist my deadly counsellor, my scepticism, which makes me doubt in the people.'[83]

Even Athena, however, ultimately failed to make it with him. Welcoming Pasteur at the Académie Française, he showed that his general scepticism remained basically unaltered: 'That poor human conscience! What efforts it makes to understand the incomprehensible.'[84] His notorious remark to Déroulède showed him equally sceptical about the future of France: 'Young man, France is dying, don't disturb her last moments.'[85]

The young men of France however did not all heed Renan's sceptical conclusions:

> 'Let us admit that in the philosophy of Renan, compounded of urbanity, cleverness and caution, we are embarrassed, ill at ease, deprived of fresh air. Come on! Let us open the windows! "My kingdom for a horse!" exclaimed an Englishman in a tragedy. We say: "All of the little Breton edifice, that delicious little edifice, for a fancy".'[86]

The fancy Barrès had in mind was the triumphant resurgence of his country. Both 'Renan and Taine died doubting in the vitality of France. They thought that the coming generations would live on the shadow of a shadow, and would die of moral starvation . . . They despaired. This is a result of their over-indulgence in analyses and cold reasoning. Why did they not trust more in their hearts?'[87]

Despite these strictures, the aristocratic traditionalism of Taine and Renan exercised a direct and acknowledged influence on the founders of French nationalism in the nineties. They must be seen as the intellectual forbears of the anti-democrats who, until 1940, will profess to be rescuing the patriotic virtues from the political prostitutes of the left.

CHAPTER FIVE

BARRÈS, DREYFUS AND PATRIOTISM:
1889–1902

WHEN MAURICE BARRÈS arrived in Paris in 1882, at the age of twenty, he was just one of many young intellectuals whose life seemed devoid of meaning.

'Our morality, our religion, our national feeling have collapsed . . . While we wait for our masters to create new certainties for us, it is proper that we should hold on to the one reality we have: the Self.'[1]

Conceived as an oasis in the midst of a hostile desert, the Self was for him the only certainty on which to build a viable philosophy. It led him, for a start, into an egocentric hedonism. Thus, while ostensibly studying law after nine hateful years at boarding schools, Barrès spent his early period in Paris savouring the pleasures of emancipation. He was an only child, and his prosperous parents gave him the means to indulge his whims. He dressed like a dandy, spent his time in cafés, played at love, and pursued a growing ambition of literary fame by editing his own review, *Les Taches d'Encre*, and finding his way into the company of Edmond de Goncourt, the Daudets, Berthelot, Anatole France, Bourget, Maurras. Like many other rudderless intellectuals of the eighties, he was seduced by Boulangism. It provided a pretext for positive action. In 1889 he was elected Boulangist deputy for Nancy. His first novel, *Sous l'Oeil des Barbares*, had been published a year earlier and had found favour with Bourget. Barrès was launched.

Sous l'Oeil des Barbares, *Un Homme Libre* (1889) and *Le Jardin de Bérénice* (1891) present the transformation of Barrès' cult of the Self into a doctrine of national solidarity. 'They describe the moment when Philippe saw himself as an instance of something

97

immortal.'[2] Having found intolerable the spiritual isolation resulting from the extreme individualism of the first volume, its author postulated a common spiritual origin for all individuals in a kind of national collective unconscious.

> 'With sincere piety, he rediscovered his origins, and he glimpsed his future possibilities. By investigating the harmony that exists between his Self and groups of men, Philippe understood the Self's real meaning. He saw it as the effort of instinct to realize itself. He also recognized that it suffered pain from floundering about without tradition and entirely devoted to the work of one lifetime.'[3]

The Self is not lost in this collective unconscious. It renews itself and expands, nourished 'by the inexhaustible forces of humanity, of universal life'.[4] Barrès did not claim any great philosophical virtues for this doctrine.

> 'In these volumes, it was a question less of constructing a logical edifice than of giving a sincere description, by means of moving *tableaux*, of certain ways of feeling. That is not scholasticism, but life.'[5]

But emotional security and spiritual strength were not the only benefits Barrès allowed his characters to derive from their instinctively felt affinities with the collective unconscious. They were also impelled to energetic action. They were 'roused by what there is immortal in things', roused enough for one of them to exclaim that 'no fever will remain unknown to me', that 'we must proscribe sin, the sin that is tepidity, greyness, lack of fever';[6] 'dear modern life, so ill at ease in its hereditary formulae and prejudices, let us live it with ardour and, damn it, it will surely in the end yield up a morality and new duties.'[7] The energy he admired in the Boulangists, and whose alleged lack among the opportunist politicians had made him despise them, this energy was for him the result of an inner harmony between the spiritual values of the Boulangists and those of the collective unconscious of France. Heeding only their feelings, the Boulangists had broken through the wordy barriers of the official ideologists of the Third Republic. They had rediscovered the ancient virtues of their country.

It is not difficult to trace the influences that had helped to lead Barrès to his doctrines.

'If we want to define, in a few words, the attitude of M Maurice Barrès towards the two masters who mainly fashioned his thought, I think one could say with some justice that his evolution consisted in his detaching himself more and more from Renan to draw nearer to Taine.'[8]

We have seen Barrès regret the playful scepticism of Renan. If this did not prevent him from adopting, at least in his early writings, a tone every bit as playful and cynical as that often found in Renan, the obvious earnestness Barrès brought to bear on the problems that really exercised him made the solid Taine a much more acceptable source of inspiration. 'M Taine is our professor of psychology, the revered ancestor of the analytic writers.'[9] Bourget and de Vogüé were, like Barrès, among Taine's acknowledged disciples. They adapted the deterministic psychology he had preached to their various needs, ridding it, in Barrès' case, of the 'slight tarnish of protestantism'[10] that was the freedom of the will on which Taine had always insisted.

'M Taine like M Renan, like all the masters who have preceded us, believed in an independent reason that exists in each one of us, and which allows us to get at the truth. Here is a notion in which I, for my part, have passionately believed. The individual! His intelligence, his ability to grasp the laws of the universe! We shall have to think again! . . . The judgments and arguments we formulate depend on the environment in which we grew up. We are not masters of the thoughts that arise in us . . . There are ways of reacting which are common to all beings placed in the same environment. It is all automatic.'[11]

Thus developed, Taine's 'return to the tradition of men like Condillac and Cabanis, justified by a fruitful meditation on the *Ethics* of Spinoza and the *Logic* of Hegel'[12] became Barrès' doctrine concerning the roots of nationalism. He expected to grasp the character of a nation in a non-rational intuition that is of the same quality as the intuition by means of which Taine had hoped to grasp the character of artists and society, both intuitions allegedly springing from an analysis of the relevant empirical data.

It is as well that Barrès claimed no great logical virtues for all this. The doctrine is obviously circular. It interprets the empirically relevant as Renan had interpreted the empirical fait accompli, in accordance with the particular characteristics he wanted to be allowed to intuit. Otherwise why should his political enemies exhibit the real soul of France any less than his allies? There is too much emphasis in Barrès on the primacy of the empirical for such an arbitrary selection of the empirically relevant not to be damning. And, frankly, if Barrès was modest about the philosophical status of his doctrines in the early years, his later insistence that he wanted them to fill the ideological vacuum from which the right had suffered under Boulangism should make our criticism appear less dyspeptic.

For Barrès, then, 'thinking in solitude leads one to think in terms of solidarity',[13] and the solidarity was to be exhibited in terms of the best qualities of eternal France. That concepts like 'eternal France' were vague Barrès realized. He conceded that one could not sensibly speak of a French race which incarnated such qualities. 'Let us say it once and for all: it is inexact to speak in the strict sense of a French race. We are not a race but a nation.'[14] But this merely transfers the difficulty to the concept 'nation', and it was to take Barrès some time to work out such precise views as he was to have on that. What he was convinced of, however, was that the neo-Kantian mentors of the young Republic were wickedly misguided in wanting to wean men from their traditions in the name of abstract principles.

The collapse of Boulangism had left Barrès angry and frustrated. But the subsequent Machiavellian attitude of the catholic hierarchy he found no more beguiling. The fate of the General, and the crushing electoral defeat of his supporters, had convinced the Church that if it was to retain any political influence in France it would have to collaborate with forces that were politically more effective than its traditional authoritarian allies. It therefore asked catholics to accept the constitution of the Republic in order, so it said, to change its legislation. This *ralliement* of the Vatican, enshrined in the 1892 encyclical *Au milieu des Sollicitudes* of Leo XIII, disorganized the authoritarian opposition even more than its defeat in the 1889 elections. The heart-searching it caused among its members split forward-looking paternalists like Albert de Mun from ineffable reactionaries like the Comte d'Haussonville. Its

effect on humbler believers is mischievously depicted in Gide's
Les Caves du Vatican.[15]

But in the year of *Au milieu des Sollicitudes* the democratic republicans – opportunists and radicals – provided their disorganized
enemy with a different rallying cry of a more persuasive order.
Predicted at least since 1888, the collapse of the Panama Canal
project became a certainty in 1892. It was soon an open secret that
it was only because all sorts of politicians had been paid substantial
sums out of the subscriptions that were to keep the project going
that the inevitability of bankruptcy had not been admitted earlier.
After 1888, therefore, thousands of small investors had invested
their money in nothing more substantial than the silence of knowing politicians. To the cry of 'down with the thieves', popular
with the opposition since the Wilson scandal, the enemies of the
régime again went into battle. But there was a most important
difference between Wilson's reluctance to pay for his own postage
stamps and the frauds apparently involved in the failure of the
Canal. Grévy's son-in-law, despite his name, was some kind of
Frenchman, and he was hunted by the opposition chiefly because
he was closely associated with the opportunists. It was said that
the men behind Panama were not as French as they might have
been. They were alleged to be mainly Jews and cosmopolitans.
The anti-democrats' sense of French decency was outraged.
Honest, guileless Frenchmen of modest means had been systematically and cynically defrauded by people who were no more than
guests in their much-tried country. Drumont had been warning
the French since the eighties of the existence of Jewish conspiracies against them. His *La France Juive* had appeared in 1886.
In 1889 he had created the Anti-Semitic League. From 1892
onwards he was continuing to watch over French interests in his
newspaper *La Libre Parole*. It was hateful that France, brought
so low by her defeat, should have her foundations even further
undermined by ungrateful foreigners, aided and abetted by the
cupidity of some of her own children. Clemenceau, together with
a number of other prominent democratic republicans, was shown
to have benefited from the generosities of international financiers.
He was a traitor, like the rest of them. 'In this immoral period',
as Barrès calls it in *Leurs Figures* (1902), the *patrie* was therefore
made even more exclusive than it had become for the *Ligue des
Patriotes*. According to people like Drumont and Barrès, only

Frenchmen of pure French birth and virtue could be patriots. And virtue, for Barrès, meant in this context 'the acceptance of a determinism',[16] the determinism of one's nation. This determinism was being naïvely defined in terms of probity, energy, courage and discipline.

With the Panama taunts still ringing in their ears, the democratic republicans went into the election of August 1893 with an understandable lack of enthusiasm. But they need not have worried. If the electorate in its turn mustered little enthusiasm for them, the royalist or anti-semitic and autocratic pronouncements of their opponents found even less favour with it. There was the Duc de Rohan who told the Barodet Committee[17] that he had made no declaration of any kind to his electors at Ploermel, while the Comte de Lanjuinais at Pontivy had everywhere 'affirmed [his] catholic and royalist opinions'.[18] If this seemed good enough for the voters of the Morbihan, who elected both gentlemen with the utmost docility, the rest of the country found such an approach to politics a little too quaint. Diatribes against Jews and Freemasons helped, or at least did not hinder, to get deputies of the Loire-Inférieure and Côtes du Nord elected, but the overall results showed that if a choice had to be made, the country preferred venal democrats to reactionary autocrats. Clemenceau, however, tainted by Panama and by Déroulède's ludicrous charge that he was in the pay of the British, lost his seat. But as in the 1889 elections, Germany – let alone Alsace-Lorraine – was barely mentioned. In the border town of Belfort, Viellard made a vague reference to it. He said that: 'Abroad, I want the national flag respected, the tricolour under which we may be called upon to fight one day.'[19] Apart from that, the nationalism of Barrès and his friends found little patriotic expression. One of the few positive achievements of the recent republican years, the as yet very unofficial Russian alliance, was commented upon with some satisfaction by several candidates.[20] In general, however, the patriotic gullibility of the masses, vociferously lamented by the socialists of Allemane, had again not been exploited by any group. Like the *Führerprinzip*, patriotism had not yet recovered from the Boulangist debacle.

It was the Dreyfus affair that marked the birth of a form of patriotism whose exclusiveness and violence had not been equalled since the Revolution. The events leading up to the trials have been exhaustively analysed by a host of writers[21] and need not be dwelt on here. It is sufficient to recall that in the year following the elections, on 15th October 1894, the French Jewish army captain Dreyfus was arrested on a charge of espionage for Germany, and that he was condemned to deportation for life to Devil's Island. Neither the anarchist outrages that culminated in the assassination of Carnot in 1894, nor the *lois scélérates* that were to curb their activities; neither the resignation of the new President of the Republic Casimir-Périer after only six months in office, nor the election of Félix Faure as his successor; neither the growth of trade unions and socialism in the nineties, nor the increasing class consciousness of the proletariat that was thus exhibited; none, nor all of these combined, can match the significance of the attitudes that crystallized out of the Dreyfus case for the future of the Third Republic.

With great patience the family of Dreyfus worked to prove the condemned man's innocence. By 1898 it had become apparent to a number of prominent Frenchmen that the evidence on which he had been convicted was not entirely convincing. This led some to attack the army for the manner in which the trial had been conducted, evidence presented and withheld, the conviction secured. Others were led to object that such attacks undermined the last bastion of French stability, that only the external enemies of France, about whom little had been heard since Boulanger, could benefit from them. They averred that the respect and dignity of the army should not be prejudiced for the sake of any individual, even at the cost of an injustice. They were seconded by those for whom Dreyfus' Jewish ancestry made the whole noisy affair doubly idiotic. For them his racial origins guaranteed his guilt.

Panama had confirmed Barrès in a belief that had first come to him during his political apprenticeship under Boulanger.

'It is through having common objects of hatred that people unite! Execrating the same man! Ah, what a powerful reason for loving one another . . . Hatred carries all before it . . . but the most intense, the most beautiful hatred is that which arises from civil wars.'[22]

Dreyfus, quite apart from constituting for him an affront to the army, was to provide Barrès with such an object of hatred. In cold blood, cynically, pitilessly, Barrès was to use Dreyfus to attempt to unite his ideologically divided countrymen in a common cause. He was to consider it his finest hour. 'My stay at Rennes is among the worthiest moments one can live'.[23] It was at Rennes that Dreyfus faced his second trial in 1899. Even if the Jew were innocent, 'there is one thing that would still have to be refused such a pitiful victim: a pardon for his defenders'.[24] For the enemy to be execrated was not merely the Jew, but whoever sacrificed the interests of France, as Barrès understood them, to abstract, universal principles. Hence his derisive definition of the 'intellectual' as an 'individual who persuades himself that society must be founded on logic, and who fails to realize that it is in fact based on determinants which are prior to and perhaps independent of individual reason'.[25]

As a first step, the French had to be made to hate Dreyfus. His method, as it appears in *Scènes et Doctrines du Nationalisme* (1902), is simple. The French would be shown to be wholly good and beautiful, the enemies of his conception of France evil and ugly.

'But, really, is it not infantile to feel ill at ease and pronounce mysterious the fact that an alien does not react to events as we would? We do not demand from this child of Sem the beautiful characteristics of the Indo-European race. He is not susceptible to the emotional stimuli that we derive from our soil, our ancestors, our flag, the word "honour". There are forms of optical aphasia where one can see graphic symbols without understanding them. In this case the aphasia is congenital; it springs from race.'[26]

'That Dreyfus is capable of treason I conclude from his race . . . The Jews belong to the country in which they find their greatest interest. As a result of which one can say that a Jew is never a traitor.'[27]

For the Barrès of those days this is all rather tame stuff, as is also the famous description of the degradation ceremony of 5th January 1895.[28] One must put it beside this kind of thing:

'Quite naturally . . . the thousand faces of the syndicate [i.e. Jews, Freemasons, etc.] showed the greenish colour of the snot that hangs from the jaws of a horse awaiting destruction.'

Or, 'often on the way out [of the courtroom] I thought I could see slime under the tables, on which the feet of these ladies and valets might slither. Perhaps these dirty people had simply spat on the floor.'[29]

Barrès summed up his aim by saying that he wanted to stir the conscience of the French.

'It is to reawaken our hereditary qualities, to stir up those *a priori* connections between ideas which lie buried in the conscience of the citizens of the same nation. Once certain spectacles, like the shameful faces of the Dreyfus gang, penetrate into our souls, they produce there . . . a response which will never be experienced by men in whom there was not previously our hereditary equipment. This has nothing to do with intelligence.'[30]

It is a resonance of the soul that cannot be shared by foreigners like Zola, whose rootless cosmopolitanism leads them into the self-interested justification of ideologies that put abstract principles before national interests. No wonder this Italian was in the forefront of the Dreyfus gang. Minorities have a vested interest in universals. So far as the apparently *bona fide* French intellectuals were concerned, who followed Clemenceau into the ranks of the pro-Dreyfus *Ligue des Droits de l'Homme*, Barrès held that they were just not intelligent enough to see the traps set for them. If France were left to them, her glorious heritage, the outcome of centuries of ancestral endeavour, would be lost in a morass of meaningless, faceless abstractions. They fail to see that they are proposing to take away the very substance of which real men are made. The *patrie* 'is the soil and one's ancestors, it is the land of our dead'.[31]

'While rejecting the intellectuals, we must pity rather than curse them. In their own way they are promoting French good sense although they themselves lack it. The brainless dog has rendered considerable service to the studies of psycho-physiology; the poor animal, despite its empty head, has more than anyone else helped us to understand the functioning of intelligence.'[32]

For Barrès, the representatives of the real France were staggeringly different. General Mercier, War Minister during the first Dreyfus trial, was honest, honourable, patriotic, cool, self-possessed.[33] Morès, whose anti-semitic, anti-British and anti-

Dreyfus exploits made him a great Frenchman (despite his Sardinian ancestry) was heroic, a magnificent example of humanity, a national force, disinterested, attractive, ever young, graceful, proud, sympathetic.[34] The women of Metz in occupied Lorraine, typical of the ordinary women of France, 'touch us through their delicacy, their infinite sweetness, rather than through their beauty . . . There is about them a downcast air, but one which awakens tenderness; there is no revolt, . . . but expectation all the same. Their eyes and hearts are entirely directed to France.'[35]

The calculated incitements to hatred on the one hand, and the equally calculated honeyed sublimities on the other were both held to be necessary for the resurgence of France.

'The generations that will have to bear in history the responsibility for the disaster of 1870–1, and had felt their immediate impact, were not greatly affected by these events; they retained their devotion to words and their insipid sentimentalities. With what execrable literature they have been proposing to amuse us for the last twenty years! They subsided into the mess they had not been able to prevent, boldly putting their feet into the dirt. Their successors, on the other hand, are animated by those violent nationalist passions that are necessary to vanquished peoples. They express them in a dozen doctrines, apparently diverse, but which complement each other: they amount to anti-semitism, anti-protestantism, a protest against the accession of foreigners to high office in the State . . . These movements, these passions must receive their justification and must be raised to the dignity of French truths.'[36]

A nationalist 'is a Frenchman who has recognized the influences that made him what he is',[37] and who accepts them. The more he has what Gambetta called 'a proper hatred of the foreigner' the better patriot he will be. The sweetness of France will be enhanced for him by the horror of all that is not French.

The 1898 elections came at a time when the agitation for a second trial was gathering momentum. They provided some astonishing manifestos. Dyed-in-the-wool royalist opponents of the democratic Republic, never renowned for patriotic declarations, joined the other advocates of strong government in tearful appeals to save the army from its treacherous detractors, for the sake of the million Frenchmen suffering martyrdom in the lost provinces.

The Duc de Broglie, after having made no mention at Chateau-Gontier (Mayenne) in 1893 either of Germany or of the army – except to protest about the military law that brought priests into line with other potential conscripts – now declared:

'For our army, for our navy, I have voted all the credits asked for, since nothing must be refused when it concerns the power and security of the country. With you I have suffered, with you I have protested when the army which is the incarnation of the honour of France was insulted and dragged through the mud by the leaders of the hateful campaign for the rehabilitation of a traitor. My votes have always been inspired by my love of the *patrie*, by my solicitude for the honour of the flag. I welcomed wholeheartedly the Franco-Russian alliance which must ensure peace in Europe, without however entailing the abandonment of just causes, and without our forgetting still open wounds.'[38]

At Laval (Mayenne) the Comte d'Elva, who in 1893 had heeded the injunction of the *ralliement* sufficiently to end his manifesto with an appeal for unity under the tricolour, but had said nothing at all about Germany or the army, now inveighed against the 'bandits . . . who seek in vain to dishonour the Army. Long live, above all, the *Patrie française*.'[39] Thus royalist absolutists joined authoritarians of all kinds – those of the left as well as of the non-royalist right – to reap what benefit they could from emotional appeals to a patriotism they could hardly have suspected in themselves twelve months earlier.

In the event, the parliamentary representation of the opponents of the régime did not change much in 1898. They obtained about a hundred seats. The opportunists – or 'moderates' as they preferred to be called – might well have remained in power under Méline. They had held office with right-wing support since Bourgeois' first radical ministry had foundered in 1896. Their orthodox financial policies had restored the national economy after a decade of depression. But they were disunited over Dreyfus, and so were their supporters. Not that very many of them allowed moral scruples to interfere with political profits. That would have meant severing the useful links with the right which had so far prevented a social and political revolution. But there were enough dissenters to make the continuation of the Méline government impossible. In 1899 Waldeck-Rousseau, a rather tougher moderate, formed a ministry which relied on left of centre support. With a small majority he steered the Republic through the next three difficult years. The right wing of his party was, however, lost to him. It had not seen in Dreyfus a sufficient reason for giving up collaboration with the conservatives and other traditionalists. In a clear show-down between Waldeck-Rousseau and the new right, on a law intended to control the activities of the Church (1901), the Prime Minister could muster a majority of only eighty. On a similar vote in 1880 Ferry had obtained a majority of over two hundred. The principles of the *mystique républicaine* were clearly at a discount.

If a good deal of right-wing patriotism was little more than an opportune smokescreen to hide anti-democratic armouries, the socialist conversion to Dreyfus offers no greater moral satisfaction. Like the radicals, the socialists began by disliking Dreyfus, not least because of their traditional anti-semitism. Barrès loved them then. It was only when they became concerned about the possibility of a military coup that they emulated the radicals and – as during the Boulangist crisis – decided to rally to the régime. Since the Saint-Mandé programme (1896) they had an additional reason for defending the Republic. Not only was the democratic régime better for the growth of socialism than a right-wing dictatorship, but they were now committed to the use of constitutional means in their bid for power. Collaboration with other democratic parties, however bourgeois, had therefore become desirable. If these parties defended Dreyfus, either as a matter of moral principle or because he had become a symbol in their struggle with the right, then the socialists would do so too. After the first trial, Jaurès could still taunt the government with the charge that anyone but a bourgeois would have been executed for treason. By the time the 1898 elections were being held, which gave the socialists fifty-seven seats, the socialist fight for justice against the right-wing militarist perverters of human values was on. It may have been this conversion that lost Jaurès his parliamentary seat. But there were compensations. The socialist Millerand, loudly and persistently supported by Jaurès, joined General the Marquis de Galliffet in the Waldeck-Rousseau government. In no time at all they seemed to have become part of the backbone of the régime. President Faure died early in 1899. The new President Loubet found himself the object of unwelcome attentions at a race meeting, where he was struck by an over-enthusiastic baron. The socialists thereupon mobilized the workers of Paris to see that the bourgeois Head of State would not suffer the same fate at similar aristocratic functions.

They had become patriotic, too. During the 1898 elections one of their leaders, Viviani, told his constituents in Paris that internationalism did not exclude patriotism:

'Moreover, the socialists stand for the international understanding of the workers. You know that when they say this, they do not deny the duties of patriotism; that they are ready to defend France because she is the material *patrie*, the glorious cradle of our race, and because she is the *patrie* of the Revolution which called for the emancipation of the oppressed wherever they may be.'[40]

Holier than the republicans so far in power, who had actually sent warships to help the Germans open the Kiel Canal, Chauvière in the fifteenth Paris constituency maintained that 'the socialists alone have held the flag of the Republic high and firm'.[41] In the nineteenth Paris constituency, the socialist Clovis Hugues was even more extravagant:

'I shall tremble with indignation, I shall wonder what the aberration of our time might be, whenever Frenchmen unworthy of the name disavow France, dragging her flag through the mud and through treachery, on the pretext that they love all *patries*.'[42]

Hugues was a poet. That some socialists did not talk in these terms merely meant that they, at any rate, would never have to explain why in 1893 not one of them had even hinted at the existence of the *patrie*.

The programme Barrès put forward to support his candidature at Nancy he summarized in three words: Nationalism, Protectionism, Socialism.[43] He defined nationalism in terms he had first used in a *Figaro* article in 1892, 'applying it to the affairs of France',[44] and made much of his belief that too many Jews and too few Frenchmen were in high positions in the land. He went on to claim that many foreign imports threatened equivalent French products, and that the latter must be protected against them. Workers and petty bourgeois too must be protected against exploitation by foreign money and the competition of foreign labour. Finally, socialism was for Barrès essentially the result of planning for the Saint-Simonian ideal of 'the material and moral improvement of the most numerous and poorest class'.[45] But socialists must be on their guard against cosmopolitan doctrines. France alone matters. – If this declaration of policy did not get Barrès elected, it at least excited the admiration of the *Action Française*. In 1900 it gave it an appreciative set of notes. By then, however, Barrès' *Patrie Française* had worked out a fuller doctrine.

Maurras has stated that it was Barrès who founded the *Ligue de la Patrie Française* after these elections. It was to counter the influence of the pro-Dreyfus *Ligue des Droits de l'Homme*.[46] Although Barrès casts himself in a more modest role in those last days of 1898,[47] the ideas the *Patrie Française* sought to represent were essentially his. From the beginning, twenty-five members of the *Académie Française* signified their support, as did many other eminent Frenchmen. This gave Barrès the satisfaction of being able to write that the intellectuals of France could no longer be said to be all on the side of the syndicate.[48] It was indeed an achievement to be able to gather such a large number of celebrated men behind such a flag. Coppée, Detaille, Forain, Lemaître, Mistral, d'Indy were among them. It was an achievement that could only have been made possible by a genuine despair over the continuing decline of political morality and its feared consequences abroad. This alone can explain the deliberate disregard of the value of generosity and good taste by such men who were heirs of a quite different cultural tradition. As Barrès says: 'What hope could there have been twelve years ago that a man like Lemaître put his hand in that of Déroulède?'[49] Even towards the end of the Boulanger crisis Lemaître's natural delicacy had prevented him from joining the right-wing agitators. His sympathy for Boulangism had been considerable.[50]

There is little point in speculating about the sincerity of these men. What is certain is that since his earliest prose essays in the *Taches d'Encre*, Barrès himself had spoken of the need to recover Alsace-Lorraine and of the national regeneration this presupposed. It may have been that conviction which had led him into Boulangism. It could equally well have been the need to let off histrionic steam. For he certainly was an exhibitionist. The *culte du moi* as it appears in his early novels is otherwise inexplicable. Those repetitious, feeble, glossily written lecturettes on politics, love, freedom and life in general are embarrassing precisely because they are the self-conscious effusions of a sensibility remarkable only for its unrefined mediocrity. At any rate, in his election address in 1889 Barrès prudently made no mention of Germany. His extreme reaction to Panama could be put down to his intense enjoyment of the corrida element in it, just as it could be accounted for by his discovery of the social and political uses of hate. The same is true of Barrès during the Dreyfus trials. But if it is as futile to attempt to discover the 'real' motives of Barrès as it is to discover those of his associates in the *Patrie Française*, certainty is at least permitted on one point. A large number of eminent Frenchmen were clearly prepared to subordinate moral to political considerations. It may well be that they were persuaded to do this by an élan of patriotic impatience. But their disregard of the moral rights of the many Frenchmen they disliked were bound to lead, quite logically, to the situation of 1940, when their spiritual heirs found that they had more in common with the equally authoritarian Germans than with a large number of their own compatriots. Ironically, Barrès predicted this evolution as early as 1904:

> 'The day will come when it will be the conservatives who will accept and call in the foreigner. Yes, those who today are the patriots, the proud, will become tired of living in a France that is decayed, a life full of humiliation, and they will call for the intervention of the foreigner who can give them at last the joy of participating in a great, collective life. And, opposing them, we shall see resistance to the foreigner personified by Jansenist demagogues.'[51]

It must have been a weird sense of humour which prompted Maurras[51a] to allege that Barrès meant the opportunists when he said conservatives; in the context, this interpretation makes no manner of sense. It was in the elections of May 1898 that the royalists demurely presented themselves for the first time as 'conservatives'.

Despite his effusiveness about Déroulède and the *Ligue des Patriotes*, the latter resuscitated to fight the defenders of Dreyfus, there now often crept into Barrès' remarks about the founder of the *Ligue* an element of embarrassment. One has the feeling that in the august presence of twenty-five academicians, Barrès was a little ashamed of the more lunatic escapades of the veteran street-brawler.

> 'While it is the function [of the *Ligue*] – so courageous, so disinterested, composed of most honest men, grouped behind a hero – to fight in the streets against the foreigners of the interior (*étrangers de l'intérieur*), I considered that it was the task of the men of letters of the *Patrie Française* to analyse the underlying causes of this anarchy.'[53]

It was the insurrectional aspect of the *Ligue*[54] that Barrès was most apprehensive about, not because he himself was above such things, but because it frightened the sedate gentlemen of the Academy. In fact, Barrès participated, if at a little distance, in the *Ligue*'s vain attempt to induce an army detachment returning from Faure's funeral to set Déroulède up at the Elysée. Like the *Ligue* in its early days, the *Patrie Française* claimed to be unpolitical. Indeed it maintained that its aims were not to be seen exclusively in the light of Dreyfus, that its chief object was the creation of national unity irrespective of the political differences that existed among Frenchmen. To that end the principles of 1789 had to be accepted, otherwise there would be chaos: 'We aim at getting the best out of what actually exists.'[55] To achieve unity, the French must go beyond conscious differences to their unconscious common heritage: 'We are the product of a community which manifests itself in us.'[56] To enable France to regain contact with this community, the rationalistic principles of rootless intellectuals would have to be replaced by the practical precepts of men rooted in the old traditions of France. 'The *patrie* is stronger in the soul of a man who has roots (*un enraciné*) than in one who is uprooted (*un déraciné*).'[57] As Brunetière put it, 'the ultimate step reason can take, its supreme victory, is its submission to something that is beyond it'.[58] No wonder Barrès hoped 'to show one day that Pascal belongs to us'.[59] The heart has reasons . . .

Going beyond reason to one's roots meant for Barrès what it had meant for Taine. Taine had been seen to hold that the feeling of patriotism was lost with the growing centralization of government and administration in Paris. Barrès and the *Patrie Française* wanted to reverse this process. They advocated a measure of regional autonomy and the encouragement of all corporations grouping men of similar interests and traditions.

'Do not be afraid to add local to national sentiment. Give everyone two *patries* to serve, to save: the great *patrie* and the small *patrie*. Men must have specific, tangible reasons for loving their country . . . French nationality is the product of provincial nationalities.'[60]

Just as Mistral sang the praises of Provence without considering himself any less a Frenchman, so Barrès constantly reminded his readers of his devotion to Lorraine.

Despite the vagueness of the programme of the *Patrie Française*, it did not succeed for long in glossing over the differences that separated many of its members. Its gentlemanly intellectuals were very unhappy about its association with Déroulède's *Ligue*, and about the militancy of the newly-founded *Action Française* which brandished a spiritual affiliation order bearing the name of Barrès. In 1900 the *Action Française* actually ignored the discretion shown by the right in 1898 and openly affirmed its desire to restore the monarchy.[61] Moreover, many members failed to observe its intended unpolitical character and spoke out against Waldeck-Rousseau's anti-clerical 1901 law. Some even presented themselves at elections with programmes no less vague than those of most other candidates. Barrès' remonstrances went largely unheeded:

'If we degenerate into being simply people who take one side or the other on this [Waldeck-Rousseau law] that is people who have candidates for the Municipal Council or at general elections, nationalism will have been no more than a momentary whiff of smoke, a political accident. Latent nationalism is something quite different.'[62]

How far Barrès himself had evolved is indicated by the fact that he passed these strictures in 1901 at a dinner commemorating his *Appel au Soldat* (1900), and in whose spirit he had regretted as recently as 1899 the absence of a Boulangist general at the time of the Rennes trial.

Perhaps it was the civilizing influence of some of the intellectuals he encountered in the *Patrie Française* that led Barrès away from insolent vulgarity to something approaching a sense of political responsibility. At all events, his resignation from the committee in 1901 marked for him a definite change of direction. His concern became more with the discovery of affinities among Frenchmen than with hunting down differences. As the war approached one heard less from him about enemies within. He will even pay tribute to Jaurès, assassinated on the eve of the struggle. In the middle of the war, in *Les Diverses Familles Spirituelles de la France* (1917), he actually wrote with evident satisfaction:

> 'Catholics, Protestants, Israelites, Socialists, Traditionalists, suddenly drop their differences. The knives of hatred miraculously disappear. Everyone says: "I shall not, even with a secret thought, stand in the way of anything that makes for the salvation of the *patrie*".'[63]

No doubt the *union sacrée* of the First War was the result of just such a truce. But it was only a truce. Long before Barrès died in 1923 it had become clear that the real power behind the nationalist agitators had passed into less conciliatory hands. It had passed into hands that were moved by the Barrès of the Dreyfus affair. The *Action Française* was to incarnate it, demonstrating the difference between the French nationalist movement and patriotism. Maurras and his friends were to work for the fulfilment of Barrès' 1904 prophecy.

CHAPTER SIX

PÉGUY: 1900–14

GAMBETTA, TAINE, Renan, Barrès, the *Ligue des Patriotes*, the Boulangist movement, all voiced protests against the suffocation of the spirit, or what they took to be the spirit, by the materialism of their countrymen. Such protests were of course not new. Already the romantics had found the air oppressive, and Stendhal had pressed the case for energetic action with every bit as much determination against the entrenched middle-classes as Renan was to do later in the century. Only the motives were different. Barrès may have the sanctimonious audacity to reproach Stendhal for 'never asking himself whether a feeling, an action are useful and fruitful, but only whether they are evidence of unusual energy',[1] as if he had not written his own early books. What matters is that out of the petty materialism of the century there grew a revolt born of frustration or disgust, a religion of action. 'Ye Higher Men, leave the market-place.' Parliamentary democracy seemed no régime for Higher Men. The contribution of Charles Péguy to this revolt was highly original, in style and in content.

He was born at Orléans in 1873. His father died soon afterwards and he was brought up by his mother and grandmother in poor working-class surroundings. He received his early schooling in his native city but finally obtained a place at the Ecole Normale in 1894 where, like many other students, he came under the influence of the socialist librarian Lucien Herr. But the ideals of socialism were to have a meaning for him that was quite different from that which it had for Herr's more bourgeois disciples. The alleviation of social injustice for a young man of his humble origins was more than a worthy abstract principle. It meant the substitution of dignity for the abjectness of the life he had shared, an end to the pointless hardships suffered by his own family, a vision of tangible happiness on earth.

'Each soul has its beauty which is particular to it. Each soul . . . achieves the highest beauty of which it is capable . . . No one has authority over the will of the individual soul.'[2]

'No work that is unhealthy, that is no work which is likely to deform the souls or bodies of the workers, can promote the material life of the harmonious city . . . The material life of the harmonious city is best provided for only by harvested natural products or by the products of work which is not unhealthy. All adult men, able-bodied and young, do that work . . . Workers choose the work for which they think themselves best fitted . . . Women do not do that work . . . Adolescents do not do that work . . . Old people do not do that work . . . The sick and the weak do not do that work, for it is not proper that the city should be the responsibility of the women, the adolescents, the old people, the weak, and the sick . . . The animals never do that work, for their souls are always adolescent.'[3]

This is not the vision of a well-meaning, impressionable young intellectual. The son of the woman who made a precarious living by mending chairs and was never able to understand what her son was doing in Paris, Péguy meant every word of it.

Universal justice is what the Republic had been said to stand for by its founders. It was the principle that the socialists said they wanted to rescue from the bourgeois who at present controlled their destinies. In 1897, the year before he had finished the opening dialogue of *La Cité Harmonieuse*, Péguy had dedicated his first *Jeanne d'Arc* to that universal Socialist Republic that Gambetta had tried discreetly to throttle in his deal with Thiers. Then began his education in political realities. Unsophisticated provincial that he remained throughout his life, Péguy could not reconcile tbe universality of socialist principles with Guesde's refusal to concern himself with Dreyfus because the Jew was no proletarian – a shortcoming, incidentally, the captain shared with Guesde. But he was momentarily reassured by Jaurès who, it seemed, had learnt to see the Dreyfus affair as a trial of strength between the forces of morality and those of blind reaction, with Jaurès strictly on the side of the angels. And, once Jaurès had made up his mind to it, there were no limits to the ingenuity of his virtuous arguments. He even maintained that it was in the interests of the proletariat to prevent too great an intellectual and moral degradation of the middle-classes,[4] and that it was consequently desirable to apply the pure moral principles of the proletariat to save Dreyfus from his immoral enemies. Another argument used by Jaurès, and which revealed his real motives for supporting the Jew at least as much, Péguy for the moment ignored: 'Who is really most threatened by the despotism of the generals, by the violence of military repression that is always praised? Who? The proletariat.'[5] That the conversion of the socialist leader to Dreyfusism might have had more to do with considerations of political expediency than with moral integrity was as yet hidden from Péguy. He thought that Jaurès was as drunk with the heady wine of total self-effacement as he was himself, that Jaurès too gloried in the luxurious, sensuous pleasures of total subservience to the ideal of universal justice, 'the most divine of all ideals'. The affair, Péguy said, required from them two kinds of courage, and from the fullness of their hearts they joyfully provided both of them:

'the first, that of publicly declaring Dreyfus innocent, to stake on him all one had, money and time, life and career, health and ruin, all possible kinds of ruin, one's whole social life, one's whole emotional life, in short: all; the second was more difficult still – psychological courage. To renounce for that man one's peace of mind – the foremost of all goods, the only good – the courage to enter for that man into the kingdom of incurable anxiety–and of a bitterness from which one was never to recover.'[6]

Soon however Péguy began to wonder about the purity of Jaurès' convictions. 'When one fails truth one necessarily fails justice: incomplete truth goes with incomplete justice, that is injustice.'[7] Péguy thought the socialist leader was beginning to fail truth. He was heard to say things that he could not, or should not, have meant, for no better apparent reason than that he wanted to be *persona grata* with bourgeois politicians. It seemed that the socialist leader had so much enjoyed the moments of power during his alliance with the other opponents of the military and nationalist conspirators that he was now ready to compromise his principles in order to retain his influence with them. It was a compromise of which Péguy thought himself incapable.

'We were the seekers and servants of the truth. Such was in us the strength of the truth that we should have proclaimed it even against our own interests . . . Now that the truth has saved us we should be depriving our recent conduct of its justice, our recent words of their truth, our recent action of its morality, if we were to drop it like a cumbersome piece of baggage . . . It would be wrong to think that distinctions can be made between truths, that in moments of crisis the great truths can be respected – those explosive, glorious truths – and that in ordinary life one can neglect the little familiar perennial truths . . . Having suffered all we have for the truth, we are not prepared to agree to give it up to be accommodating . . .'[8]

It was to defend this uncompromising attitude that, in 1900, he founded the *Cahiers de la Quinzaine*. They were to reflect the intellectual preoccupations of the French until 1914, for there was no major political, social, and philosophical problem that was not aired in the *Cahiers* while Péguy was their editor.

The first significant betrayals of the Dreyfus spirit came, according to Péguy, with the elections of 1902. Jaurès, who had lost his seat in 1898, was returned to the Palais-Bourbon with his stature and ambitions enhanced by the defeat of the anti-democratic groups, and he allowed himself to be elected Vice-President of the Chamber. As a reward for political dishonesty that was bad enough. But the utter disregard by the electorally successful left-wing coalition for the sanctity of minority opinion was for Péguy an unforgivable violation of the most fundamental principles of justice. Although less than a quarter of a million votes separated the two sides, the voting system gave the socialist and radical republicans a majority of about 150 seats. The campaign had been bitter, and the victors intended to have their pound of flesh. Their attitude had been expressed by the radical Léon Bourgeois in an address to his constituents at Châlons-sur-Marne:

'Under the disguise of nationalism you have recognized from the first the eternal enemies against whom on 25th May, on 16th May, and during the Boulangist period the Republic has always had to defend herself. You are republicans and patriots. You remember the disasters into which autocratic power had dragged the *patrie*, and you know what the Republic has done to save its honour, to restore its military power; you will not permit that the army of the nation be raised up against the Republic, you do not want the flag of France to become the flag of a party.'[9]

In Paris, the socialist Cardet put forward a similar case, if in more direct language, and this showed how a more flexible approach to politics had made the electoral alliance between socialists and radicals possible:

'Loving his country like every other Frenchman, but the declared enemy of the charlatans of patriotism, he will fight that heterogeneous gang composed of clericals and reactionaries who, through their lies and hypocrisy, have succeeded in imperilling the Republic while disguising themselves deceptively as nationalists.'[10]

Péguy was to find the results of this flexibility as little to his liking as the inflexibility of Marcel Sembat in the 18th Paris constituency. There was to be, the candidate had said, no collaboration whatever with bourgeois parties, for this could only serve to prolong the period of their rule. He summed up the sole important aim of socialism as:

'International understanding and action of the workers; political and economic organization of the proletariat in a class party to conquer power and bring about the socialization of the means of production and exchange, that is to say the transformation of capitalist society into a collectivist or communist society.'[11]

If the left saw the right-wing combination of ex-opportunist 'moderates', ex-royalist 'conservatives', and nationalists as a conspiracy of clerical reactionaries, the latter now reciprocated by casting themselves in the role of sole custodians of the patriotic virtues. With sad, unconscious irony moderates like Albert Le Moigne (Cherbourg) were to claim with much justification that they were the true heirs of the Gambetta-Thiers tradition:

'France has to choose between two policies. The first, which is in the republican tradition, was also that of Thiers and Gambetta; it is the policy of progress . . . liberty, tolerance . . . The second, which is in the Jacobin tradition, wants to reform society by force.'[12]

True to the first tradition, M Le Moigne managed to dismiss the question of old age pensions by saying that they were no doubt desirable but too difficult to finance, and also to justify the electoral alliance of his group with the more extreme right. For the likelihood of a political reorientation in the event of a right-wing victory bothered the true descendants of the opportunists far less than the possibility of an economic and social reorientation in the event of a left-wing victory. Hindsight tells one of course that they need not have worried, since the economic measures they dreaded were just as unpopular with the bourgeois radicals in the left alliance as they were with the right.

As for the more extreme right, its manifestos were less mellifluous. The department Meurthe et Moselle, which includes Barrès' old haunt Nancy, provided a particularly expressive crop. At Lunéville, C. des Essarts began: 'I come confidently to ask you to unite your efforts with mine so that the Republic can be saved from the domination of Jews and Freemasons.'[13] If the Comte Ferri de Ludre in the second Nancy constituency could bring himself to appear as a republican without losing himself in cheap jibes, and even go so far as to hope for France's 'natural' frontiers,[14] the other two future deputies for Nancy reserved their patriotic fervour for the internal enemies of the syndicate. 'Nationalist, yes! I am a Nationalist,' proclaimed L. Gervaise. 'I am one of those good Frenchmen who want to defend France against the enemy within, preserve her territorial integrity, have her respected abroad',[15] in that patriotic order. It is one of the marks of the self-appointed post-Boulanger patriotic crusaders that their thunderbolts are mainly directed against the political enemy at home. One can understand what moved Barrès to predict their traitorous future.

In terms of votes the left of centre coalition had little to crow about. Perhaps because of that, but certainly because of the immense bitterness created between the two camps since Dreyfus, the victors decided to deal with their enemies with no less firmness than Waldeck-Rousseau had shown them before the elections. Indeed, after Combes had become Prime Minister in June 1902, the final assault on the allegedly most audacious citadel of reaction, the Church, was becoming inevitable. So petulantly and pettily, with such a robust vulgarity was the Church persecuted already before the law was passed which separated it from the State (1905), that even convinced anti-clericals were nauseated enough by the hardships caused to nuns, monks and other catholics to protest against Combes' policies. It was in keeping with its ethos that the government finally fell when it was discovered that André, the War Minister, was secretly investigating the political and religious beliefs of his officers, and that promotions depended on what he found.

Péguy's reaction to this aftermath of the affair can easily be imagined. His wrath was reserved not so much for Combes, from whom few had expected the highest spiritual performance, as for Jaurès. Péguy, in common with many other observers, saw the Vice-President of the Chamber as the real power behind the throne. He found it difficult to square the persecution of the Church, for whose authoritarian outlook he himself had little sympathy, and the prying into the private beliefs of officers, with Jaurès' protestations of moral purity during the fight for universal justice at the high noon of the Dreyfus affair. The socialism Péguy valued concerned itself with economic problems and left the individual's liberty intact. He never seemed to see the paradox of that distinction.

He wrote of Jaurès: 'You believe strongly that unity is the *sine qua non* of everything, that unity must be promoted above everything else, that from unity all else will follow. From dualism, from pluralism you expect nothing except the victorious tyranny of the one over the enslaved other . . .'[16]

'My Republic is in a sense above all a Republic in which people are left in peace . . . The revolution [I want] will do away with all authority. . . .'[17]

The metaphysical monism Péguy saw lurking behind the socialist leader's attitudes offended his sense of philosophical honesty. 'In you', Jaurès was told, 'sincerity, philosophical probity give way to monism, as political probity has given way to unity.'[18] 'Unhappy is he who has not at least once . . . called everything into question.'[19] In fact Péguy here understated his case. He wanted everything to be called into question all the time. Like his first Joan, everyone should forever tremble at the uncertainty of everything, should constantly doubt the veracity of his voices. From which it follows that the imposition of specific views on others, or the persecution of others for their beliefs, merely amounts to base bullying. Be it from ambition or from philosophical arrogance,

Jaurès had betrayed socialism as Péguy thought they had both conceived it during the Dreyfus affair.

The growing despair one encounters in the writings of Péguy is the result of his growing conviction that it is not only the *Cité Harmonieuse* which is a utopian dream, but that even the much more modest hope of the alleviation of the misery of the poor is likely to go unfulfilled. The monistic price demanded by the socialists of Jaurès was too high, even if they had been serious about their principles. Others, like Daniel Halévy, who had in the eyes of Péguy for a while remained true to the highest ideals, were unlikely to be much use in the fight. Their personal fortunes prevented them from understanding the problem.

'We must not forget, Halévy, that we belong to two different classes, and you will grant me that in the modern world, *where money is everything*, that is certainly the most serious, the biggest difference, the greatest gap that could exist.'[20]

From the proletariat, on the other hand, nothing could be expected either. It appeared to Péguy in no rosier a light than it had to Allemane. It was fickle, violent, vulgar, ungenerous, intolerant. It eagerly followed any demagogue who preached hatred, jealousy, envy.

'It is beyond itself with happiness if it can be given the illusion that by falling on the weakest it sacrifices itself nobly for some great cause, for some conception of human salvation.'[21]

The proletariat had misery but no insight. Halévy had insight but no misery. Péguy alone appeared to have both. And both are necessary for the perception of truth, 'that genius which is born of the continuous experience of misery'.[22]

Rationalist doctrines purporting to demonstrate the truth of moral precepts meant nothing to Péguy. The moral mechanics of materialistic utilitarians he thought an insult to the sensibility of man. They ignored the deeper validation true morality receives from the intuitive perceptions of honest hearts. That ultimately for Péguy only his heart was honest, the cynical reader will already have concluded. As towards the end of his life the *Cahiers* lost more and more subscribers, the anathemas of their editor fell thickly about the ears of even the most modest critic. The loneliness he had made for himself would have been unbearable had he not found a means of transcending it. Like Barrès, he found it in the cult of France.

1905 is a date that marks the end of an epoch not merely for Péguy but for France as a whole. Germany, resenting increasing French encroachments on Moroccan sovereignty without there being any apparent compensation coming her own way, as was customary in the colonial horse-trading at the turn of the century, had turned on the heat again. She protested in a speech delivered by the Kaiser, much against his will, while briefly in Tangier during a Mediterranean cruise. All German resources would be used to maintain the independence of Morocco, his Chancellor, Bülow, had prompted him to say. Abruptly France was reminded that she had problems more vital than anti-clericalism. With the two countries suddenly brought to the brink of war, narcissists like Péguy changed mirrors. Civilians saw themselves in uniform, the proletariat they despised became sublime cannon-fodder, a God held to be immoral was transformed into a benign deity with a pronounced weakness for the French.

Delcassé, who had been at the Quai d'Orsay since 1898, thought the Germans were bluffing. Unlike his predecessors, he had got his priorities straight from the moment he took office. Arriving at the Quai in the middle of the Fashoda crisis, in which Franco-British colonial rivalries were dramatically highlighted, he realized that Britain and Germany could not be faced simultaneously. He also recognized that the temperamental French see-saw that elevated Berlin to the position of a potential ally when Paris was displeased with London, but elevated London when Paris was displeased with Berlin, that this unstable apparatus was no substitute for an intelligent policy. It would ultimately alienate both powers. 'While the Germans are in Strasbourg,' Delcassé is said to have written to one of his ambassadors,[23] 'France has only one enemy.' He therefore systematically worked for an understanding with Britain. If it lost France face through her withdrawal from Fashoda, it also gained her the Entente Cordiale of 1904. And only just in time, because the military uselessness of the Russian alliance was demonstrated by the ease with which the Japanese triumphed over the Tsar's forces, from the moment they sank his fleet at Port Arthur in February 1904, two months before the Franco-British negotiations were successfully concluded.

The Rouvier government which had replaced that of Combes did not share Delcassé's optimism over the Tangier events. The Prime Minister thought the Germans were trying to profit from the obvious weakness of the Russian alliance and that, though no doubt useful at sea, the British would not be much help when France had to face the Germans on land. The Foreign Minister's tears were no substitute for dragon's teeth, and not only did the cabinet decide to submit to the German demand for an international conference, but they got rid of Delcassé as well. The popularity of the Foreign Minister's resignation reflected the relief with which the subsequent relaxation of pressure was greeted. But hindsight shows that this crisis was one too many. From the moment the British had given concrete proof at the Algeciras conference (1906) that they were in earnest about the Entente, and staff talks had begun between Britain and France, the French position hardened to the extent of making a showdown inevitable.

'Within the course of one morning', wrote Péguy, 'everyone knew that France was under the threat of an imminent German invasion.'[24] This dramatic, if not theatrical, realization wrought an equally dramatic change in Péguy. The fragility of his moral and political utopianism had just again been demonstrated to him by the ferocity and moral heedlessness of the Russo-Japanese war. Tokyo had not even gone through the gentlemanly motion of declaring war before sinking the Russian fleet at Port Arthur. But the threat to civilized life as he understood it was now much nearer home. It was no longer merely a few forgetful Dreyfusards who prevented the socialist paradise from being established on this earth. Barbarians by the million were now conspiring against it. Péguy's hopeful little flame of civilization seemed about to be extinguished by a storm of unprecedented violence.

'It is not up to us to decide whether it will happen, but it is up to us to accept our responsibilities. . . . When a people of culture is threatened with a military invasion by a people of barbarians, or by a government of barbarians that has always had its people on the march; when a free people is threatened with a military invasion by a people addicted to servitude, the people of culture, the free people has only to prepare perfectly its national military mobilization . . . It is not up to us to decide whether that event will occur. But it is up to us to do our duty.'[25]

Grim watchfulness was to be one of his main themes from now on. Thus, in April 1913:

'Since we came under the German menace, that is since 1905 . . . it has been incumbent upon us to raise ourselves to a point of maximum exasperation and firmly to remain there, without ever relaxing in any way. Without ever resting . . . This is in fact a state of war in peacetime . . . I do not believe that since the beginning of the world there has ever been a situation like that through which we are living now. It is an armed vigil without end.'[26]

France as a whole, in the eyes of Péguy, was now to be seen as the embattled bastion of civilization and culture. He was no longer alone.

When one recalls Péguy's pessimistic invective against his compatriots, this apparent reconciliation with his contemporaries in the face of the barbarian threat may strike one as a display of the kind of opportunism he had always decried. It was not. Priests as well as priest-eaters, nationalists as well as internationalists, materialists as well as idealists, all continued to receive their periodic punishment in the *Cahiers*, with a vigour undiminished by civilized considerations. It was not in them that Péguy was discovering the virtues of France. The real France, whose features he distinguished only faintly in 1905, and for whose defence he invited the aid of all Frenchmen, the real France is made of the stuff of Dreyfusism. It was the guardian of the eternal values of liberty, charity and honour. Joan of Arc and Corneille's Polyeucte were used to epitomize it. Before he had come to those conclusions, however, the elections of 1906 helped to encourage Péguy in his withdrawal into myth.

The Second International, meeting at Amsterdam in 1905, had decreed that French socialism was in a disgraceful state. It was split into a diversity of factions, as a result of which it was ineffectual as a political force. And some of those factions had seen fit to collaborate with bourgeois parties and politicians, as a result of which it was ineffectual also as a class force. It was decided that the French socialists must reform. They were to unite, and to resist the temptations of political power under a bourgeois régime. From Péguy's point of view the results of Amsterdam discipline were not cheering. Not only did the socialists fail to speak with one voice in the 1906 election, but among the many professions of faith that emanated from them only that of someone like Viviani could possibly find favour with him. The soothing sonorities of the deputy for the fifth Paris constituency (first district) did at least include a profession of patriotism:

> 'They say that the socialists want to destroy the *patrie*. That is a lie . . . They love the *patrie*, which is the mother of us all. If the *patrie* has not so far distributed justice equally among all its children, they nevertheless count on the *patrie* to bring that justice about . . . And if the frightful calamity of a war were to occur the socialists, like all the other citizens, would defend France without arguing about the origins of the conflict.'[27]

No other socialist had gone as far as that, any more than any other socialist had managed to declare: 'They say that, as a socialist I am with the rest of my party the enemy of property. That is a lie . . .'[28] Most socialists adopted the ambiguous line of Jaurès which, without saying anything about what they would do in the event of war, proclaimed their desire for peace.

> 'But how could this great effort [towards greater social justice] succeed, if the nation were thrown into the horror of war? That is why we socialists detest and condemn adventures. That is why we want to maintain and ensure peace through the harmonious union of the workers of all countries, through the growing practice of international arbitration which is a prelude to the simultaneous disarmament of the nations. That is why ever since the still obscure beginnings of the Moroccan conflict I pointed out the danger, denouncing the financial calculations of one side and the megalomania of the other.'[29]

Arthur Rozier not only followed Jaurès in not mentioning the *patrie*, but affirmed a resolute pacifism: 'We are very decidedly pacifists; peace alone offers the workers guarantees.'[30]

If the socialists took Tangier merely as a warning for greedy capitalists, the ex-royalist conservatives did not seem to have been moved by it all. Their manifestos suggested that the threat to the nation came not from an enemy abroad but from political adversaries at home. The law of separation was what exercised them. Tangier, Germany, the army, they often did not even mention.

That veteran royalist, Mackau, at Argentan (Orne), in a very subdued declaration, merely regretted that 'the legislature that has just come to an end has been very severe [to us].'[31] Henri de Hercé, in Mayenne: 'My candidature is a candidature of catholic protest,'[32] a sentiment echoed by the deputy for the second Mayenne constituency. The Vicomte Villebois-Mareuil, successor of the Duc de Broglie at Chateau-Gontier, began: 'Like all of you, I am a Catholic before everything else.' He then affirmed his love of France, without however detailing what that love might entail – no one had loved France more than the émigrés – to end with a curious, 'Long live God! Long live the *patrie*.'[33]

No doubt Péguy would not expect to find himself seconded by more or less rallied royalists. He found Barrès, in the first constituency of Paris, more to his liking. In a declaration couched in the moderate terms one would expect from a man who had forsaken the *café* for the *coupole*, Barrès asked that 'the French should become reconciled with each other around the idea of the *patrie*', though he seemed to exclude from this the Freemasons.[34] To obtain the real flavour of the old Barrès one now has to go to the ex-Boulangist Lucien Millevoye, in the sixteenth Paris constituency:

'Patriots, . . . we do not forget that many hands have vied with each other to sling mud at military judges, the high command, the general staff, and that under the pretext of proving a condemned man innocent, reptilian slime, foreign filth have been heaped on the most eminent heads of our Army.'[35]

In the other constituency of the sixteenth arrondissement, Paul Beauregard's electors were assured that their candidate had fought all those who had 'supported . . . that unfrocked priest [Combes]; . . . Pelletan, the disorganizer of our national Navy; General André, the ill-starred puppet who has handed our officers over to the police spies, disarmed our frontiers, and deliberately weakened our country'.[36] This is language Péguy understood, and was himself to use with increasing frequency. He was to treat as traitors socialists and left-wing radicals like Caillaux, with their internationalist doctrines, their pacifism, and their anti-militarism.

The patriotism of the centre, like its attitude to social reform, was too pale to be politically important. Jules Cosnard (Paris, seventeenth constituency, second district) was against the internationalists and anti-militarists, against aggression, for peace, for military readiness.

'*From the social point of view*, I shall associate myself with all practical proposals which, without compromising the interests of commerce and industry, could improve the fate of the workers.'[37]

Hearts were unlikely to beat faster . . .

Despite the charge of anti-patriotism levelled against all the supporters of the law of separation, they won the elections with an increased majority. Péguy's dramatic tirades about Tangier had impressed the intellectuals as little as the nationalist agitation had impressed the electorate at large. The right obtained only 174 seats. The fact that the year of Tangier had also been the year during which military service had actually been reduced from three to two years, and left there, damned the governmental coalition no more in the eyes of the electorate than the growing volume of anti-militaristic literature with which the right tried to associate it.[38] No doubt it was to take the electorate as well as its representatives some time to appreciate the new situation created by Tangier on the one hand, and by the Algeciras-born confidence on the other. The elections of May 1906 came barely two months after the end of that conference. Three years later Radolin, the German Ambassador in Paris, was to write to Chancellor Bülow that 'the politicians, the intellectuals and businessmen who had made no secret of their desire for better relations with her [Germany] were now asking themselves if war were not preferable to a perpetual state of uncertainty'.[39]

Had Péguy been a leader he would now have come into his own. But, unlike his Joan, he was not. Joan too had her moments of doubt, but they were followed by moments of resolution. And Joan had charm enough to let her followers forget the moments when she had chided them, while Péguy never let up. If he was not complaining about his financial worries, he was insulting his friends and enemies with awful impartiality. As those who had respected and admired him found themselves one by one, often incomprehensibly, cast out of the nemetic presence, they left behind them a bitter fury that soon had only itself to feed on. By 1907 Péguy was writing lyrical poetry. 'Pouvoir me taire.'[40] He saw it himself.

While France knew a period of social unrest rare even for her in intensity, Péguy had withdrawn from the world. He was actually trying to get rid of the *Cahiers* at a time when, after the Amiens charter (1906), the now more than three-quarters of a million strong trade union movement (Confédération Générale du Travail) had decided to go over to direct industrial action, dissociating itself from the whole political machinery of the Republic. With Sorel's *Réflexions sur la violence* (1906), they cherished the myth of the omnipotence of the general strike. The proletariat seemed to have set itself up against the bourgeois Third Republic. Certainly that is how the radical Clemenceau saw it in 1906, once he had exchanged thirty years of Jacobin opposition first for a long awaited place in a ministry, later for the premiership. Although the period between Algeciras and the outbreak of war in 1914 was one of steady economic progress there was, around 1908, a wave of unemployment and, throughout the period, a good many strikes. While the deputies voted themselves an increase from nine thousand to fifteen thousand francs after the 1906 elections, most of the rest of the population was not similarly rewarded. There was unrest in the vineyards that now had to face competition from capitalist wine growers. There were postal strikes (1909), a teachers' strike (1910), and there was a railstrike (1910) which the erstwhile syndicalist hero Briand broke by the simple authoritarian device of mobilizing the railwaymen. But these were merely the more spectacular manifestations of popular discontent. And the moment the results of the 1906 election had propelled them into positions of direct political responsibility, both Briand and Clemenceau had lost much of their reformist dash. This showed itself also in the infinite solicitude and splendidly opportunistic *combinazione* with which they pulled most of the teeth of Combes' separation law, until it amounted to little more than the emancipation of the catholics from State interference.

Throughout this time Péguy cultivated his emotional garden. When suddenly, on 20th June 1909, his pen again exploded in the *Cahiers*, the years of comparative silence seemed to have done nothing to calm him. Far from it. As if a safety valve had burst, the lone guardian of the *mystique républicaine* hissed out his anger at the moral degeneracy of his countrymen with undiminished energy. 'Sons of defeated fathers, born into a defeated people, we have been defeated ourselves . . . Even in our very homes. Even in our very hearts.'[41] Péguy cannot suffer defeat. 'Defeat engenders defeat. And until the revocation of defeat this [remains] a vicious circle. . . .'[42] The origin of this lamentable degeneration is 1870, a defeat which Tangier forced back into reluctant memories.

> 'Tangier reminded us, as always brutally, bitterly, as always, that military realities have a fundamental importance, as a foundation of the other realities of the spirit; intellectual and mental realities; of moral realities too; even – I dare say it: of religious realities.'[53]

1870 killed the moral fibre of the French, and their one supreme hope of regeneration, the Dreyfus spirit, they sold for political favours, or worse, for a quiet life.

> 'The personal defeat . . . the scandalous failure of the Dreyfus affair . . . I shall never reconcile myself to that . . . A unique opportunity presented itself to regenerate this people . . . A stroke of luck. An opportunity that does not come twice in the life of a people . . . The fraudulent bankruptcy of the affair in political double-dealing, the biggest swindle of the century, the crime that initiated us into public life, into our whole life . . . I shall never be silent about it. I shall always remain inconsolable.'[44]

For Péguy it was a sign of the times that it was that alleged traitor to the cause of universal justice, Jaurès, who had arrogated to himself the re-opening of the Dreyfus case in 1903, to bring about the final rehabilitation of innocence.

If defeat had plunged France into this state of degeneration, only victory would be able to rescue her from it.

> 'It is in vain: it is useless trying to make oneself believe it: the taste of defeat is not the taste of victory. Whoever swallows his defeat . . . the saliva he swallows has not the same taste as that of victory . . . It is a taste that cannot be got rid of. *UNTIL DEFEAT ITSELF HAS BEEN GOT RID OF.* . . . Neither in himself, nor in his own country, nor in his own blood, nor in his own people can the defeated speak the same language as the victorious . . . *UNTIL THE DEFEAT HAS BEEN MADE GOOD.*'[45]

The doctrine of the purifying influence of war, the war of *revanche*, had thus been given a new twist. For Péguy patriotism had become something other than the frustrated expression of hurt national pride that it had been for Déroulède, or the pretext for energetic self-affirmation that it had been in the early Barrès, or the cover for political authoritarianism that it had been for the followers of Maurras. For Péguy, at this stage, it fulfilled a moral need.

Péguy went out of his way to exhibit the differences between his own outlook and that of others with similar preoccupations. Taine and Renan are taken to task in the course of many lengthy disquisitions.[46] They are accused of 'intellectualism', of wanting 'to transfer *en bloc* modern scientific methods into the domain of history and man'.[47] A whole generation had been perverted by them: 'these two names, Taine, Renan, these two men, Taine, Renan, welcomed us, greeted us on the threshold of researches, . . . since then they have never ceased, they will never cease to accompany us.'[48] For worse. But what Péguy does not seem to recognize when he accuses Taine and Renan of a 'dogmatism infinitely more authoritarian than that of catholicism' is that he is guilty of the same offence, that their 'positivism' was based just as much on an intuition as the intuitionism in terms of which he so dogmatically condemns them. There is no qualitative difference between Taine's intuitive positivism, Renan's intuitive scepticism, and Péguy's intuitive messianism. All, in fact, lead to forms of nationalistic irrationalism precisely because of their basically intuitive character. Sorel's general strike possessed the same ontological status as Taine's *race-milieu-moment*. Péguy should have been grateful to his influential predecessors for having prepared the ground so well for his own fictions.

He was safer when he dissociated himself from some of his contemporaries on other grounds. Maurras and his nationalist friends clearly had much in common with Péguy, and it is not surprising that they should have shown an interest in him. But Péguy thought as little of their anti-semitism as he did of their royalism. In *Notre Jeunesse* (1910) he showed why his Joan of the same year was called *Le Mystère de la Charité de Jeanne d'Arc*. It was because charity was still for him the most important Christian quality. That is why he felt compassion for all who suffer:

'Being poor myself, I shall bear witness for the Jews who are poor . . . They are like us, they are among us, they are our friends, they have been tested, they have suffered, they have been maltreated as much as we, more than we.'[49]

If he rather despised Dreyfus, that was not because he was a Jew but because the poor man fell, understandably, rather short of the saintly myths woven around him. But Julien Benda remained his close friend when most others had been shown the door, and Bergson was his main philosophical inspiration. Both were Jews. As for royalism, Péguy thought it a non-starter. On the other hand, when the nationalists actually threatened the régime Péguy warned them that they 'would find out what we are still capable of doing for the Republic'.[50] Like Barrès, Péguy accepted 1789, and there lies the main difference between them and the followers and imitators of Maurras.

Barrès, indeed, promoted Péguy's candidature for the *Académie Française* after the publication of his second Joan and *Notre Jeunesse* (both 1910). But Barrès' motives were not altogether pure. He did not think much of Péguy as a writer. According to the Tharaud brothers[51] he said that, 'when I read Péguy I look at my watch'. It was far more likely that, like the other nationalists, Barrès wanted to lure the now famous Péguy into the right-wing camp. The points that divided them worried Barrès no more than did Maurras' rejection of 1789. On the other hand, the editor of the *Cahiers* had no high opinion of Barrès.[52] This was not improved when Barrès failed to get him elected.

The general elections of May 1910 again showed how little the patriotic effusions of Péguy and the nationalists had stirred the public. The most discussed issue was whether voting by lists and proportional representation should replace the single member constituency system as it had operated since 1889. Only the radicals, who had evolved a most persuasive constituency machinery, were whole-heartedly devoted to the old system. Most other politicians averred that the changes they envisaged would make people vote for ideas rather than for personalities, and would thus lead to a fairer representation in Parliament of the political views of the country. Even as near the frontier as Reims, Lannes de Montebello[53] devoted his manifesto of two and a half sheets almost entirely to this issue. At Verdun, Albert Noël made no reference either to the army or to foreign affairs.[54] The same was true of other constituencies near the frontier, for example Chaumont and Langres (Haute Marne).[55]

The grateful complacency into which the country had relapsed after the stir of Tangier was faithfully mirrored by the successful candidates in their preoccupation with purely internal matters. Even Barrès (Paris, first constituency) apparently despaired of making political capital out of patriotism in this election. He proclaimed his 'cult of patriotism' as briefly as he then demanded 'liberty of conscience, a better financial administration, a constant and practical improvement of the fate of the least privileged'.[46] Lucien Millevoye was one of the few exceptions: 'For France first of all! For France above all else! For France always! For France in spite of everything!'[57] But it was a Lorrainer, Raoul Méguillet at Lunéville, who summed up public sentiment: 'I love my native soil. I do not forget, however, that peace is indispensable to the industrial and commercial prosperity of a nation.'[58]

Paradoxically, the socialists dwelt on foreign affairs. With Jaurès setting the tone, they warned against colonial adventures that could easily lead to open hostilities among the great powers.

'The socialist party has constantly watched and constantly denounced the intrigues, plots and imprudent acts which could endanger international peace. I venture to say that my friends and I have helped to circumscribe the dangerous Moroccan enterprise which the colonial speculators sought to enlarge and which would have set fire to the whole European powder keg.'[59]

But as in previous elections there were some socialists who went out of their way to affirm their patriotism. Meslier, at Saint Denis, pointed out that the 1910 Stuttgart congress of the Socialist International had pronounced itself against war, but not against the perpetuation of nation-states, thus again giving the lie to those who wanted to identify socialism with anti-patriotism.

The fact is, however, that only a handful of successful candidates laid any stress on patriotism, foreign affairs, or the army during these elections. One wonders where M Jacques Chastenet got the idea that the results showed that the *mystique républicaine* had been replaced by 'perhaps a patriotic faith more clearly affirmed than before'.[60] As regards the new Chamber, with the exception of an increase in socialist seats from fifty-nine to seventy-five, nothing much was changed in its political complexion. In October, having looked through his subscription list, Péguy wrote despairingly that the *Cahiers* seemed to have no future. It was clear that if the French, in fact, wanted a patriotic watchdog they wanted one that was less troublesome.

During these months of literary silence, which also included a period of illness, what Péguy called the 'deepening' [*approfondissement*] of his catholic faith continued. It was, indeed, the only consolation left to him, since he had become estranged even from his family. While the radical-socialist Prime Minister Caillaux alienated the socialists by his hostility to electoral reform, and the centre and right by his desire to introduce a progressive income tax, and while a new Moroccan crisis flared up with the arrival of the German warship *Panther* at Agadir (July 1911), Péguy continued to work on his religious profession of faith. The contrast with his reaction to Tangier could not be more complete. It would be wrong, however, to put this down to sudden indifference. The Agadir crisis was finally to convince a large number of Frenchmen that a show-down with Germany would have to come, be it military or diplomatic, and that whether it be the one or the other the balance of power between the Triple Entente and the Triple Alliance would have to be tenaciously defended if France was not to get the worst of it. It was largely because Péguy had been convinced since 1905 that the struggle was inevitable that he failed to be particularly excited by Agadir.

The *Cahier* in which he broke his silence (19th September 1911) was ostensibly an answer to Fernand Laudet's review in the *Revue Hebdomadaire* (17th June 1911) of Péguy's recent Joan. For one idiotic moment Péguy even hoped for the support of the Church to vindicate his belief in the possibility of direct personal contact with God. But, with or without that support, poor Laudet had become an unenviable target.

> 'You do not seem to doubt for a single instant, M Laudet, that when one speaks of the voices of Joan of Arc one speaks with precision . . . The voices of Joan of Arc, M Laudet, are Saint Michael, Saint Catherine and Saint Margaret. Visions, M Laudet, do you know what they are? Well, they are visions. They are direct communications.'[61]

Péguy soon recognized the isolation such views imposed upon

him, first because they involved constant soul-searching, and second because they contravened orthodoxy. But he put on a brave show: 'nothing is as beautiful as courage in solitude . . . Nothing is as beautiful, nothing is as great as he to whom the post of solitude has been entrusted.'[62] Péguy was not impressed by the charge that these doctrines involved him in sin. 'When a man does not sin, cannot sin, it is then that he is not a Christian; that man does not enter into the Christian system.' And to prove that his identification of the faith of Joan with the virtues of France had lost none of its conviction he concluded:

'[Christianity] is a city. A bad citizen belongs to the city. A good foreigner does not. A bad Frenchman is a Frenchman. A good German is not a Frenchman.'[63]

When Poincaré, after the fall of Caillaux over Agadir, became Prime Minister (15th January 1912), his decision to take over the Quai d'Orsay as well symbolized the growing awareness of the French of the seriousness of the international situation. The political effervescence in the Balkans threatened at every moment to involve either Austria or Russia or both. Thus, through the system of alliances, war between the central powers (Germany, Austria, Italy) and the Triple Entente (France, England, Russia) was a real possibility. There were of course those who felt that to involve France in war with Germany over unpronounceable Balkan places would be criminal folly.

'We Frenchmen would be without justification if we permitted ourselves under any circumstances to be drawn into this adventure. Not a French soldier, not one, should be risked . . . in the conflict caused by the aggression of the Balkan League.'[65]

It was an attitude typical of that expressed by middle-of-the-road radicals during the 1910 elections. Radical-socialists like Caillaux, as well as the socialists of the SFIO (Section Française de l'Internationale Ouvrière), continued to press for an understanding at all costs with the central powers. Neither the middle-class electors of the radicals, nor the lower middle-class electors of the radical-socialists, nor the working-class electors of the socialists had anything to gain from war. The terms in which the right of centre parties saw the situation, as a potential threat to the sovereignty of France if she failed assiduously to observe her obligations to her Entente partners, these terms seemed unreal to the left. It had little faith in the balance-of-power theories of Poincaré and his friends. To the radicals of the centre they seemed at least dangerous if not treated with the utmost prudence. So much, indeed, was Russia alarmed by the lack of enthusiasm for her cause in the Balkans that she resumed her subsidies to French newspapers, suspended in 1907, to the tune of 300,000 francs. But by 19th July 1913, when Barthou managed to get army service extended from two to three years, most of the leaders of public opinion had rallied to the policy of the maintenance of the balance of power at all costs. Only the socialists and Caillaux's radical-socialists voted against the bill. The hand of the advocates of the Triple Entente policy had already been strengthened when, in January 1913, Poincaré had succeeded Fallières at the Elysée.

How much the criterion of patriotism had changed since 1870 emerges from the obituary notices on Déroulède (31st January 1914).

> 'He was the last witness who continued to relive the *année terrible*; it seemed that the tragic memories which he defended were disappearing with him.' (*Figaro*).
>
> 'For the last ten years he was the object of an ungrateful silence.' (*Journal des Débats*).[65]

Revanche, which had been the touchstone of patriotism since the treaty of Frankfurt, had already lost its ability to stir the French by the time Boulanger blew his brains out in 1891. Since that time it was what the *patrie* stood for in the minds of individual Frenchmen that determined whether they would be moved to fight for it. *Revanche* had provided a rallying point of an appeal so universal that it was only the fear of an even more crushing defeat that had dissuaded the majority of Frenchmen in the seventies and eighties from embarking on a holy war for the recovery of Alsace-Lorraine. That twenty years of frustration and the turmoil of the political and social scene should have created a vast number of other preoccupations is easily explicable. So is a natural reluctance to go to war under any circumstances. If in the midst of the political and social upheavals of the Third Republic Alsace-Lorraine receded into the background, it was understandable that after Tangier and Agadir Frenchmen should ask themselves what the *patrie* they might now again have to fight for amounted to, and whether the need to fight for it was indeed inevitable. After over fifty years of socialist propaganda, of internationalism and anti-militarism, it was no longer enough to demand blind obedience, or to appeal to primitive patriotic reflexes. Similarly, after over fifty years of economic progress, the middle classes had to be persuaded that, economically, war would at least not be a disaster. To a progressively less gullible society, national sovereignty need not be the most important desideratum. Poincaré's belief that France could only be saved from becoming a German satellite if she resolutely stood for the preservation of the balance of power was probably sound. As yet, few were prepared to say openly that national sovereignty did not matter. But socialists and radical-socialists were clearly wondering how high a price it was worth paying for it. They were opposed to the balance of power politics of Poincaré because they alleged it would lead to war. They preferred a direct agreement with Germany. They were even prepared to forget about Alsace-Lorraine, particularly if the proposed autonomy of the area within the German Empire were to be made a reality. Few of them however went so far as to say that, as a last resort, they would not be ready to defend their country.

From the point of view of the Triple Entente, it was as well that France also had a right wing. However positivistic the *Action Française* and other right-wing groups pretended to be, they had a vested interest in irrationalism. Reliance on reason, they said, made for materialism, and materialism made for democracy, which made for stagnation and weakness. Whether they primarily detested stagnation, or democracy, or materialism, they were agreed that only some form of idealism could do away with it. If one listened to one's heart instead of one's reason, they argued, generosity would get the better of egoism, the good of the community would be put before narrow self interest, and mere number would seem to be less important than quality. Democracy would, therefore, yield to oligarchy or monarchy, and patriotism would be recognized as a sacred duty which would keep the country united. The early Barrès had already preached the merits of a common hatred. Poincaré in his first speech as Prime Minister had made no mention of social legislation.

But even during the general elections of 1914, when the prospects for peace were already dim, few candidates were chauvinistic.

Those of the right contented themselves on the whole with self-congratulation on having voted the three year military law, and with the demand that France should be ready to face all contingencies in a patriotic spirit.[66] Louis Puech put their case very concisely: 'The [three year] law had become indispensable as a result of . . . the formidable increase in German forces. The security of the frontier was no longer certain.'[61] For the extreme republican right Henri Galli made the point rather more volubly:

'The first duty of a Frenchman as our fathers understood it in 1792, is to serve France, that is to be ready to defend her as a soldier. The French Republic, faithful to the glorious past of the nation, must not let itself down, it cannot connive at violations of Justice; it can only accept a dignified and proud peace; it must have the force to inspire respect. That is why the national Army, which guarantees our independence is our most important preoccupation.'[68]

As one moves towards the centre one encounters less specific emphasis on the demands of patriotism. Indeed Waldeck-Rousseau's *Parti républicain démocratique* put the stress on economic policy: 'We have made our choice between the French revolution and the social revolution,' it said tersely. The social revolution entailed income tax, the French revolution liberty, that is freedom from having one's finances pried into for income tax purposes. They therefore chose the French revolution.[69] At the centre Briand, Barthou, and Millerand, grouped in the *Fédération des gauches*, talked about the desirability of improving the hygiene of the nation, as indeed Barrès did also as a good national-socialist. Like the various right-wing groups they continued to support their three-year military law and, at the second ballot, ended with the rather lame patriotic appeal:

'Republicans and patriots! You will vote only for men who do not separate the interests of the Republic from those of the *patrie*.'[70]

The sting in the tail was meant to hurt the socialists, for the radicals and radical-socialists at least paid lip-service to patriotism by insisting on peace with dignity. 'We want to be strong in order to command respect.'[71] But their main preoccupation was no more with foreign affairs in 1914 than it had been in 1910.

They concentrated on flogging two horses, one of which was dead (laicism) and the other too much alive for electoral comfort (the introduction of income tax).

The socialists alone spoke out as a group against the three-year military law. It is significant, however, that – with the exception of Dejeante at Belleville – they rested their case on the alleged uselessness of this increase in military service. They maintained that a return to two years would strengthen rather than weaken national defence. They did not – Dejeante again excepted – imply that national defence did not matter. Jaurès was most eloquent on this point:

> 'With all my strength, aided by the whole socialist party and too small a section of the radicals, I have fought the bad three-year law. With all my strength I shall take up the fight against it again from the very beginning of the new legislature. It is so absurd, so contrary to the true interests of national defence, so enfeebling for the army itself, so ruinous for the budget, so crushing for industrial and agricultural production, so hard on the peasants whose manpower already barely suffices for the land . . . It is in the truly democratic organizations of the nation-at-arms that France will find the guarantee of her independence, of her just and human self-respect.'[72]

These views, which Jaurès had earlier expressed at rather greater length in his *L'Armée nouvelle* (1910) and which entailed the abolition of a standing army in favour of a national militia, his fellow-socialists proclaimed up and down the country. Among them was Pierre Laval at Saint Denis.[73]

The socialist Dejeante, however, went further. He succeeded in getting himself elected in Gambetta's Belleville on the bold declaration that national sovereignty was an outdated concept. 'To urge a war nowadays for the sole aim of ethnic unity . . . is a monstrous crime and a mark of stupidity.'[74] France, he added, should make the same efforts to negotiate an entente with Germany as she had made towards the entente with Russia and England. The evolution of political thinking in Belleville since Gambetta is intriguing. In 1889, Tony Révillon had been elected in the same constituency on a programme stating that 'as patriots, we await the hour of *revanche* without fear, though without provoking it.'[75] In 1893 the candidate for Belleville made no reference to either Germany or *revanche*. It is not until 1906 that there is again any significant reference to foreign affairs. Dejeante then advocated a 'purely defensive policy; the maintenance of international peace'.[76] The rest of the programmes through these years were concerned with internal socialist reforms. In 1910 Dejeante made no mention whatever of either the army or of foreign affairs. This development in political thinking is typical of the growing lack of interest at least among the working-classes in patriotic attitudes.

The coming of the war coincided with the crystallization of Péguy's religious thinking. At the beginning of 1914 the works of Bergson were threatened with the catholic index. Péguy, in an effort to vindicate his philosophical idol, set out to show that Bergson's intuitionism was a necessary condition of true faith. He had always held that the most detestable aspect of catholicism was the 'mystical complacency'[77] of the catholics. For him catholicism was the religion of the rich, the satisfied, of those without problems. He now dwelt on the belief that only free personal choice could guarantee true faith. But it must not lead to Montaigne's endless scepticism. That was a cowardly abdication of responsibility.[78] Descartes was nearer the mark, particularly when in the second maxim of the *Discours* he commended action even when the truth of the principles on which it was based was not demonstrable.[79]

'Anything is to be preferred to going round in circles – To set out, *walk straight on*, arrive somewhere. Arrive somewhere else rather than not arrive at all. Arrive where one was not going rather than not arrive at all. Above all, arrive.'[80]

Arrive, yes, but not to remain there, but to set out again, free, to explore more corners of the earth, 'a heart and a spirit perpetually alert, a heart and a spirit perpetually pure'.[81] 'The most honest man is not he who complies with the obvious rules. It is he who remains in his place, works, suffers, is silent.'[82] And that is how Péguy hoped to convince Rome.

When the *Note sur M Bergson*, which was largely about Descartes, had manifestly failed in its purpose – for Bergson was put on the index in June 1914 – Péguy returned to the charge in *Note Conjointe sur M Descartes*, which was largely about Bergson. The familiar themes recur, but they are amplified.

'[Bergson] takes us literally back to the point of Christianity, the point of view, the point of life and the point of the existence of Christianity. For he puts us back into the realm of the precarious, the transitory, the naked which truly is the condition of man.'[83]

Neo-Thomists like Maritain, who had published his attack on *Bergsonian Philosophy* in 1913, are taken to task for their 'static Christian theology'.[84]

'They are not Christians. They constantly lose sight of that precariousness which is for the Christian the most real aspect of the condition of man . . . They are at peace, contented, modern.'[85]

Let them have no illusions about their future. Bergson's loss will not be their gain. The positivism of Spencer will gather up whatever fugitives there might be from the intuitionists:

'Saint Thomas will have nothing. And he will have no one. And he will be as he was before Bergson . . . A great doctor, esteemed, celebrated, honoured . . . Buried.'[86]

The honest search for truth, for God, cannot therefore according to Péguy be reconciled with a belief in ready-made orthodoxies. 'There is something worse than a bad soul: a ready-made soul.'[87] Life must be a perpetual crusade for truth, for its discovery and its defence, and the crusade is endless because certainty endlessly eludes us. But freedom is a prior condition for the very possibility of this crusade. This freedom France incarnates, and of this freedom Germany is the implacable enemy.

'It is for that reason that we do not delude ourselves when we believe that a whole world is interested in the resistance France puts up against German encroachments. That a whole world would perish with us, and that that would be the world of liberty itself.'[88]

That, in the centuries of struggle between the protagonists of these two principles, the principle of liberty has never entirely succumbed proves for Péguy that God is on its side: 'God wants to be loved freely'.[89] The argument is meant to be efficacious against both the Thomists and the Germans. It is also directed against the socialists: 'While life is alive, while liberty is free . . . it makes war',[90] it fights for its survival. All else is cowardice.

The *Note Conjointe* was not published until 1924, for Péguy had been mobilized before he could see it through the press.

'Praying, fighting. The first not without the second. The second not without the first. But the first and the second together, both.'[91]

When Poincaré's balance-of-power fixation finally led France into war on 4th August 1914, Péguy's arch-enemy Jaurès had already been assassinated (31st July 1914), and he could depart with 'savage exultation'.[82] On the first day of the battle of the Marne, 5th September 1914, he died in action.

Péguy's enthusiasm for the war found few immediate echoes in France. Even on 1st August Poincaré refused to summon Parliament. According to Carroll,[93] this was because he wanted to avoid a show of chauvinism, but it is much more likely that the President was afraid of the reverse. When the hours that followed showed that the machinery of the alliances had inexorably been set in motion by Austria's reaction to the Serajevo murder, *revanche*, a concept carefully hidden from polite society since Boulanger, was anxiously coaxed back into the political limelight. It was meant to add an element of nobility to the absurdities of power politics, to unite the country in its reluctance and bewilderment. It just about did the trick.[94]

CHAPTER SEVEN

THE *ACTION FRANÇAISE* AND THE FIRST WORLD WAR

ONE OF the interesting questions about the political climate at the outbreak of the war is why the noisiest 'patriots' seemed no keener for the show-down when it was obviously imminent than anyone else. On 1st August the nationalist *Presse* wrote 'no one in France has desired war, it will be accepted as a cruel test'.[1] Jacques Bainville, whose admiration for Maurras was equalled only by Maurras' admiration for him, viewed the situation with the coolest detachment. He confided to his *Journal* that only the Republic could have been foolish enough to expect peace from the international mores of the period:

> '27th July 1914 . . . But what stupidity could have led anyone to believe that Europe divided into two formidably armed groups competing with each other in an armaments race offered solid foundations for peace? It is clear today, though perhaps rather late, that the European balance of power through the Triple Entente and Triple Alliance was mere verbiage, concealing the reality of the situation which the ministers and spokesmen of the government of the Republic will be seen to have dangerously obscured.'[2]

Maurras may claim that the mobilization proceeded smoothly in Paris only because his strong-arm men kept the anarchists at bay,[3] but it is clear from the writings of most of the members and sympathizers of the *Action Française* that they already thought of themselves as an élite outside the framework of the republican *patrie*. Even at the worst moments of the war Bainville's *Journal*, with implacable monotony, labours three points. One: the excellence of absolute monarchy; two: the decadence of democratic republicanism; three: the need for naked self-interest in international affairs. It was typical of the priorities of the *Action Française* throughout its existence that it was more concerned with the political enemy at home than with the national enemy abroad. The patriotism its spokesmen forever claimed for it had less to do with the blindly passionate defence of the native soil than with a most exclusive doctrine about who, and in the name of which principles, should govern France. It thus helped to atrophy the normal patriotic reflexes from the right, as class-consciousness and economic self-interest were creating similar effects from the left.

The political development of Charles Maurras provides an effective insight into the mentality of the *Action Française* as a whole. Born in 1868 at Martigues, he came to Paris in 1885. His father had been a supporter of Thiers after Sedan, and Maurras himself was no royalist in his early years in Paris. But from his lower middle-class background he had inherited its anti-semitism:

> 'The moment I took my very first steps in Paris, on the morning of 2nd December 1885, I was struck, emotionally affected, almost wounded by the physical appearance of those beautiful streets and those great boulevards that were decorated from top to bottom with a multitude of foreign signs, filled with those names containing K, W, Z which our printing workers wittily call the Jewish letters. *Were the French still at home in France?*'[4]

He was seventeen, had been stirred by Lamennais' *Paroles d'un Croyant* but had allowed Schopenhauer to fill the void created by a growing agnosticism. Taine, Le Play, de Maistre and Bossuet had led him to Comte and Renan, the positivist convincing him of the futility of thinking in terms of class-war, the sceptic persuading him of the social and political efficacy of élites.

> 'Comte put to flight the pernicious and artificial doctrine according to which there is an opposition between the interests of the ruler and the ruled, for the latter derives his greatest benefit from being directed and guided . . . Renan finally made me aware of the service any élite, when it sincerely concerns itself with the highest considerations, renders and must render to the multitude, even unconsciously.'[5]

Maurras was struck by what he took to be three social facts. First, man's apparently innate desire to transform his environment. Second, the differences that exist between men in the mastery they have achieved over this environment. Third, man's desire to transmit his mastery to his descendants, thus perpetuating the differences already created.[6] Capital and tradition are expressions of mastery achieved and Maurras wonders, rhetorically, whether 'the unity of mankind could exist without that capital which the revolutionaries of my youth called *infamous* and which I, for my part, called *divine*'.[7] The conclusions he drew from these postulates are worth quoting more fully. They inform all the thinking of the *Action Française*:

> 'This pre-existing capital brings men fortune and honour, equips and refines them from the moment they come into the world, without anything having been done about it by these happy animals . . . Whatever brings together this beneficent capital is therefore a good thing; whatever dissipates it is less good. Work is good, saving is good . . . It is in the closely knit and stable circle of the home that production, acquisition, conservation have the greatest chance of success, for the personal instinct is there moderated and regulated by immediate affection, and generosity balanced by healthy egoism. Thus strength, duration and heredity are related and linked; so are also the constitution of great families, the accumulation of vast possessions, the possibility of education and culture.'[8]

Communism, Maurras continued, could conceivably apply its egalitarian doctrines to an ephemeral and rootless society. But the moment this society encountered difficulties, the natural inequalities among men would assert themselves, and natural hierarchies would emerge.

Although he took inequality as a basic social datum, and as such deemed it an inescapable starting point for all social and political theory, Maurras was aware of the abuses that power in the hands of the few could entail. But if the accumulation of moral, cultural, and material capital was the supreme good, and Maurras never seems to have doubted that it was, then he was prepared to accept the evils of inequality rather than have his supreme good compromised by inhibiting the action of the élites which alone could promote it. He consoles himself with the thought that the benefits of capital, even if initially monopolized by the élites themselves, would eventually also percolate to the rest of society:

'No one is disinterested. Man is an heir. The beggar who devours his black bread sitting on the edge of a milestone benefits from the work of the centuries that preceded him, he is an aristocrat seated on the savings of thousands of ancestors . . . It is the seed of the strong which creates the capital through which everything progresses.'[9]

Maurras is adamant on another point. His doctrine, he says, owes nothing to Nietzsche. The author of *Zarathustra* lacked generosity, according to Maurras, while his own social conscience, formed by Plato, Aristotle, Pascal, Bossuet, Comte, and Renan, was in his opinion highly developed.[10] He will always regret being accounted a member of the right. 'When we are being treated as men of the right it must be recognized how many of that right were heart and soul the good friends of our worst enemies.'[11] He is here thinking of those conservatives who had rallied to the Republic after 1892, and of the fact that the good friends of the Republic were not always the most conscious of social evils.[12]

It was the Wilson scandal that had brought a reluctant Maurras to political action. He was nineteen. '2nd December 1887, Place de la Concorde, with 200,000 other Parisians, and the unanimous cry "Down with the thieves", to overthrow M Grévy.'[13] He did not care much for Boulanger, but he was impressed by the growing conservatism of the General, and the national awakening the Boulangist movement seemed to promote. At a moment when other nations arrogantly proclaimed their putative rights and vaunted their strength, France was in a state of political anarchy. The smallest sub-groups of the Slav world, Japan, China, the Philippines, all were beginning to assert themselves as nations. What he thought important about this phenomenon was that 'nationalism, wherever it can, breathes conquest and absorption, pacific or warlike'.[14] If France was to hold her own in this free-for-all, she had to think out her policies scientifically. It was too late for pragmatic muddling. As Renan had shown, democracy is the great dissolvant of the military institutions of a country. If only for that reason, democracy had to go if France was to survive. But what was to replace it?

It was on a French ship in the spring of 1896, after his first trip to Greece, that the ostentatious self-assurance of the descendants of the victors of Trafalgar and Waterloo led Maurras to his answer.[15] Again it is worth quoting him at some length.

'We were on a boat from Marseille. The company, captain, crew, all belonged there. Among the passengers only a few were French. Was it then for the sake of other races that we were ploughing through the sea of Theseus and Ulysses, of Pytheas and Duilius? But the cook, who must have hailed from the Saint-Jean district, had written the menu in an Anglo-French that was so reassuring that the rumpsteak appeared on it as *ronstec*. I abandoned myself silently to the joy of a free and beautiful translation when on the other side of the table a ruddy-cheeked lady with big teeth grabbed the gold pencil that adorned her skinny bust. The ferocious image of Great Britain truly mistress of the sea, she struck out with one determined stroke our provençalism, replacing it with the outraged insular formula. Let it not be said that I could have hit a lady, but, across the glasses, the plates and the flowers, I sent her the look of the man who is ruined, despoiled, who is being evicted from his home . . . The fact is that, from that moment, the destiny of my country began to be clear to me; I pictured our nation endowed with so many worthwhile qualities still intact, still sparkling with so much charm, but reduced to the position of a real orphan. In what way are, or were, those proud English better than we?'[16]

Maurras was twenty-eight, and one might fervently hope he had his tongue in his cheek. Nothing is more unlikely.

With that hard, objective, positivistic look that Maurras had decided to take at political realities, he found that the reasons for British superiority lay in the settled political and social climate of the island. How different things were in France. There, democracy had produced leaders who were merely out to make their packet, before returning to the obscurity they should in all decency never have left. In England, indeed in any country that amounted to anything, what ensured the settled conditions indispensable for greatness was the existence of a ruling dynasty:

'In London and in Berlin, at the time when Berlin and London flourished, the government was *dynastic*; it was so in Paris when Paris flourished. Dynastic succession creates the coherence of all the strength of an empire. Etymology would tell one that, in the absence of history. Not only because dynasty does without the exhausting system of electoral and parliamentary competition, but because it is good and beautiful that the authority of the sovereign authority should not be a force fashioned by human hand, that it should come to us from the most ancient times, and that the centuries should have created it for us and transmitted it to us, named it and imposed it on us *ready-made*, helped as it were by its legitimacy, that *right* of the leaders which is based on the fact that they played the major part in the creation of the country.'[17]

For a would-be political realist these lines contain a quaint interpretation of the powers of Queen Victoria. But within the contemporary French context one clearly sees what Maurras meant: 'That France may live, the King must return.'[18]

The political evolution of Maurras was almost complete. He merely had to rid himself of the optimistic hope that the changes he envisaged could be effected from below. By 1897 he was not only a convinced royalist, but had also concluded that universal suffrage was so mindless that its salvation had to be imposed on it from the top.[19] What it is difficult to fit into this doctrine is Maurras' federalism. One would have thought that the decentralization it entailed would have weakened the power of the central government he wanted strong. It is however not of major importance for his doctrine.[20]

The Dreyfus affair and its aftermath forced Maurras and his friends to examine their position in relation to other anti-republican groups. From this examination the *Action Française* emerged as a distinct movement. Maurras began, on 3rd November 1897, with an article *A quoi servirait un monarque*. There, with the most brazen but characteristic disregard for the truth, he maintained that the republican democrats who defended Dreyfus were merely trying to avenge their treatment at the hands of the army in 1871:

'The old republicans are drunk with joy. The army, their enemy, had once been their judge (for, after all, those people got close to, if they did not actually appear before, the courts-martial of 1871). . . . No monarchic state, of whatever kind, would allow that.'[21]

The implication is clearly meant to be that the republicans of 1870-1 had been traitors to their country, and that the army had acted as the patriotic avenging angel. The lie is too obvious to need refutation. Even if one were to disbelieve the patriotic protestations of the communards, it would be hard to forget that it was the imperial armies which had surrendered and that it was the Republic which had fought on. The more genteel representatives of the right will find Maurras' readiness to subordinate everything to his political ends, including the truth and good manners, a rather distasteful characteristic.

One might have respected Maurras more if he had admitted that the kind of monarchic rule he dreamt of could only establish and maintain itself with the help of a strong army, and that it was for that reason that he wanted the army inviolable. His lack of real concern for *revanche* is adequately epitomized by the fact that one encounters no reference to it in his history of the *Action Française* (*Au Signe de Flore*) until one reaches page forty-two. Like the rest of the right, he is far too concerned with internal political questions to worry much about foreign enemies. But this does not prevent him, nor his friends, from blaming the Jewish-Freemason syndicate for having promoted anarchy in the army which, they further allege, was to be the cause of the heavy French casualties of the First World War. Léon Daudet even put the syndicate in the pay of the Germans:

> 'Solely restrained in the Republic of Bismarck-Gambetta (1871-97) by the French military element, [the Germans] had succeeded, thanks to Jewish complicity, in completely disorganizing that military element in the Republic of Bismarck-Dreyfus (1897-1912). The roads were free, the ministries accessible; so were the bribes.'[22]

Disavowed by the monarchist *Soleil* whose valued contributor he had often been, ignored even by the *Libre Parole* of the arch-anti-semite Drumont, Maurras allowed his hatred of the syndicate to explode in an hysterical apology for Henry, who had committed suicide when his forgeries, meant to confirm the guilt of Dreyfus, were exposed. 'Colonel,' he was permitted to write in the *Gazette de France*, 'your blood . . ., according to the newspapers, was quickly wiped away on the orders of the governor of the Mont-Valérien. But that is a great error. You should know that there is not a single drop of that precious blood, the first French blood shed in the Dreyfus affair, which does not run hot wherever there beats a French heart.'[23]

For Maurras, Henry's death at the end of August 1898 marked the beginning of national revival, although it took some months before many of those of the right, who had earlier turned a deaf ear to his diatribes, began to join the bandwagon. It was then that the *Libre Parole* collected one hundred thousand francs to fight Joseph Reinach's pro-Dreyfus campaign; that the *Ligue de la Patrie Française* was formed with a similar aim; that 'legitimate hope opened its wing'. Maurras, so far mainly known as a literary critic, was now fast acquiring fame as a political polemicist. Amouretti, Lucien Moreau, and Gabriel Syveton were his close collaborators. At the office of the *Soleil* he met that matinée idol, Barrès, to organize the opposition to Dreyfus among the intellectuals. It was a great blow that Anatole France, whom he held in great esteem, joined the defenders of Dreyfus. Instead, he recruited Henri Vaugeois and Maurice Pujo, whose renown at that time was no greater than that of his other collaborators.

The two main nationalist movements of the moment, Déroulède's *Ligue des Patriotes* and the *Ligue de la Patrie Française*, made little appeal to Maurras. He recognized both for what they were: the first worthy but politically inept, aggressively wedded to a republicanism that was supposed to be tightened up by plebiscitary appeals to universal suffrage; the second, in its efforts to recruit as many intellectuals as possible, too woolly to have any real meaning.[24] He and his friends therefore decided to launch a more incisive and vigorous campaign of their own. After much argument Maurras managed to persuade those who had since April 1898 formed with him the group of the *Action Française* that constitutional means were inadequate to deal with the situation. 'There was only one remedy: that of insurrectional force.'[45] Or, as he was to put it later, the ideas of the *Action Française* had to win 'by the use of any means, even legal ones'.[26] Time, he said, was running out. France was rapidly being led to the slaughter by the syndicate, abetted by a blindly complaisant electorate:

'The very *being* of this *patrie*, the *body* of this nation, the real *object* called France . . . had to matter to us far more than the French . . . In short . . . if angling has to be defended against anglers and hunting against hunters, there may be something to be said for defending France against the French.'[27]

Thus was conceived the distinction between the *pays réel* and the *pays légal*, the first the true France as interpreted by the so-called élite of the *Action Française*, the second the France of universal suffrage, fickle, gullible, selfish, brainless. *Réaction d'abord* was the theme of Vaugeois's article in the bulletin of the movement, 1st August 1899. Moreover, Maurras' *Enquête sur la Monarchie* (1900), commissioned by the *Gazette de France*, had shown that the restoration of the monarchy no longer seemed the crazy dream it had been even five years earlier. By 1902 Vaugeois, Pujo, Montesquiou, Lucien Moreau had helped to make the *Action Française* royalist as well as openly reactionary.

Despite the pretensions of Barrès[28] and the *Ligue de la Patrie Française*, Maurras also felt that it was left to his own movement effectively to organize the opponents of the democratic Republic by providing them with a clearcut guide to belief and action.[29] To that end, in January 1905, the *Ligue de l'Action Française* was founded. The declaration that every member had to sign read:

'As a Frenchman by birth and sentiment, by rational conviction and deliberate choice, I shall carry out all the duties of an alert patriot. I undertake to fight any republican régime. The Republic in France is the reign of the foreigner. The republican spirit disorganizes national defence and promotes religious influences directly opposed to traditional catholicism. France must be given back a régime that is French. Our only future is therefore the Monarchy as it is personified by HRH the Duke of Orléans, heir of forty kings who, in the course of a thousand years, made France. Only the Monarchy ensures the public good and, being responsible for order, prevents the public evils denounced by anti-semitism and nationalism. The Monarchy, which is the necessary organ of all the general interests, restores authority, liberty, prosperity and honour. I associate myself with the work of monarchic restoration. I undertake to serve it with all available means.'[30]

The *Action Française* gained little from the disintegration of the *Ligue de la Patrie Française* after its electoral failure in 1902. It is surprising that Maurras should have expected it to do so. The gentlemen of the *Ligue* who laced their innocuous patriotic generalities with an occasional pious tear were hardly likely to be attracted by the crude, allegedly scientific, violence of the *Action Française*. Maurras, nevertheless, lamented that the majority of the right did not support him, and enviously contrasted this absence of enthusiasm with the fervour shown by the right-wing parties in Italy and Germany towards the fascists and nazis after the First World War.[31] But his movement did make headway, particularly among young intellectuals. Its proselytizing activities increased still further with the founding of the *Institut de l'Action Française*, where 'the teaching was based on what, in practice, there was in common between the ideas of de Bonald and Comte, de Maistre and Renan, traditional catholic dogma and the experience of history'.[32] Moreover, in 1908, the bulletin of the *Action Française* became a daily newspaper under the direction of Vaugeois, with Léon Daudet as editor.

But the most visible impact of the *Action Française* was made through its systematic recourse to violence. For a movement that was deliberately anti-constitutional such conduct was to be expected, and it is with loving detail that Maurras describes the street fights and other forms of rowdyism in which it was involved at every possible opportunity. For example:

'Thalamas [who had spoken ill of Joan of Arc] . . . had turned up again, no longer in a modest secondary school, but in the midst of the Sorbonne . . . What a scandal! It was not allowed to pass unnoticed. We were equipped to put that right. Led by Maurice Pujo – whose audacity, common sense and sure touch, from the beginning to the end, from 1908 to 1939, had always made him the obvious person to undertake and execute all the real "actions" of the *Action Française* – Maurice Pujo, seconded by Maxime Réal del Sarte and Marius Plateau, led, I said, by them, the patriots of Paris, first the students, then all, young and old, inaugurated those famous Thalamas days which have not received their renown for nothing. On eleven consecutive Wednesdays, led by Pujo and the *Action Française*, the Latin Quarter rose in revolt, booed the emulator and successor of Cauchon, invaded the University, once took the lecture room by assault, on another occasion spanked the professor at the rostrum and finally drove him from it, without mentioning the detour past the Place Vendôme which allowed a sally into the very chancellery of Briand.'[33]

Perhaps it was simply the vanity of an old man, but recalling, in 1943, this and similar 'actions', Maurras makes them the cause of Briand's Périgueux speech (1910), in which he had asked for the reconciliation of the political factions in France. The vulgarities of the *Action Française* might have been a nuisance in Paris; to claim that 'these words of reconciliation were therefore imposed by us'[34] is, at that time, megalomaniac nonsense. Even Maurras had to confess in his less sanguine moments that his 'judicious mixture of brain and fist',[35] his 'violence . . . in the service of reason'[36] could not count on success until 1950.[37]

Maurras alleged that his 'integral nationalism' was meant to counter the kind of patriotism that was confined to the defence of a particular image of France. Disapprovingly he quoted Ranc's, 'Yes, France must be great and the Republic strong, but it must be the France of the Revolution, and the Republic that represents Right and Justice in the world.'[38] Maurras averred that the *Action Française* stood for unconditional patriotism, and it would seem from the attitude adopted towards his movement immediately before the First World War, and during it, that this affirmation was taken at its face value by a considerable number of his compatriots. It therefore appeared logical that he should attack Péguy for his attachment to the ideals of 1789, just as he had attacked Ranc, and even Barrès, though the last with some circumspection. All three reserved their fervour for a particular vision of France. But even before 1914, Maurras' unconditional patriotism can be seen to have been a pose. The distinction between the 'real' France of the *Action Française* and the 'legal' France of universal suffrage was already then of fundamental importance to him. His quarrel with Ranc and Péguy was, in fact, a quarrel among sectarians.

It is true, however, that when the First War came his movement, like most of its rivals, was still old-fashioned enough to rally to the defence of the State regardless of its political constitution. Yet his claim that France could only go to war because it was propped up by the *Action Française* is as fantastically unreal as his account of the reason for Briand's Périgueux speech:

'The three-year military service law had indeed been voted (it could not have been, said M Barthou,[39] without the Camelots du

Roi[40] who prevented the anarchists from coming down to the Place de la Concorde) . . . In mid-July 1914 Jaurès was talking about proclaiming a general strike in the face of the enemy. At the end of the same month 'additional police', our Camelots du Roi, were needed on the *grands boulevards* to cut to pieces the anarchist bands of Almereyda and ensure the smooth functioning of mobilization in Paris. If therefore our stupid Democracy did not die, it had been seriously wounded, and remained contained and supervised by us.'[41]

Even if the *Action Française* had the wide appeal among youthful intellectuals that *Les Jeunes Gens d'Aujourd'hui* attributed to it in 1913,[42] Poincaré would have managed manfully without it.

Despite all the patriotic clamour generated by the *Action Française* before, during, and after the war, there is no evidence that it seriously meant to arrest the growing disunity of France in the face of the threat from abroad. On the contrary, it contributed all it could to increase this disunity, making its internal enemies the main target for its activities. Even Maurras' *Kiel et Tanger* (1910) was little more than an indictment of the Republic whose degeneracy, he alleged, prevented it from effectively waging war. The acid detachment of Bainville in July 1914, which made him ask whether 'the government of the Republic [has] sufficiently considered the consequence of the Russian alliance,'[43] is not effaced by the *Action Française* of the same day when it expressed the hope that, as in previous similar cases, arbitration would resolve the conflict between the two blocs. It is a moot point whether its professed opinion that the democratic Republic was no match for the Germans justified such attitudes towards what to most Frenchmen appeared as insolent provocation, or whether its subsequent support for the war effort atoned for them.

Maurras had made much of the suppression of the Statistical Section of the War Office, which was a direct result of the Dreyfus affair. He had maintained that it had seriously weakened military intelligence, as André's witchhunts had seriously weakened the army's morale. Indeed, military intelligence was poor. It was responsible for many of the early disasters of the war. Joffre, Chief of the General Staff since 1911, had grossly underestimated the strength of the enemy, and it was largely this error which turned early French successes into the rout of the end of August, costing the French, and the British Expeditionary Force that had begun to arrive at the front in the third week of August, 300,000 casualties.

The Germans had sent patrols into France on 2nd August, the day after French mobilization, and had declared war on the 3rd. By the beginning of September they had got as far as Chantilly, and had won a considerable victory over the Russians at Tannenberg. That France did not suffer the fate of 1870 all over again was largely due to Joffre's nerve. At the end of the first week of September, he had begun the battle of the Marne, and with it the recovery of France. But the country had received a severe jolt, not least by the government's removal to Bordeaux on the forty-second anniversary of Sedan. By 15th November the front had been stabilized, the long trench-war of attrition had begun. The government returned to Paris on 9th December 1914.

The growing numbers of the B.E.F. did not, however, compensate for the strategic superiority of the Germans. They held most of the high ground of the line and were consequently in a good position to deal with the many offensives Joffre's military preconceptions imposed on them. In spite of the bloody failures of these methods, and the ill-starred Dardanelles adventure for which he bore less responsibility, Joffre was made Commander-in-Chief of all French armies at the end of 1915. By then 600,000 Frenchmen had died. The war clearly was not going to be as short as everyone, including the Germans who had not had a Dreyfus affair, had expected, and not only politicians were beginning to wonder about its cost in lives and wealth.

The government of Sacred Union (*Union Sacrée*), formed by Viviani on 28th August 1914, had so far had the support of most politicians. Even Guesde had joined it, with Delcassé back at the Foreign Ministry and Millerand at the War Office; at the Interior was Malvy, the protégé of Caillaux, himself debarred from office through the unfortunate conduct of his wife who, in a fit of conjugal loyalty, had shot down the editor of the *Figaro* because he had said unkind things about her husband. But after over a year of the apparently endless struggle murmurs of discontent began to be heard. Was Joffre's manner of waging the war, so costly in French lives, really the best? Was the army being properly and speedily enough equipped? Were the appalling conditions in the trenches inevitable? Was the best way of paying for the war really by means of loans as distinct from increased taxation? Were the British pulling their weight or were they and the Americans simply enriching themselves by supplying the French with loans, and with war-materials that France could not manufacture herself in adequate quantities because the Germans occupied the industrial regions in the North and North-East? More seriously, socialists like Merrheim were beginning to say openly that the French proletariat had no obvious stake in this war, even if the socialist party, on 14th July 1915, unanimously voted a resolution stating that the only hope of freedom lay in the defeat of Imperial Germany. None of this, however, was strong stuff, and the fact that Viviani resigned in October 1915 had little effect on the continuation of the political truce. But with Viviani went Millerand, who had allowed Joffre a very free hand in military matters. The new team headed by Briand saw in their Commander-in-Chief no more than the victor of the Marne; they were not particularly impressed by his performance since.

The Germans upset Joffre's plan for a July offensive in 1916 by a series of attacks on Verdun, lasting from 21st February until 12th July. Joffre could see little point in holding the fortress and would have withdrawn had he not been reminded of its sentimental value. Difficult to defend, particularly since the French were still short of heavy artillery, and militarily useless, Verdun became a graveyard for both armies. When the fighting there ceased in the middle of July, the two sides had lost about 300,000 men each in casualties. It had, however, brought to public attention the name of Philippe Pétain, who had taken over command at Verdun after the first German attack. He had shown himself a resolute but humane leader, under whom soldiers would fight with great devotion.

Regardless of the massacre at Verdun, punctually on 1st July 1916, Joffre launched his Somme offensive. It dragged on into November, achieved nothing of any consequence, and again brought heavy casualties. Meanwhile Nivelle had recovered, at little cost, most of the losses around Verdun. The politicians in Paris felt that Joffre had outlasted his usefulness and Briand, after making him the first Marshal of France since 1870, replaced him with Nivelle. To show that a new era was beginning, military headquarters were moved from Chantilly to Beauvais. The rumblings of discontent among the working population were silenced by means of wage increases at about the same time. But the apparently endless butchery extended the appeal of pacifism in the socialist ranks, particularly in Paris. The following year was to be the most crucial. It provided the seeds of victory. But it also provided the seeds of France's post-war political plight.

Nivelle's plan for 1917 was one of quick victories. By a more judicious disposition of artillery, he thought, he would defeat the enemy at little cost. He promised that if after two days an attack was not successful it would be stopped. There would be none of the disastrous drawn-out battles that had characterized Joffre's operations. Briand fell in March 1917 and was followed by Ribot, whose War Minister, Painlevé, had no high opinion of Nivelle nor of his plan. But after a threat of resignation the Commander-in-Chief was given his head and, on 16th April 1917, the offensive was launched. By then, however, everyone seemed to be in the secret and the Germans, who had air superiority in any case, were not greatly troubled by the onslaught. It is not saying much that Nivelle gained a little more than Joffre had done at the Somme. He had kept neither of his promises. In mid-May he had still won no victory, nor had he ended the battle. Ribot replaced him with Pétain, who made Foch his Chief of Staff. The government had acted only just in time.

The thirty-two months of hardship that many soldiers had experienced, the repeated promises of swift victories that seemed forever to go unfulfilled, the lack of confidence in their leaders and a growing feeling of the pointlessness of so much carnage had led to a number of mutinies in May 1917. No doubt some were politically inspired; the March revolution in Russia had reinforced pacifist propaganda in France. But although there were rumours about a march on Paris, the mutinies themselves were not violent. Still, the fighting spirit of the army was inevitably weakened while soldiers undermined its discipline, and it was lucky for the allies that the Germans had no idea of what was going on. Pétain, the new Commander-in-Chief, restored order by remedying some of the main material grievances – food, lodgings, leave, allowances, launching a few successful small offensives, paternally touring the whole line, and executing twenty-three trouble-makers. But no sooner was the army on the point of emerging from its moral ordeal than there came a political crisis that threatened to eclipse it.

Among the government's propaganda efforts was the payment of subsidies to newspapers. The *Bonnet Rouge* was one which received such support. When, however, that paper appeared to become a mouthpiece for pacifist agitation, the government subsidy ceased. It was promptly replaced by a German subsidy. Although this fact seems to have been generally known, no official action was taken because, it was rumoured, the *Bonnet Rouge* enjoyed the protection of Malvy, who was the only minister to have retained the same office since 1914. But the politicians were no longer the docile upholders of national unity they had been in the first two years of the war, and Ribot was not the man to bring them to heel. It was bad enough that Nivelle should have been allowcd to carry out his allegedly crackbrained scheme. When the mutinies broke out they felt that the time for action had come. Did the government intend to win the war? If so, how could they reconcile that intention with the tacit support given to pacifism by one of their chief ministers? Daudet, in the *Action Française*, characteristically went to the extreme of accusing Malvy of treason, of having betrayed Nivelle's secrets to the enemy. On 22nd July Clemenceau attacked Malvy in the Chamber. Malvy was forced to take a holiday. At the end of August he resigned. It was also the end of Ribot.

Painlevé, who succeeded Ribot, indeed took action against the *Bonnet Rouge*. But the military situation was now so grave, and the political situation so delicate, that someone more imposing than Painlevé was required. The British had suffered severely at Passchendaele, after the October revolution Russia was out of the war, the Italians had been routed, more German-subsidized pacifists were uncovered in France. In mid-November the President and Chamber grudgingly recognized that Clemenceau, the politician they most detested, was the most likely to pull them through. At the age of seventy-six, the man the Germans called France's last card set to work with Jacobin resolution. One of the few grounds for optimism he had was the promised influx of fresh, if raw, American troops, for the United States had declared war in April.

That Clemenceau would seek to annihilate defeatism was to be expected. Some shady characters were executed. Malvy was taken at his word and put on trial for treason, but only found guilty of official misconduct and condemned to five years' banishment.

Caillaux was arrested on no precise charge. But these were Clemenceau's only early victories. For the campaign of 1918 was opened by Ludendorff, in the third week of March, with an attack on the British which at first threatened to cut them off completely from the French. In such an event the fate of both allies might well have been sealed. It seemed that proper co-ordination between the allied armies, so far often talked about but never implemented, had now become vital and, on Haig's suggestion, Foch was appointed to undertake it. The French then came to the aid of the British and, by the end of the month, the immediate threat had disappeared. On 14th April, Foch was made commander of the allied armies, with Weygand as Chief of Staff.

But further German offensives followed, against the British, then against the French lines, and they took Ludendorff again up to the Marne. Some politicians in Paris were already talking about removing Clemenceau. But the Germans were rapidly becoming just as weary of the war as the French and British, and they had not the prospect of being joined by hundreds of thousands of fresh American troops. In July the tide was turning at last. On the 18th, Foch counter-attacked the Germans after they had attempted yet another offensive, and defeated them. For the next two months allied superiority asserted itself in almost every encounter, and the Germans were gradually being pushed back to their own border. The armistice Ludendorff was refused by his government at the end of September was finally signed on 11th November 1918. One and a half million Frenchmen had died since that first day of August 1914 when President Poincaré had told his countrymen that mobilization did not mean war.

Despite noisy opposition from the *Action Française* and other right-wing groups, the peace treaty, signed at Versailles on 28th June 1919, was probably the best the French could get. Their demands, based on their interpretation of the needs of military security and economic recovery, often met with no less hostile a reception from Britain and the United States than from the Germans. The hostility of the Germans was understandable, that of France's allies was based on a mixture of high idealism and narrow political and economic self-interest. The imminent abandonment of France by Britain and America to her fate in a Europe numerically dominated by the Germans had little to do with idealism.

The French desire to acquire the left bank of the Rhine, beyond the obvious recovery of Alsace-Lorraine, made admirable sense in terms of military security. If the British and Americans could afford to be moved by idealistic considerations – they had not suffered two major invasions by an aggressive and numerically superior neighbour within fifty years – the French had necessarily to be more practical about their fate. For nearly half a century the Empire created by Bismarck had been France's most dangerous enemy. It would have been unpardonable if after the four-year massacre France had not looked to her future safety. But so much talk was there of French imperialism that Clemenceau had to content himself with occupying the Rhineland for a period of fifteen years, and a clause perpetually demilitarizing both sides of the Rhine. The British and Americans also guaranteed France's border, and this was of capital importance in converting Clemenceau to the Anglo-American view.

But Wilson did not persuade his countrymen to honour that guarantee, and the British followed this by releasing themselves from their own promise. No wonder that thinking Frenchmen were beginning bitterly to talk about going it alone, collecting such guarantees of German good behaviour as they could while Germany was still weak, outside the League of Nations that Wilson had expected to safeguard the future peace of the world. Moreover, when it came to reparations the same incomprehension was shown towards France, although the full extent of this was not to become clear until the twenties. The French, however, were as much to blame as anyone for the unrealistic demands made on the Germans in the name of economic atonement. They thought in terms of £40,000,000,000. Economically this was, of course, ridiculous. But the Germans had deliberately and systematically destroyed the countryside and industries of the large and prosperous areas they had occupied. It seemed fair to the French that the Germans should pay.

In 1919, however, not many Frenchmen were prepared to go along with the *Action Française* in its refusal to rejoice at the ending of the war:

'The war policy of the *Action Française* having since 1914 demanded a return to the Germanies of the 1866 or – why not? – of 1648, the *Action Française* has always stated it clearly in all its detail during the diplomatic negotiations and parliamentary debates . . .'[44]

Only the jealousies of party politics, Maurras maintained, prevented the politicians from admitting the soundness of his doctrine. The fact of the matter is that when, on 16th November 1919, the first post-war general elections were held, Germany was no longer the most important concern of the electorate.

CHAPTER EIGHT

THE BOLSHEVIST SPECTRE:

1919–29

THE MOST important single issue of the elections of 16th November 1919 was bolshevism. It took precedence even over the gradually dawning realization that, as the *Temps* mildly put it, 'the end of hostilities has settled nothing'.[1] Clemenceau might exhibit captured German war material in the Place de la Concorde, the peasants still prosper, the working man still consider himself an indispensible member of society. The illusion of a victor's peace was soon to disappear in the dust of the old alliances. But the new situation created by the Russian October revolution posed an apparently more immediate threat than the recently defeated Germans. Thus demobilization was slow not only because parts of Germany were being occupied, but also because Foch intended to use French forces to crush the Red armies. The worst fears of the government seemed more than justified when the 156th division was sent to the Crimea at the end of 1918. Its fighting power was strangely inhibited. If this was less because the soldiers sympathized with the bolshevists, and rather more because they wanted to get back home, it was not quite the same with the French fleet. Off Sebastopol, the *France* and *Jean-Bart* hoisted the red flag. French sailors and Russian workers fraternized in the town, while the crew of the *Waldeck-Rousseau* was suborned by French prisoners from another mutinous ship. The biter was bit. The *Revue des Deux Mondes* was beginning to wonder whether 'the end [of the revolution] is as near as one might wish'.[2]

No doubt there was genuine revulsion in France against the assassination of the Tzar and his family, and anger at the revolutionaries' separate peace with the enemy. But the *Union des Intérêts Économiques*, the employers' association whose first programme was published on 3rd April 1919, was the declared enemy of bolshevism for less sentimental reasons. Its notorious election poster – a bloody, hideous head with a dagger between its teeth – was the more visible part of its contribution to the resources of those who, in 1919, asserted that bolshevism constituted the most serious national and international problem. In a speech at the Salle Ba-Ta-Clan the ex-socialist Millerand expressed the need for a *Bloc National* against the socialist left, if the Red menace was to be defeated in France. Although the radicals were divided among themselves in their attitude to the *Bloc*, many joined it, along with liberal catholics like Sangnier and the more traditional enemies of the left.

The election address issued by the *Bloc* in the first Seine constituency fairly reflected its attitude:

'Speculating on the misery created by the war and the difficulties of peace, the bolshevist agitators, who only listen to their appetites, preach violence and prepare disorder without asking themselves if they are not criminally digging the grave into which France, now in glorious convalescence, might fall without ever being able to rise again . . . Remember that our programme would be no more than a scrap of paper if the most important condition were not to be fulfilled: the rout of bolshevism.'

Their positive programme contained the usual *ordre moral* pieties: evolution not revolution; help for the needy; rights imply duties, nation and army constitute a single moral whole. It ended with the double determination to prevent future wars and to ensure the carrying out of the provisions of the Versailles treaty.[9] In the second Paris constituency, Barrès and Millerand were among the signatories of a rather more pungent declaration:

'The cartel we are submitting to the votes of the electors . . . is dominated by this single thought: the desire to combine in one vigorous group those workers, employees and employers who refuse at all costs to suffer bolshevist tyranny.'[4]

Maurras blamed Marcel Habert, Déroulède's spiritual heir, for the exclusion of the *Action Française* from the *Bloc*. Habert, he alleged,[5] had persuaded Millerand to make the *Bloc* exclusively republican, and thus break the *Union Sacrée*, because he was afraid that the royalists would become too powerful. Maurras even hinted darkly that Habert might be a Freemason. In any case, it is likely that the supporters of the *Bloc*, who paid such exquisite electoral lip-service to democracy, would have been acutely embarrassed by Maurras' frank contempt for the masses:

'Demos does not know how to bear good fortune. He has never been properly enlightened nor morally elevated except by blows, those that he receives.'[6]

With clairvoyant hindsight Maurras included in his disdain the politicians who, in this post-war year, failed to see that the future belonged to men of his stamp:

'Already the Europe of 1918 was evolving towards its critical dates . . . 1922 for Italy, 1923 for Bavaria, 1930 for Berlin, 1936 for Spain.'[7]

Despite the catholicity of its aristocratic contempt, the *Action Française* put up its own candidates in a number of constituencies. Only Léon Daudet was successful. Addressing his electors in the third Paris constituency, Daudet returned to the misdeeds of men like Malvy and Caillaux, and made them responsible for the state of military unreadiness in 1914. He also blamed Tardieu, who had negotiated much of the detail, and Wilson for the unsatisfactory peace treaty. This had allowed Germany to pay too little and to remain united under Prussia, so that her position in relation to France was only very temporarily weakened. France must, therefore, avoid internal revolution through national reconciliation, an aim furthered by the *Action Française* when it now grandly opened its arms to royalists and republicans alike.

The more detailed policy statement published by Daudet asked for a 'considerable reduction of military service', which was to be made possible by a more efficiently organized and equipped force. Then the family received its usual conservative attention, both as a potential demographic cornucopia and as the basic social unit; Daudet even proposed the family vote. The call for cheap government, through the reduction of the number of ministries and deputies, echoed a more widespread right-wing opinion, and drove civil servants ever more firmly into the opposing camp. This was followed by a restatement of the confused *Action Française* doctrine on decentralization, which demanded a degree of regional self-government (without saying how much) in the name of economy (*sic*), while clamouring at the same time for a greater concentration of governmental authority in the case of assistance to the devastated regions, presumably in the name of efficiency. The address ended with a plea for the restoration of diplomatic relations with the Vatican at ambassadorial level, and the payment of subsidies to catholic schools, whose freedom from State inter-ference should be guaranteed.[8]

Between the *Bloc* and its various left-wing opponents was the *Union Républicaine*, formed by left-of-centre politicians who, for one worthy reason or another, wanted to avoid being identified with either side. It included the radical leader Herriot and the two independent socialists Painlevé and Viviani. Proclaiming their rejection of the reactionaries as well as of the revolutionaries, they recommended the complete laicization of the schools, a crusade against bolshevism and all other forms of dictatorship, support for the League of Nations, unspecified social reforms with equally unspecified reductions in army service.[9] It would not be unfair to say that most members of this group were expecting sooner or later to reap the political benefits of their abstemious wisdom.

That the *Bloc* should have confounded socialists and bolshevists in one grand anathema astonished only the simple-minded. The truth was very different. Marxism, pacifism, internationalism, patriotism, bolshevism had all made their impact on the socialist movement, and it is hardly surprising that the delicate balance within the unified party should have been disturbed by the two great European convulsions, the war and the Russian revolution. Socialists had to decide anew on their priorities. These would depend very much on the answer to questions such as whether Clemenceau had the eight-hour day voted before the elections merely as a fast move, or whether the vote indicated that French bourgeois society was after all able to transform itself peacefully into a progressive, welcoming host to the rest of the nation. Paul-Boncour was inclined to take the latter, more favourable view. But, like Léon Blum and Pierre Dormoy, he thought the party would have to push as hard as it constitutionally could to achieve its aims. Transport, insurance, large steel plants were to be among industries to be nationalized; education was to be free at all levels; general disarmament was to be achieved. In the programme they issued in the second Paris constituency, and from which these details are taken, they very properly point out where 'orthodox'

French finance had led the country. Having refused to tax directly those who could have afforded to contribute more to the war effort, successive bourgeois ministers had sought to finance the war through public loans. As a result of this fiscal tenderness – with its short-term political advantages – the national debt had risen from twenty-eight milliards, which it was before the war, to the present total of 205 milliards: 'There is the balance sheet of a victorious war.' The manifesto poured scorn on the hypnotically repeated slogan that Germany would pay. Like the few non-socialist realists who were amused and dismayed at the mounting reparations demands, Blum and his friends were wondering where the claimants thought the Germans might find the money.[10]

The socialist programme in the first Paris constituency differed from that of Blum in its priorities and emphasis. It thus helped to exhibit the lack of unity of the party. Blum had declared his solidarity with the bolshevist revolutionaries but had stated explicitly that the socialist party (SFIO) did not want to see a revolution in France. Marcel Cachin, Arthur Groussier, Sembat, and Raymond Lefebvre said in the other manifesto that they neither welcomed nor condemned the bolshevist revolution; yet they ended most ambiguously: 'as Marx has said, you have nothing to lose but your chains'.[11] Earlier they had happily endorsed comments from Lloyd George and Clemenceau, according to which the war had hastened the disorganization of capitalist society. They thought this was especially true of France, where bourgeois governments were apparently unable to extract enough money from those who had it in order to run the country. They were equally convinced of the unwillingness or inability of those governments to alleviate the hardships caused among the less well-to-do by increasing inflation and the housing shortage.[12] Rather less anti-revolutionary than Blum's, this programme was nevertheless also issued with the SFIO imprint. In the Seine department, Pierre Laval stood as a candidate of the SFIO because, he said, '[I] preferred to stand by my political friends and run on a party label which had no chance of being accepted, rather than agree to the offer which had been made to me to head the national block which was overwhelmingly successful at the elections.'[13] He was not the only socialist candidate who was unhappy about the party's chances.

The electoral defeat, which duly came, was well deserved.

Despite Paul-Boncour's assertion to the contrary,[14] the socialists were not united; the two electoral programmes analysed above showed a marked difference in tone and emphasis. Moreover, instead of trying to ensure that they were not being outflanked on the left, both sides would have had to be far more circumspect if the *Bloc*'s charge of bolshevism was not to stick. And bolshevism was not merely a dirty word. For the majority it had sinister implications: 'the fools repeat the word with fear, without understanding it'.[15] One is almost back in 1871, with the socialists in the role of the communards. Only, their subversive activities are now said to be aimed at the subordination of French interests to those of the enemy, for bolshevism is often presented as a German phenomenon.[16] The accusation was made the more plausible by the brazen internationalism of many of their less tactful members, whose rapturous welcome for Wilson and the League of Nations struck quite the wrong political note on the morrow of a hard-won victory. Nor did their aggressive scepticism about German reparations endear them to a public that was determined to forget the hardships of war in a German-subsidized peace.

The vast number of small employers and self-employed people in agriculture and industry were even more afraid of bolshevism than the few big industrialists and property owners who had financed the anti-socialist campaign. Their very number, and their inveterate distrust of each other, prevented them from acting together effectively to counteract socialist threats of nationalization. Although in 1924 there were to be cases where small property owners vote for the extreme left as a protest against the large proprietors, as in Lot-at-Garonne, in 1919 their fear of the bolshevists sent many of them scurrying for shelter in the *Bloc*. The full advantage taken of their scarcity value by skilled workmen in some trades was taken as a typical example of the growing self-assurance of the socialist-organized working-class. If still more had been needed to frighten these people, the impressive socialist procession of the first Sunday in April 1919 would have provided it. It was a protest against the acquittal of the assassin of Jaurès. The trial had been delayed for five years in order, it was said, not to exacerbate feeling during the war. The verdict seemed an insult, particularly when a few days later an unsuccessful attempt on Clemenceau resulted in the death penalty for the would-be assassin. Led by Paul-Boncour and Anatole France, stretching from the Etoile to the Trocadéro, the socialist procession marched to the bust of Jaurès at the Bois de Boulogne. There the war-wounded placed their decorations at the foot of the pedestal. Speeches having been forbidden by the authorities, Anatole France apparently contented himself with murmuring, 'Long live the International'.[17] It was really all quite peaceful.

More disquieting for the middle-classes were the demonstrations of 1st May 1919. Riots broke out in various parts of Paris, charges were made by the Republican Guard which was attacked in its turn with the iron surrounds of trees and other weapons, often from behind barricades of overturned tramcars. It may never have looked like a real revolution, if only because of the overwhelming force of police and troops, but the fear of bolshevism among most of the electors was certainly increased by it. For these riots were becoming part of a pattern of unrest. Thinking French-men who had hoped for an era of peace and plenty after the war that was to end wars were beginning to feel dismay at so much violence. Some, like Barbusse's *Clarté* group, saw the remedy in revolution, without which peace seemed impossible to them. Others were driven into the *Bloc* by just such talk.

Apart from the bolshevist spectre there was another important cause for the defeat of the extreme left, and that was all its own work. In the name of fairness on the eve of the war, the long discussed principle of proportional representation had finally been voted. It allegedly presided over the first post-war general election. The old single-member constituencies had been replaced by larger multi-member constituencies, in which the seats were allocated proportionately to the votes cast. But if a particular party or combination of parties obtained a majority then, with a marvellous interpretation of fairness, all the seats would go to that majority. It was hoped that this device would promote the growth of larger political groupings, and thus of stabler political conditions. However, at the national congress of the SFIO in July 1919, Bracke had a motion passed which forbade all electoral alliances. Given the new electoral law this was clearly suicidal. The socialists must have known that it was. Their refusal to listen to the overtures of the radicals must be taken to mean that they had no desire to participate responsibly in the government of their country. They seemed to wish to perpetuate the cleavage between their pro-letarian clientèle and the rest of France. That some of their number, including Paul-Boncour and Laval, deplored this attitude does not alter the fact that an important part of the population had thus been led to declare its lack of interest in the reconstruction of the country. For the party continued to represent about a quarter of the voters, as was shown by the 1919 results, and the electorate had been told often enough of the decision to refuse not only electoral alliances but also – in keeping with Guesdist doctrine – participation in bourgeois governments.

There was, of course, no equitable relationship between votes cast and seats gained under the new electoral law. The results are adequately characterized by the fact that a quarter of all the votes gave the socialists only about one-eleventh (sixty-eight) of 610 seats. In 1914, with slightly fewer votes, they had obtained 104 seats. 338 seats now went to the *Bloc*, the rest were divided among groups – largely radicals – whose support of the *Bloc* was not unconditional, though likely on major issues. For example, the budgets for 1920–1–2 were opposed by only 68, 87 and 48 votes respectively.

The victorious *Bloc* had no desire to work with Clemenceau. Not only had he recently flirted with the CGT, but he was also suspected of hatching sinister plots against private enterprise. When, in January 1920, his name was put forward at the election for the Presidency of the Republic he was beaten by Deschanel. The devaluation of the Presidency, begun with Grévy, was clearly continuing, for Deschanel was nothing if not insipid. It is, however, hard to believe that Clemenceau was as dismayed by his defeat as he affected to be – he had often boasted that he had no friends, and he was too old a hand at politics to expect gratitude – but he promptly resigned as Prime Minister. Millerand, the architect of the *Bloc*, succeeded him. Nine months later, when Deschanel had to enter a mental home, Millerand went to the Elysée. The triumph of the right seemed complete.

According to Léon Blum, France received her inoculation against fascism during the rule of the *Bloc*. There is a little truth in this over-optimistic remark. The *Ligue Civique*, constituted at the end of 1918, had advocated presidential government on the American pattern. Millerand went a long way towards showing that he believed in even stronger government. Not only did he put a nonentity, Leygues, at the head of an otherwise unchanged ministry when he migrated to the Elysée – thus retaining his own

F*   169

hold on the executive – but he had shown great ruthlessness in dealing with the extensive labour troubles while he was still Prime Minister. He had even tried to have the CGT dissolved. In the summer of the same year (1920) he had sent Weygand to Poland to help drive the Russian revolutionaries back eastward. This would have the double advantage of being a blow to Russian communism and of isolating Germany so far as was possible from the bolshevist infection. Some of the basic ingredients of fascism were therefore present. But if they constituted an inoculation it was a very short-lived one. By January 1921 it had become clear that acutely short of leaders as the *Bloc* was – Millerand's election to the Presidency had deprived it of the only generally acceptable head – it was sufficiently imbued with the 1877 phobia about authoritarian Presidents to refuse its consent to presidential government. And once the Chamber had taken over again, all fears of strong government could be discounted.

In fact, the only thing all members of the *Bloc* could ever be counted on agreeing upon – apart from their fear of bolshevism – was their attitude to Germany. Their passionate execration of the former enemy was, however, closely bound up with their financial requirements for reconstruction and development, which their political prudence prevented them from obtaining from their own countrymen. It is legitimate at least to wonder whether all the moral talk about responsibility for the war, in the name of which Germany was being coerced into making huge reparations payments, was not merely an excuse for getting easy money for an easier life from an apparently already bankrupt nation. Certainly the enormous deficits of the immediate post-war years would not have been regarded with quite the same equanimity if the *Bloc* had not rashly anticipated large reparations payments. Lavish amounts had been spent on compensation, reconstruction and re-equipment in the devastated regions; by the beginning of 1923 these had added up to 97,740,000,000 francs. In return France had received 1,541,000,000 francs from Germany, which even failed to cover occupation costs. It is understandable that with, additionally, an alleged budget deficit of 3,000,000,000 francs in the same year, the *Bloc* was getting restive.

There were, however, less suspect reasons for the *Bloc*'s sensitivity about Germany. It was very conscious of having to face a compact population of sixty million Germans with only about forty million Frenchmen. Constant vigilance alone could prevent Germany from again becoming the most powerful single nation on the continent. At the many disarmament conferences of the twenties, French objections to cuts in their forces were not merely based on cynical calculations about how many troops might be needed from time to time to encourage the Germans in the fulfilment of their reparations obligations. So far as that went, the *Action Française* had warned its countrymen on 17th November 1921 that 'good sense requires that you should understand that the [German] war spirit will evolve in direct proportion to your coercive measures."[18] It was a question of survival. Even Briand, who had taken over from Leygues in January 1921, and already had a reputation for being 'soft' towards the Germans, said at that time that France must remain armed and alert. Since her former allies had refused to guarantee her security, Briand argued, they could not reasonably deny France the right to do so herself. But Briand, in his fear of finding France isolated, lacked firmness, and the supporters of the *Bloc* were becoming very angry at the interminable succession of wordy international conferences at which France seemed forever to be asked for patience on reparations, and concessions on disarmament. They were not appeased by a directive to the courts from the Minister of Justice that the word *boche* was henceforth to be avoided. In January 1922, a year after taking office, Briand handed over to Poincaré, who was expected to see to it that French rights under the Versailles treaty would be vigorously defended.

After having vacated the Elysée for Deschanel in 1919, Poincaré began to re-emerge as the upright, juridical, aloof, somewhat dessicated politician he had been before the war. Not even the right found him lovable; the Presidency had not been a stronghold of firm leadership under him. As for the left, it quite simply accused him of having been largely responsible for the war. But his imperturbable inflexibility which aroused the dislike of the more sophisticated was just what the *Bloc* now wanted. Only implacable obstinacy and complacent self-righteousness would ensure that Germany would pay up and that France could face the world in her refusal to disarm. And Poincaré was one of the few Frenchman who could adopt a high moral tone on both points without having to fear the accusation of hypocrisy. There was no doubt that he truly believed in the expiatory role of reparations, that France had what he called a 'sacred duty' to make Germany atone for the wrongs she had inflicted on his country. Of him, at any rate, it could not be said that moral precept ministered to economic greed:

'You who witnessed these horrors, you who saw your parents, wives, children fall under German bullets, how could you be expected to understand and stand idly by if today, after our victory, there were people sufficiently blind to advise you to leave unpunished the actions of such outrages, and to allow Germany to keep the indemnities she owes . . . That kind of behaviour . . . was encouraged or tolerated by all Germans; all Germans abetted the sacking and firing of the unfortunate provinces in the North and East . . . We shall see to it that they repair the damage.'[19]

Passions were, in fact, running so high by the middle of the year that there was a good deal of talk about war. Poincaré's War Minister Maginot had conscription extended to eighteen months. At Bar-le-Duc, on 24th April 1922, a week after the Russians and Germans at Rapallo had agreed to waive their reparations claims against each other, Poincaré appealed to the country for a new *Union Sacrée*; the situation, he said, was as perilous as it had been in 1914. But among all France's former allies only the Belgians had any sympathy for her. The French liked to think that this was because of all her former allies only the Belgians knew what German invasion and occupation meant.

Perhaps it was mere coincidence that the militant morality preached by the Prime Minister, and warmly applauded by the *Bloc*, came at a time when it was assumed that the budget for 1923 would have to show a deficit of four milliards. On 28th May 1922 the *Temps* added fuel to the already lustily burning fire by reminding its readers that France owed war debts that would have to be paid: eighteen-and-a-half milliard gold francs to the United States, fifteen milliards to England. If there was humour in the situation the French failed to see it: the Anglo-Saxon countries clearly had no doubts about the morality of collecting their debts from a deficitary France that had borne the main burden of the war, but they professed to be appalled by France's determination to recover what she could from the enemy who had attacked her and laid waste her land. In mid-November the Germans, admittedly suffering great economic difficulties, asked for a moratorium on reparations payments of three to four years. The explosion of anger this request elicited in France is adequately illustrated by a single quotation from that usually most sedate daily, *Le Temps*: 'Enough. Since we shall only get what we grab, let us grab.'[20]

Clemenceau who, like Briand, had little faith in the ability of France to face up to Germany alone, sought to obtain President Harding's arbitration. It was too late. The *Bloc* was set on collecting. Poincaré rejected a last-minute offer of a non-aggression pact with Germany, going to the intemperate lengths of adding that even an Anglo-American guarantee of her borders would no longer be adequate. On 11th January 1923, forty thousand troops began to enter the Ruhr to protect, it was said, a mission of some forty engineers.

France now learnt a lesson she was not to forget. Even while the right-wing press was still echoing the feelings of the supporters of the *Bloc* in its vituperation against Germany and its demand that 'accounts should be settled once and for all while the claws of the enemy are still short',[21] it was becoming clear that Clemenceau and Briand had been right and the *Bloc* wrong. In the face of hostile world opinion, and the unexpectedly effective passive resistance of the Germans, France had no prospect of successfully going it alone. There were limits to what even the *Bloc* was prepared to do. Without an electorally disastrous recall to the colours of a large number of reservists, the millions of unco-operative Germans of the Ruhr could not have been turned into obedient French tools. As on several later occasions, the government was not disposed to incur the displeasure of the voters to that extent. It is not even certain whether, on reflection, the majority of the right would have been willing to use the force required – had it been available – at a time when the League of Nations was still the centre of idealistic hopes all over the world. Exact figures have never been compiled, but it is fairly certain that the French, as distinct from the Belgians who alone joined them, actually lost financially in this adventure. It was a political defeat of the greatest magnitude. And it was complemented by a resultant drop in the franc which shook the already unbalanced economy with such severity that even Poincaré had to persuade the *Bloc* to increase taxation. Whether the result of outraged patriotism or mere greed, the Ruhr expedition marked the end of the illusion that victory might have restored to France her pre-Bismarckian continental position. Whoever still wanted France to count as a 'great' power had to think in terms of alliances. That such thoughts should not always turn to the now ironically named *Entente Cordiale* is understandable. France was reinforcing her links with Poland and the Little Entente states, Czechoslovakia, Rumania, and Yugoslavia.

The success of the opponents of the *Bloc* at the elections of 11th May 1924 is as much an indication of the latter's dramatic decline in popularity as of the former's resilience. The splits in the SFIO and CGT in the immediate post-war period had hardly permitted great hopes of early political successes. The differences of emphasis during the 1919 elections have already been noted. But on 20th December 1920, there opened at Tours a socialist congress which within six days managed to liquidate fifteen years of effort towards union.

Cachin, who had been an ardent patriot during the war, and Frossard, the secretary of the party who was to become a member of the *Conseil National* under Vichy, had both been sent to Russia to study the situation there. On their return they demonstrated their complete conversion to the militant and exclusive views of the Third International in their articles in *L'Humanité* and, subsequently, at Tours. It was however objected, by many socialist deputies, that the requirements of the Second Congress of the Communist International seemed to entail the subordination of non-Russian parties to Russian interests. At least, the conditions of membership, such as the formation of clandestine organizations and the fostering of discontent among the armed forces, clearly intended to convert socialist parties into subversive bodies. Accusations of treason made by the Communist International against many of the SFIO leaders seemed however to have stuck, and Marcel Sembat's tired prophecy of a massacre of the proletariat worse than the Commune failed to convince the majority of the adequacy of the old policies. By a majority of three to one they voted to join. The minority withdrew. The party was split. The CGT divided along similar lines in February 1922, after a congress in December 1921. Ironically, Jaurès' *Humanité* fell into the hands of the Tours communist majority.

That despite these divisions the socialists were able to increase their seats in 1924 from sixty-eight to the 1914 figure of a hundred and four is due to at least three factors. First, there were the well-founded grievances of the workers and the lower grades of the civil service; if it is more likely that the former contributed to the election of the twenty-six communists rather than to that of the socialists, the civil servants certainly increased the socialist vote. Secondly, Léon Blum's constant well-reasoned opposition to the Ruhr escapade turned his unpopularity at the time of the invasion into respect at the time of the retreat. Thirdly, and in the final analysis no doubt most important, the socialists had softened on the question of electoral alliances; the increased number of seats reflects better electoral tactics rather than a major increase in votes. Socialist federations in the various departments were allowed to campaign jointly, and appear on the same lists, with the radicals and other left-wing groups wherever they could not hope to win alone. The *Cartel des Gauches*, as the alliance was known, swept the discredited *Bloc* from office.

It was almost too easy. One has to assume that the *Bloc* really did think that it could frighten the electorate into voting for it by rehashing the dreadful tales of 1919 and the pre-war days.

'Do you, like the communists, want to push France along the road to bolshevist Russia, following in the footsteps of Lenin and Trotsky? Do you, like the *Bloc des Gauches*, want to take France back to the time of disreputable stagnation, of [André's] index, of Combism, of religious struggles and anti-militarism, under the auspices of a Caillaux or a Malvy? Or do you prefer to entrust her again this time to patriots, to men of order, determination, and good sense, who will defend tomorrow as they have defended yesterday the policies of the great Frenchmen whose names are Alexandre Millerand and Raymond Poincaré?'[22]

Bravely they went on to claim that the occupation of the Ruhr had forced Germany to pay up, that while the League of Nations deserved support, France must nevertheless remain strong herself. At least they were frank in their statement on economic policy. The currency, they said, must be strengthened by making money dear, and by planning production in terms of what money was available. They added that the alternative was still higher prices.[23] They did not add that their policy entailed unemployment and lower wages. The electors put the right back into the lowly position of 1906, after having raised it up in 1919 to the heights of Thiers'

Chambre Introuvable. The thinking contained in its policy statement hardly merited even that.

The programme of the *Action Française* showed that its putative élite had given up all hope of collaborating with parties that were prepared to work within the framework of the Third Republic. Its statement was uncompromisingly authoritarian and openly paid tribute to Mussolini's recently created fascist state:

> 'Our peril resides chiefly in the fact that there is no authority. Parliament is merely an anonymous and shameful dictatorship, it is not authority . . . France must be given a leader who can see things clearly, plan, know, give orders, act, endure. Events and men call for the leader who is independent of the caprices of Parliament . . . For parliamentary intrigue we . . . must substitute method, authority, continuity, all that dictatorship alone can bring about, all that Italy has found in Mussolini, all that our France is still lacking . . . We need a leader who will be the Foch of Peace.'[24]

Abroad, Germany must be made to pay and remain disarmed; the *Action Française* proudly pretended to responsibility for the Ruhr expedition, 'an action we advocated and made possible'.[25] At home, foreign influence must be eliminated, the civil service must be cut but better paid, monopolies and nationalization avoided, and income tax must be seen to be undesirable. Léon Daudet, the *Action Française*'s only deputy, lost his seat despite a slightly increased vote. This electoral failure of the movement cannot be put down to the refusal of the *Bloc* to work with it in an electoral alliance, which is what the *Action Française* certainly wanted in 1919. In all the four Seine constituencies put together, it only polled just over half a million votes, a total smaller than the smallest number of votes in any single Seine constituency obtained by the SFIO when fighting alone in 1919.

The communists, campaigning under the title *Bloc Ouvrier-Paysan*, made their simple appeal in disarmingly simple terms:

> 'Only the workers' and peasants' Republic of the Soviets of Russia is working for the maintenance of peace . . . while the *Bloc National*, in the vanguard of world reaction, pursues its work of death . . . Abroad: [we want] the cancellation of the Treaty of Versailles, an alliance with the Union of

Socialist Republics, the organization of the United States of Europe.'[26]

Among those elected in the Seine on this programme was Doriot, who was to prove a great asset to the Germans in the thirties and early forties.

The declaration of the *Cartel des Gauches* was sober in tone and, beside that of the *Bloc*, largely realistic:

> 'We want a durable peace through the League of Nations, the alleviation of military expenditure through the organization of a national militia (*La Nation Armée*). We want the payment of reparations due from Germany, but by substituting for the sterile methods of violence joint action with our allies and the aid of world opinion.'

At home, the statement envisaged the extension of direct taxation, the complete laicization of education and the abolition of fees, the franchise for women, and a boost for the birthrate.[27] Among those elected in the Seine on this programme was Laval. In the Nord department, where they stood alone, the socialists demanded a reduction of military service to eight months.[28]

The electoral results, however, tell a very incomplete story. True, the *Cartel* filled 266 seats out of a possible 568, the *Bloc* running second with 229; and the Centre groups (47 seats) could on many internal matters be relied upon to vote with the *Cartel*, thus giving it an overall majority. But not only was that majority largely statistical, its political ineptitude did more harm to the Republic than a thousand abortive Ruhr expeditions. No doubt it is easy to exaggerate the hopes which the electorate, after half a century of republican depreciation, might still have placed in its politicians. But it did turn out in large numbers to record its views, and on the victorious *Cartel* these enjoined the liquidation of the Poincaré line. This, as has been seen, consisted mainly of the attempt to force Germany into making good France's budgetary deficit, and France into accepting the results of the disinflationary measures allegedly required to save the franc after the Ruhr fiasco. To reverse these policies of the right, which were supported by most professional patriots, industrialists, and bankers, the left needed all the strength and determination it could muster.

Instead, the socialists decided to play the kind of ambiguous game for which they reproached the communists a decade later. They refused to participate in the government, but assured it of its support in the policies on which they agreed with it. One can believe Paul-Boncour when he suggests that for many socialist electors this deliberate refusal to help shape the future of the country at such a time was too subtle by half. After their electoral flirtations with the radicals, these maidenly concessions to Guesdism may have pleased the prudes of the extreme left, particularly since it eased their consciences that were already troubled by their exclusion from the communist sanctum. But for most of those who had voted for the *Cartel* it merely reinforced the old conviction that what you voted for bore little relation to what you got:

> 'When I went back to the Tarn department the first words I heard were these: "We elected you together, you should have taken power together." Most of my colleagues of the left must have heard these same words. A potential cause of disaffection from the régime was thus introduced by the lack of correspondence between the composition of governments and the wishes of the electorate.'[29]

The only thing to quarrel with in that quotation is the word 'introduced'.

Not that the *Cartel* had only failures to record. On some matters of little consequence for the future of France most of its supporters were sufficiently agreed to make positive action possible. Thus its most spectacular triumph, at the very beginning of its rule, was the enforced resignation of Millerand. The ex-socialist authoritarian President would no doubt have had a difficult time at the Elysée with a *Cartel* majority at the Palais-Bourbon. He might even have been a unifying influence on it. But the left treated him as the opportunists had finally treated Grévy. They refused to form a government under him. But the brittleness of the *Cartel* was immediately exhibited. Painlevé, third of the Trinity, with Herriot and Blum, that led it, failed to win the presidential election. Although the radicals had a Senate majority, and could thus have ensured Painlevé's success, it was clear from this result that the senators, at any rate, did not consider themselves bound by the *Cartel* alliance. It was Gaston Doumergue who succeeded Millerand, a pale neutral. The Senate went on to give itself a right-wing President, M de Selves.

There were, however, other irrelevant successes. The *Bloc National* had treated the regained lost provinces with gingerly consideration, particularly when it came to applying the anti-Church legislation of previous republican governments. Led by Herriot, the *Cartel*, in happy union, gleefully decided to deal with the schools and priesthood of Alsace-Lorraine as their spiritual predecessors had dealt with them in the rest of France. But so noisy was their anticipatory smacking of lips that sufficient opposition could be aroused in time to frighten the motley *Cartel* into foregoing the traditional feast. The much-mooted diplomatic break with the Vatican, actually voted on 2nd February 1925, had the same result. When, therefore, the Pope revealed in 1926 that some of Maurras' writings had been put on the index as early as in 1914, and proceeded to deal with the rest of his writings and the *Action Française* newspaper in the same way, this was hardly because the Church thought it had cause to fear renewed persecution from Herriot's government. To have the trumpeted support of Maurras and his friends, with their mixture of vicious prose and quaint royalism, must have been as embarrassing for the new progressive image of the Church under Benedict XV as it seemed to have become for the Pretender when, in 1937, he too finally disavowed it.

If the policies on which the supporters of the *Cartel* were agreed had such meagre results, one can imagine what happened to the others. Once they had decided to accept the Dawes plan, which promised the resumption of German reparation payments, but scaled down, and after a moratorium, they had certainly relieved international tension. But they were still faced with the same economic difficulties that had led Poincaré into the Ruhr. France's internal debt alone amounted to over 270 milliards, of which forty milliards had to be repaid in the near future. Since her annual budget ran at about thirty-four milliards it was clear that she would have to borrow in order to repay, or increase taxation to a punishing rate. Since the latter course was out of the question, the government had to maintain confidence in its creditworthiness. For a government subsisting on socialist support that was not easy. On the other hand, strong measures to coerce potential creditors into assisting the State, though no doubt popular with the socialists, would hardly have commended themselves to the radicals, wedded as they were to the liberal principle of the *minimum de gouvernement*. The Bank of France was by no means alone in offering good advice to the government which, like that emanating from other right-wing sources, dwelt on the need to reassure potential creditors. The feeling of instability caused by measures the government had already taken – for example, the legalization of civil service trade unions – or by those it was contemplating – for example, a tax on capital – was likely to have a quite different result. On 10th April 1925, the Senate voted against the *Cartel*'s continued increase of note circulation. Although the Senate was no doubt right to be concerned about the inflationary effect of this increase, it was probably more concerned about the Finance Minister's inordinately candid admission that he expected to raise a loan to cover it which, in its turn, might be transformed into a tax on capital. As a result of the adverse vote Herriot resigned.

A left-of-centre government, tainted rather than strengthened by half-hearted socialist support, had clearly been no match for those who held the purse strings. It was not only the failure of the socialists to join the government which contributed to the ever-growing political cynicism of the electorate. It was even more the subsequent realization that money was more powerful than a democratically elected majority. As yet, however, the cynicism managed to be largely good-natured, for although the economic difficulties had caused a certain amount of hardship – for example some wages had decreased – there was little unemployment; indeed France had succeeded in absorbing three million immigrants since the war.

Painlevé, second member of the Trinity, took over from Herriot, giving the Foreign Ministry to Briand and calling Caillaux out of his political exile to serve as Finance Minister. It was certainly a quixotic gesture to set the alleged war traitor who was well known for his radical economic views – he was for instance a staunch advocate of a graduated income tax – against the right that was still full of patriotic slogans and sheltering behind 'the wall of money'. But he was also unpopular with most socialists, if only because he refused to tax capital. When he failed in his bid to postpone repayments on the American loan, and the socialists threatened to break with the *Cartel* over him, the government resigned and re-formed without Caillaux. He had lasted six months, during which time the franc had dropped from around ninety to the Pound to about 109. There now followed a succession of more or less ephemeral ministries, each coming to grief over proposals to deal with the increasingly catastrophic economic situation, until the point was reached towards the end of July 1926 where the franc had dropped to 250 to the Pound. To put it mildly, the *Cartel* had been unable to create confidence. Doumergue, with a left-of-centre majority in the Chamber of Deputies, called on Poincaré to form a government. Bowing to the inevitable, the Chamber gave him a majority.

Even two days before he announced his plans, Poincaré had the satisfaction of seeing the franc rise to 199. It was scarcely, however, because he had formed a national coalition government that confidence rallied to send the franc up to about 120 by the end of the year. To see Herriot, Painlevé, Briand, rubbing shoulders with reactionaries like Tardieu and Marin was of course quite a spectacle. But what really reassured potential lenders was the certainty that Poincaré would never threaten whatever capital they had. His programme did not disappoint them. Five milliards, the experts said, would be needed to make the economy healthy. Poincaré decided on getting six milliards. To reassure the right still further, the extra revenue was to be raised by an increase in indirect taxation. Once again, therefore, the less prosperous majority was to make most of the sacrifices. 'And now let's make way for the misunderstood ex-servicemen' Forain had captioned a drawing the previous year.[30] He had epitomized a feeling of increasing popular disillusionment.

In foreign affairs the *Cartel* was more successful. Cynics may say that this was because it asked for nothing. But this would be unfair. It was courageous of Briand, who remained at the Quai until shortly before his death in 1932, to advocate and work for a Franco-German *rapprochement* after so many decades of bitterness. Whether the conciliatory policy was based on idealism or on the realization that the numerous Germans would not remain unarmed forever, it was an honourable one while it relied on mutual respect.

When Briand arrived at the Quai d'Orsay in April 1925, an imminent *rapprochement* with the Germans seemed unlikely. Hindenburg had been elected President earlier in the year, despite the fact that the French had branded him as a war criminal whose punishment they had demanded as late as 1919. The excuse proffered by the Marshal's apologists that his election amounted to no more than a patriotic protest against the Ruhr expedition was unlikely to appease any French critic. The latter already felt uneasy about what to him looked like a French defeat at the hands of a few unco-operative German coalminers. But within six months the treaty of Locarno was signed. This, unlike Versailles, was the result of a German initiative happily taken up by Briand, and it recognized the Rhine frontier. German entry into the League of Nations in 1926 was no doubt facilitated by the detente created at Locarno. The left saw all this as the dawn of a new era, even if Poincaré's return as Prime Minister was as badly received in Germany as that of Hindenburg had been in France.

Not only the left had reason to be pleased with Briand. France as a whole enjoyed a world prestige she had not known since the war, nor was she to know it again before the next. 1926 was the year in which Briand obtained the Nobel Peace Prize for his services to the League of Nations, and Poincaré achieved the stabilization of the franc. At the beginning of 1927 the *Entente Cordiale* looked alive again during the President's visit to England, and in April Briand made his dramatically appealing but depressingly empty proposal that the United States and France should outlaw war. Although this last proposal was less idiotic than its adaptation by the American Senator Borah – Briand had at least a vision of a League army capable of enforcing League decisions, while the Senator was just full of hope – it showed that the grip on realities was in danger of being lost. That the American Secretary of State Kellogg should take up the idea, and suggest that the whole world should be allowed to renounce war, entailed no reversal of United States policy. It was pious and committed her to nothing, except further disarmament which was not entirely unpopular politics in the United States. On 27th August 1928, Germany, Belgium, England, Italy, Japan, Poland and Czechoslovakia signed such a renunciation, the Americans having done so on 6th February.

The elections of 22nd April 1928 again confirmed that the right was as sceptical about abstract concepts in international as in national affairs. The feeling expressed in a drawing by Faivre in the *Journal* of 23rd May 1926 was characteristic of it: 'Spirit of

Locarno, where are you? – In France, and nowhere else.' While no successful right-wing candidate actually spoke ill of the League of Nations, all thought that complete reliance on its ability to avert war would be crazy. If there was any difference between them it was one of tact. Malinger, in Paris, was diplomatic:

'Faced particularly with the continued arming of Italy and the absence of Russia from Geneva, a strong army for defensive purposes is still necessary.'[31]

On the other hand, Maurice le Corbeiller, also in Paris, was brutal:

'France will be listened to all the more in Geneva if she has more respectable forces at her disposal.'[32]

De Tastes was even more frank. He reminded his Parisian electors that, despite the Briand-Kellogg euphoria, Germany had still not recognized the borders of Poland and Czechoslovakia, and that it would be useful to clear this point up while French troops were still on the Rhine.[33]

It was no use. While most Frenchmen now seemed happy to have their international future settled by League diplomats, rather than face renewed isolation and the demands of unilateral action, the nationalist element of the right was in eclipse. After all, even Poincaré now supported Briand. In the circumstances, the electoral programmes of the right devoted most of their attention to internal matters. At about the same time Hitler's national socialists increased their votes in Germany from seventeen thousand in 1927 to one million; two years later this was to rise to six million.

The large measure of agreement on international affairs did not extend to internal questions. The return to single member constituencies and two ballots having been voted just prior to the dissolution, the country was given the record choice of over 3,700 candidates from whom to select 612 deputies. The electorate showed that it was no more homogeneous than the candidates, dispersing its votes at the first ballot in such a way that only 187 deputies were elected at it.

The right, whether royalist, ex-royalist or neo-opportunist, attempted to perpetuate its image as the champion of national unity. Even those who, like Taittinger, were merely continuing the crude nationalism of Barrès were greedily hauled to the bosom of the *Union Nationale*, successor of the *Bloc*. Clamouring for 'order, liberty and social progress', Taittinger said he was 'continuing the political work begun by Barrès, to bring about the complete reconciliation of all the spiritual families of France'. The declaration ended with the early Barrès formula: 'Long live the National-Socialist Republic'.[34]

President of the *Jeunesses Patriotes* who, with their blue raincoats and berets, had been enjoying themselves since 1924 after the manner of the *Camelots du Roi*, Taittinger was elected at the first ballot by the small shopkeepers of the first Paris constituency. Perhaps there is no better way of illustrating the feverish anti-*Cartel* promiscuity of the right than to state that in the adjoining second constituency, Paul Reynaud was prepared to campaign under the banner of the same *Union Nationale* as Taittinger. But, like Le Corbeiller,[35] Reynaud belonged to the *Union* because he supported Poincaré's economic and laic orthodoxy, and not because of a weakness for power-hungry toughs. In fact, the *Union Nationale* really staked its electoral appeal on the reputation of Poincaré. It was the daily *Echo de Paris*, whose Propaganda Centre had been providing a training and publicity institute for the whole of the right since 1927, which had done more than any other single body to make such a unified front possible.

The attitude of the parties that had composed the *Cartel* showed little change. Less compromised by the inclusion of extremists than the right – the communists' averseness from participation was no disappointment to the socialists and radicals – the left continued its equivocal game. For electoral purposes it tried to present a common front, particularly at the second ballot, but radicals and socialists issued different policy statements. And the socialists, while clearly ready to collaborate with bourgeois parties at elections, were still not prepared to collaborate with bourgeois parties in forming a government. The socialists and communists were thus effectively disenfranchising two and three-quarter million electors, over a third of the total. Their continued alienation from the State was justified to them in terms of class interest and internationalism. It was inevitable that, within this political framework, the government of France would have to be carried on by right-of-centre groupings. For even if the *Cartel* obtained a majority, the radicals would not have enough seats to govern alone. The legislation of such a coalition could be expected to exacerbate class differences still further. Nor must it be thought that this alienation affected only the industrial areas. Goguel[36] has shown that while since 1919 the communists had tended to supplant the socialists in the industrial areas, the latter increasingly supplanted the radicals in rural areas.

The election marked a slight swing back to the right, largely because of the results of Poincaré's success with the investors. It could, therefore, be expected that the Prime Minister's policies would continue to have their way. Since France was now also beginning to enjoy some of the benefits of the sacrifices she had made for reconstruction and re-equipment, Briand's renewed tenderness about German reparations did not elicit quite as much hostility at home as usual. The Dawes plan had envisaged that German payments would reach their maximum annual figure in this election year of 1928, provided Germany was then able to bear the burden. After the retirement of Poincaré in July 1929 Briand, in his double capacity as Prime Minister and Foreign Minister, accepted the Young plan. This scaled down German payments still more and spread them over a longer period, ending in 1988. There were no guarantees other than the word of the Germans that Germany would fulfil her obligations even now, for it was assumed that there were by 1929, in Briand's words, 'neither victors nor vanquished'. Moreover, it was also agreed that the French should evacuate the Rhineland before the end of 1930. As if to emphasize France's imminent nakedness before Germany, the British and French poisoned the atmosphere between their countries for several years by their haggling over the exact division of such reparations as the Germans might make in the future. But Briand battled on. On 15th September 1929 he proposed his United States of Europe, which were to begin with a measure of economic union. Even if Maginot conceived his fortified line as a more practical answer to the proposed French evacuation of the Rhineland, a decade after Versailles the majority of Frenchmen seemed prepared to base their future security on German good faith and the promises made at Locarno. If anything exercised them it was not the growth of aggressive German nationalism, but the rights and wrongs of bolshevism.

CHAPTER NINE

THE GROWTH OF FASCISM:

1929-36

1929, THE YEAR Poincaré resigned, was the end of an era.
France was yet stable and at the height of her post-war prosperity.
But in America there was the Wall Street crash, caused by alleged
fears of overproduction. When it hit France, later than most other
countries because of her Poincaré financial soundness, a new
generation of politicians had to cope with the tragic problems it
created. They lacked the stature of the man who had saved the
franc in the twenties, and they failed to unite the country in their
efforts to alleviate the economic, social, and political miseries the
depression brought with it. Already in 1930, despite Tardieu's
lavish spending of the accumulated surpluses, foreign trade was
declining. The United States and Russia were among the countries
that were importing less wine. Luxury products were increasingly
difficult to sell in Central and Eastern Europe. With the progressive stagnation of international trade and the devaluation of
various moneys came a shortage of foreign currency, so that the
tourist industry also suffered, particularly after the decline of the
Pound from 1931. The excellent French harvest of 1929 did not
help, because it merely added the peasants to the list of those who
suffered hardship, the collapse of world markets meaning low
home prices. In one respect France remained luckier than most
other industrial countries. The comparatively low rate of foreign
trade – one of the results of her traditional policy of protection –
insulated her from the worst dangers of unemployment. While
England at one time had to cope with nearly three million workless
and Germany with six million, France never quite reached even
the half-million mark. In fact, in the early days of the slump,
France actually helped the United States and Great Britain with
loans. Laval, Prime Minister in 1931 when the loan for England

was arranged, even had his daughter claim that her father's love of the country of MacDonald was thus proved.[1] But when France did succumb, she took much longer than Britain and America to recover.

If the end of Poincaré's political career coincides with the beginning of the French economic decline, the departure of Briand from the Quai d'Orsay in January 1932 marks the end of whatever serious hopes anyone might still have had of the League of Nations. Tardieu and Laval, who had the real power in France between 1930 and 1932, were not to be less tender to Germany than Briand had been, but were to prefer directly negotiated agreements rather than League resolutions. As for the disarmament talks that opened in Geneva in February 1932, after having been prepared with benign procrastination since 1926, the League did not enhance its status by the hypocrisy of the member nations who were guided by narrow self-interest. As Léon Blum ponderously put it in the *Populaire*, 10th March 1930:

'We cannot permit that . . . any power whatever shall take its *needs*, of which it is necessarily the only judge, as the criterion for the armaments it is to have.'

No wonder Briand died a disappointed man.

It did not take a cynic to recognize that there seemed to be some causal connection between French conciliatory moves towards Germany and fresh German demands. Even Briand however was shaken by the news, in March 1931, that the Germans and Austrians were proposing a customs union. It was natural for the French to fear the possibility of a subsequent political union, which would put their country at a still more serious demographic disadvantage by increasing their already numerous neighbour to nearly twice their own population. Even when the International Court at The Hague pronounced against the Austro-German plan in September, the right continued with its vociferous condemnation of what it saw as another proof of the stupidity of the policy of Franco-German conciliation. They did not have to wait long for more grist. Within a year of the coming into force of the Young plan, the Germans pleaded for a further postponement of reparations payments. On 6th June 1931 the German Chancellor Brüning declared that his country was unable to meet its liabilities under the agreement. However well founded such a repudiation of responsibility might have been on economic grounds, it is difficult to believe that, had Germany seriously intended a *rapprochement* with France, sufficient funds could not have been found. When Hoover took up the German case a fortnight later, this proved to the French no more than that he wished to do his best to save American investments in Germany. The moratorium he proposed for a year cost France two milliard francs. It would hardly cripple her, any more than the earlier German repudiation of her obligations had prevented French post-war recovery. It was the principle that mattered, and the Germans knew it.

Laval, disdainful of the League, thought himself smart enough to derive some tangible benefits from the German economic collapse. When Brüning passed through Paris on his way to the economic conference in London in mid-July 1931, Laval offered credits to the tune of 150 million dollars, to be granted by France, England and the United States. In exchange, Germany was to refrain from increasing her military expenditure for the next ten years and to sign a non-aggression pact with France. The British did not care for Laval's suggestion, if only because they did not have the money with which to give it effect, and Brüning – no doubt mindful of the increasing power of nazism in his country – received Laval's plan with polite evasiveness. However, the crowds that turned out during the Briand-Laval visit to Berlin two months later, crying out for French help to overcome the miseries of the depression, those crowds were hardly *revanchards*. It is doubtful if nazi sentiments would have prevented them from eating French bread. As it was, German nationalists clamoured for equality with other nations, the abandonment of reparations, the right to rearm, while in Paris the nationalists exulted over the state of affairs that could make Germans beg for French help. Since politicians on both sides refused to ignore their more poisonous countrymen, it is not surprising that the only result of the Berlin visit was the setting up of yet another commission which achieved nothing. If, in both countries, extremists were about to rise to positions of national importance, this was not because the populations of these countries had become extremists, but because non-extremist politicians had failed to take timely action. In France, where the results of the depression were making themselves increasingly felt, the Senate threw out a bill giving workers a week's paid annual holiday. It had been the

Chamber's sop to the section of the population that had only rarely felt an integral part of the Republic, and that early in 1932 saw its livelihood threatened through increased unemployment and the reduction of the average working week to about forty-three hours. The elections of May 1932 could not have come at a more depressing time.

Despite mounting feelings against the politicians who had allowed prosperity to decline and Germany to default, the electorate did not betray any positive discontent with the régime as such. It had almost as great a choice of candidates ready to play the parliamentary game as in 1928. But the number of candidates is no index to popular political interest. Any Frenchman could be a candidate at either ballot, provided only he was twenty-five years old. He did not have to be nominated nor pay a deposit. Although there was no significant change in the abstention rate in 1932, a contemporary observer plausibly suggested that voting had become divorced from political expectations, that although the electorate went through the motions of political activity, it had little faith left in the determination and ability of its chosen representatives to carry out its wishes.[2]

In an attempt to recreate the *Bloc National*, the groups to the right of the radicals made common cause at the second ballot. They presented themselves as supporters of the Tardieu-Laval line, proffering Poincaré as their Patron Saint. Taittinger summed up their programme in terms of the sacredness of France's frontiers, the need for adequate defence budgets and alliances. At home, the crisis was to be resolved by the collaboration of all men of order, the expansion of colonial markets, and the determination that 'expenditure must be geared to receipts and not receipts to expenditure.'[3] As in the previous election, Paul Reynaud was prepared to subscribe to a programme similar to that of the heir of Déroulède and Barrès in the neighbouring Paris constituency.[4] Some supporters of Tardieu made touching if logically incoherent appeals to the workers of France. Thus Jean Lerolle, also in Paris, after arguing that the budget ought to be balanced without recourse to additional taxation, went on to proclaim the end of the class war. He said:

'The crisis has once again demonstrated the intimate solidarity which binds together employers and workers. The class war is not only a crime against the *patrie* and society; for the workers themselves it brings misery and can only lead to anarchy and ruin . . . England's recent experience of socialist government has exhibited to all the danger of collectivist utopias.'[5]

In yet another Paris constituency, Le Corbeiller got rather close to the bone in his evaluation of the cartel of socialists and radicals:

'The radicals say they are attached to the principles of private property, individual freedom, and the *patrie*. So they are. But they are unable to separate themselves from the socialists of the SFIO who want to destroy property, individual freedom, and the idea of the *patrie*. Does that make sense to anybody?'[6]

There, with some exaggeration, is one of the main dilemmas of internal French politics in the inter-war period.

The trouble with the radicals was the gap between their words and their deeds. Ideologically they were on the side of the progressive angels, and that made their alliances with the socialists morally entirely satisfactory. In practice, however, the well-worn saying that the Frenchman has his heart on the left and his purse on the right applies most neatly to the radical party. As a result, electoral marriage with the socialists was usually followed by parliamentary divorce. Young radicals like Bergery might show some impatience with their more worldly wise party elders, it affected the majority of Herriot's friends very little. Gaston Bonnaure, in Paris, put out a programme which is almost a caricature of the *fumisme* exhibited by too many of his fellow radicals:

'Not words, but principles: Honesty in politics. Independence in action. Energy in execution. First of all economy. Tolerance and good order thereafter. Justice and Peace always.'[7]

It is true that he went on to mention some specific measures he would like to promote, free education at all levels for example, but they were not elaborated in any detail.

The socialists, on the other hand, showed much more concern with specific problems of the day. It was a socialist, for example, who was the only one of the successful Paris candidates to mention Hitler during these elections. Graziani, in the second constituency of the fourteenth arrondissement, asked his electors to vote against the Tardieu-Laval coalition because its alleged nationalism added fuel to Hitler's incendiary fury and could thus lead to war. He also warned against the dangers of anti-democratic movements, citing attempts by Mandel and de Tastes to reduce the number of parliamentary parties in an effort to facilitate government. Like his communist rivals he advocated the forty-hour week, and proposed unemployment insurance which the radicals also asked for but, characteristically, wanted to be based on the Friendly Society principle. After the fate of Herriot's Cartel government in 1924, the further socialist demand for state supervision of the banks came as no surprise. Nor did the repetition of their proposal for the nationalization of the railways, mines, of oil, and insurance.[8] The one area of agreement between radicals and socialists which was not largely linguistic was still that of anti-clericalism. But this was no longer a practical political issue. Church influence in the State was now reduced to a level that could annoy only the doctrinaire. This suggests that its persistence in the electoral almanac must have been due to a remarkable facility for engendering heat on abstract issues.

The communists continued to plough their lonely furrow. Their social demands went understandably further than that of the socialists. Since they did not even remotely consider taking part in government they had little to lose in making impossible demands. Thus Monjauvis asked that workers be allowed to retire with a pension at fifty-five – at fifty if they were in unhealthy jobs – should receive twenty francs a day and be absolved from paying rent and taxes if they were unemployed.[9] Rather more amusing was their approach to foreign policy. It was all still very much along the lines of the workers of the world uniting to supersede the system of nation states.

'Against imperialist war, for the defence of the USSR and for peace . . . For the abolition of the system created by the Versailles treaties, the Young plan, the Hoover plan. For support of the revolution in Indo-China.'[10]

For good measure they also demanded that career soldiers be dismissed from the army and, as a last anti-patriotic fling, it was proposed that all French soldiers and administrators should be withdrawn not only from the French colonies but also from

Alsace-Lorraine, where the communists were supporting the autonomist movement. In political opportunism the party had obviously nothing to learn from the radicals. To prove it, within less than two years the communists had transformed themselves into the most fervent defenders of Versailles, the most punctilious patriots, the staunchest supporters of a socialist and radical coalition.

Between the two ballots the President of the Republic was assassinated at an ex-servicemen's book sale. Tardieu tried to exploit the fact that the murderer was Russian, but the electorate was sufficiently sophisticated to be able to distinguish between the act of an apparently unbalanced wretch who happened to have been born in Russia, and a deeply laid communist plot against the State. The figures given by Lachapelle[11] indicate that the combined socialist and communist vote was slightly up on 1928, while the radicals did very much better. The result was that the Cartel's seats increased from 253 to 323, giving it a majority in the Chamber. Lachapelle wrily points out that under proportional representation sixty-one seats would have gone to different parties.[12]

What, one may wonder, could have been expected from the government that Herriot formed soon after the elections, in early June 1932? In an interesting analysis of the intellectual climate of the thirties M Jean Touchard[13] has collected enough evidence to show that the generation which grew to maturity after the war could be just as hostile to the parliamentary system as was a large number of ex-servicemen. The former resented the privileged position claimed by the latter, and tended to despise them for the flabbiness with which they used it, while the ex-servicemen felt let down by the politicians who had promised them the things politicians promise servicemen. However, the disagreements among the anti-democrats were as numerous as those among the democrats so that, unless total anarchy was to be courted, the régime had to survive. When therefore the new President, Lebrun, called on Herriot to form a government, little optimism was understandably displayed. With the financial position deteriorating at a time when it was beginning to improve in other countries, it could be taken for granted that Herriot could expect as little socialist support for his 'orthodox' measures as he could expect right-wing support for his conciliatory foreign policy.

The budget deficit of about ten milliards could not be made

good by increasing taxation without offending the right, nor by
reducing expenditure without alienating the socialists. The old
habit of trying to cover extraordinary expenditure by loans was
carried a disastrous stage further by making the loans short-term
ones. The consequent snowball effect on later governments can be
gauged from the grotesque speed with which ministries came and
went over the remaining few years of the Third Republic. Budget
policy was not, of course, the only cause of ministerial instability,
but it was a main one. The Lausanne conference, held shortly
after the elections, put an end to all hope that any more reparations could be expected from Germany.

On one thing at least the Chamber could agree. It reduced the
defence budget by 1½ million francs at about the time when
the German War Minister Schleicher announced that Germany
could no longer consider herself bound by the military limita-
tions put on her at Versailles. At the end of the month (31st
July 1932) the nazis obtained 230 seats in the Reichstag, thus
more than doubling their representation. Chancellor von Papen,
after having been unsuccessful in obtaining Hitler's participation in his government, appealed for a gesture from France to
enhance his own standing at home. He wanted Herriot to recognize
Germany's position as an equal at the disarmament marathon still
being fought out at Geneva. Faced with Herriot's polite refusal,
and an unmanageable Reichstag, he called for new elections in the
middle of November. The nazis lost thirty-five seats. To those who
had opposed defence cuts because of the apparent successes of the
German nationalists, Blum had soothingly prophesied that 'Hitler
is henceforth excluded from power, he is even, if I may say so,
excluded from all hope of power.'[14] In mid-December France
agreed with England and Italy to grant Germany the equality of
rights von Papen had been refused only a few weeks earlier. Now,
however, Schleicher was Chancellor, and France's gesture
coming with that show of reluctance with which she had accom-
panied most of her earlier conciliatory moves – was unlikely to
bring about a drastic German change of mood. Three days later
(14th December 1932) Herriot used the Chamber's aversion from
paying war debts to the United States while Germany paid no
reparations to France to resign from office. Already the new
Chamber had shown itself as recalcitrant as the old. National
expenditure now exceeded receipts by seventy-five per cent. Inter-

G   193

nationally France was more isolated than she had been for many years. It was she who was blamed for the obvious failure of the disarmament conference, at a time when England in particular went through a stage of enthusiastic pacifism. The Germans certainly did not feel very drawn to her, and the United States did not care for her reluctance to pay up. The government of Paul-Boncour which followed Herriot's could not cope either. It only lasted forty days. It fell on 28th January 1933. Two days later Hitler came to power in Germany.

Blum's continued obtuseness greatly contributed to the now daily more evident disintegration of the democratic Republic. It was the same lack of perception which had pronounced Hitler a dead duck two months before he became Chancellor that prevented Blum from seeing that the Cartel's comparatively progressive policy was doomed unless the socialists supported the new radical Daladier government. No doubt it takes two to make a bargain, but the principal reason for the failure of the radicals and socialists to collaborate in the post-war era is to be found in Blum's unimaginative Guesdist orthodoxy, not in radical aloofness. That this socialist attitude would lead to right-of-centre government, and would thus further exacerbate the bourgeois antipathies of a third of the population, should have been a matter of concern to a democratic party. Its disastrous effects on French stability at a time when the traditional enemy across the Rhine was again becoming menacing had apparently not entered Blum's head. But he was no more influential than his party allowed him to be. Socialist party congresses were as fully capable of fiddling about with anachronistic principles as those organized by the rue de Valois. But now the world was beginning to burn again, and neither party seemed able to recognize that fact. Meanwhile the right, already impressed by Mussolini and the orderly government fascism apparently brought with it, was viewing Hitler's transformation of Germany with mixed feelings. Nazi stability would no doubt exorcize the ghost of a German Marxist revolution, and strengthen France's defence against bolshevism. But Hitler had said in *Mein Kampf* that France must be annihilated.[15]

Daladier's tough exterior concealed the same lack of incisiveness and decision that anatomically less misleading heads of government had worn on their sleeves. In foreign affairs this showed itself in the manner in which he dealt with Mussolini's plan for a four-power agreement between Italy, France, England and Germany, which was to have more positive results than the interminable exchanges of views at Geneva. Had he seriously examined the likely outcome of the talks (June 1933), Daladier could not have gone into them with such equanimity. Nothing had happened to suggest that England under MacDonald was prepared to put undue energy into European affairs. Mussolini was clearly on the make and Germany, despite Hitler's pacifist lapses, was no francophile. What did France have to gain from Mussolini's plan? Certainly no guarantee of the *status quo* that Locarno could not better. A common front against communism, no doubt. But the isolation of Russia had been complete for some time, and the advent of nazism in Germany completed the physical containment of the Marxist threat. In fact, the results of these four-power discussions were entirely detrimental to France. The countries of the little Entente felt that France was letting them down in her private tête-à-tête with the Germans. The Poles had similar suspicions. The Russians, who were the only really useful military counterpart to the Germans on the continent, were made to feel still more resentful against the West as a whole. At home, the opposition to the talks from the left – embittered by fascist and nazi persecution of Italian and German socialists – and from the nationalist right divided the country further. In short, at the end of 1933 the position of the forty-one million Frenchmen had considerably worsened in relation to their sixty-five million neighbours. And there were no compensations at all, for the trivial results of the four-power talks were never ratified. To make things worse the world economic conference held in London in June 1933 had underlined the rift between France and the United States over the question of war debts, and Germany had walked out of the disarmament conference and the League of Nations, thus making any kind of foreign pressure on her more difficult to exert.

Meanwhile, at the Palais-Bourbon, the politicians' private game continued, untroubled by world events. Except by the slump. Daladier tried to bridge the budget deficit by devices such as a six per cent reduction of State salaries and pensions. Socialist opposition to these measures led to the fall of that government too. But this time there was a new element in what would otherwise have been a routine crisis. Thirty socialist deputies, led by

Marquet, Déat, and Renaudel voted for the government. The sterility of Blum's opposition had led them to form a neo-socialist group. They felt that internationalist socialism had had its day. They even said that the concept of the class war was outdated and elaborated a programme which Blum described as fascist. A few years later they were to constitute the contribution of the left to Franco-German collaboration apart, of course, from that of the communists. After the Daladier government, that of Sarraut lasted a mere three weeks. It, too, fell for the lack of socialist support. Chautemps, another radical, was to have the same fate eight weeks later. But by that time the situation in the country had become very ugly, not only because of the bitter derision the Palais-Bourbon merry-go-round now elicited from a large number of electors, but also because of the revolutionary atmosphere created by the right on the occasion of the Stavisky affair.

The discovery of shady financial deals perpetrated by a Jewish crook, who seemed to have enjoyed official immunity as a result of well-paid friendships, gave the *Action Française* the opportunity to bring out Maurras' favourite Wilson-Panama war-cry 'Down with the thieves'. With the same nose for scandal that had given the *Libre Parole* a head-start in reporting the beginnings of the Dreyfus Affair, the *Action Française* came out with innuendoes about the Stavisky crowd a month before the scandal came into the open. As usual the press cared little about the truth of its allegations, provided they were likely to be politically useful. In *Rire*, January 1934, Picq had a lady saying to her servants: 'Tonight we shall be entertaining a minister and two deputies. Count the silver.' The whole parliamentary system seemed to stand accused, and the fact that Chautemps was a Freemason was for many prima facie proof of his guilt, too. When, at the height of the row, Stavisky was found dead, the *Action Française* went so far as to accuse the Prime Minister of having ordered his assassination to prevent the truth from being revealed. An unprecedented number of Frenchmen seemed at least to be intrigued by its editor's belief that 'Democracy means political infection', for the circulation of the paper rapidly exceeded the half-million mark, about five times its former figure. The democratic régime was now not only presented as inefficient and brainless, it was also again alleged to be dishonest. On 11th January 1934 fighting broke out near the Palais-Bourbon between the police and demonstrators shouting: 'Down with the thieves.' This set the pattern for the next few weeks, during which violence in the streets rapidly assumed revolutionary proportions. At the end of January Chautemps resigned, unable to deal with the situation.

Three days later, 30th January 1934, Daladier formed another ministry. Lebrun had discovered that something rather dangerous was happening, and had sought to apply the usual republican remedy by requesting a father-figure – this time the former President of the Republic, Doumergue – to come out of retirement and lead a government. It was only when he refused that Daladier was asked. At least he still had a reputation for toughness and integrity. One of his first acts was to dismiss the Paris police chief, Chiappe, who was supposed to have had dealings with Stavisky as well as a tenderness for the right-wing rioters. The various right-wing organizations, already on the boil, suspected that Daladier had dismissed Chiappe as a prelude to their own dissolution. The demonstrations they had planned for the day the Chamber returned after its recess, 6th February, were likely to produce fireworks. That Chiappe had been very popular with his police was not going to help the government preserve order.

Right-wing organizations that were prepared to argue their case in the streets, as violently as the left had been doing it since the Revolution, had multiplied considerably since the war. What they had in common, ideologically, was a revulsion from parliamentary democracy and a craving for strong, orderly government. There were, for example, Taittinger's *Jeunesses Patriotes*, created as some kind of answer to the *Cartel des Gauches* in 1924. They worked with concepts inherited from Déroulède and Barrès and had, by 1934, collected ninety thousand members. That patriotism had now become a matter of defending France against what were held to be her internal enemies was made clear by the official statement of the movement.

'The *Jeunesses Patriotes* are a group of French citizens determined to defend the National Territory against the dangers of internal revolution, to increase public prosperity, and to improve our public institutions.'

It was not for nothing that the movement first came to the attention of the public in 1925, when it violently protested in the streets against the transfer of the ashes of Jaurès to the Panthéon.

Déroulède had at least begun by stressing foreign perils. Of these, in 1934, the Soviet Union was not the most obvious. Perhaps M Taittinger's wealth had something to do with his choice of enemy. But Marshal Lyautey, much revered for his legendary exploits in Morocco (rather less for his disastrous spell as War Minister in 1916–17), also joined the movement, as well as people like Clemenceau and Maginot. If this proves anything, it is that all kinds of men were sufficiently obsessed by the prospect of a bolshevist revolution to welcome the alternative of a right-wing dictatorship ushered in by street gangs. Just as Thiers had preferred to work with Bismarck rather than with the communards, so the Taittingers of France were shortly to prefer Hitler to the prospects of a Popular Front. On the other hand, had it not been for the Taittingers' growing strength, it is unlikely that there would ever have been enough agreement among the radicals, socialists, and communists to make the imminent Popular Front possible.

Coty's *Solidarité Française* was formed in 1933. The perfume maker's active interest in politics goes back at least to the immediate post-war period, when he bought the *Figaro* to publicize his Bonapartist views. From the mid-twenties onward he gave increasing evidence of being not merely an anti-parliamentarian but also an anti-communist. While the circulation of the *Figaro* declined as a result of his unsophisticated propaganda, he decided to launch a new paper, popular in character, to sell more cheaply than its rivals, in order to influence the proletariat. It first appeared in 1927 as the *Ami du Peuple*. Within two years it claimed a circulation of 700,000. There is little evidence that the paper exerted any real political influence. In 1933, after having lost most of his money, his political activity was reduced to the organization of the *Solidarité Française*. This propagated the same mixture of anti-communist and authoritarian views as Coty's other enterprises, except that it had at its disposal some two thousand storm troopers to add weight to them in the streets. They were to be responsible for the first burst of firing by the police on 6th February 1934.

Unlike the *Solidarité Française*, the *Croix de Feu* of Colonel de La Rocque was largely a middle-class organization. Formed in 1927 as an ex-servicemen's movement, it soon grew into an anticommunist crusade, disdainful of the parliamentary system that could allow weak governments to tolerate the Red conspiracy in France. No doubt because of its particular composition, the demonstrations of the *Croix de Feu* were generally little more than shows of potential strength, rather than the riotous outrages of the more proletarian movements. But it had not refused the offer of headquarters at the *Figaro*, made by Coty in its early days. In the beginning of 1934 it claimed a membership of 33,000. Alexander Werth[16] added this significant point:

'De la Rocque, a friend of Foch and Lyautey, has many friends in the army, and he has also many Reserve Officers among his followers.'

It will be seen that he could do even better than that.

The instructions conveyed to the members of the *Action Française* through its newspaper, to demonstrate on the evening of 6th February in front of the Palais-Bourbon, were repeated by a host of organizations besides the *Solidarité Française* and the *Croix de Feu*. The official inquiry later held by the Chamber showed that there was little effective co-ordination between the various groups. The sheer magnitude of the demonstrations, however, was quite enough to put the fear of God into the government and most deputies, and into anyone who cared about democracy in France.

'Soon after four o'clock the Place de la Concorde was already crowded with people, many of them shouting '*à bas les voleurs*'. At five o'clock the first stones were thrown at a police lorry; and by six o'clock, after the closing of the shops and offices, the Place de la Concorde became a howling mob of about a hundred thousand people. All over the square, and in other parts of Paris, battles broke out between rioters and police'.[17]

Shortly before eight o'clock the police fired their first shots at members of the *Solidarité Française* who were attempting to break through the cordon guarding the Palais-Bourbon. Six rioters were killed and forty injured. Another six were killed and seventeen wounded in a second burst of firing at about eleven o'clock. The following morning Lyautey increased the pressure to get rid of the Daladier government by threatening the President of the Republic with a march on the Palais-Bourbon by the *Jeunesses Patriotes*. A plan was also being worked out to set up a provisional government at the Hôtel de Ville. In the afternoon the government resigned.

There is even today a remarkable tendency to play down the importance of these events. Chastenet engagingly maintains that the rioters merely wanted to beat up the deputies to teach them a lesson, that they had no intention of promoting a revolution. His evidence is one statement by one member of the *Jeunesses Patriotes* at the official inquiry.[18] M René Rémond suggests that there was nothing fascist and barely anything resembling a riot about the 6th. It was perhaps Boulangist, he admits. No doubt it all depends on what one means by fascist. M Rémond dismisses altogether the contention that there was any fascism in France worth speaking of, on the grounds that for him fascism means disturbances and that the French right wanted stability.[19] It is hard to believe that M Rémond has forgotten the march on Rome and the nazi riots, before the stability imposed by the dictators could be achieved. The right-wing organizations in France certainly envisaged a permanent state of effervescence no more than those in Italy or Germany. But they were clearly not averse to employing riotous means to achieve their stable end. The essence of fascism is a ruthless sectarian authoritarianism and an ambivalent attitude towards capitalism. Most French right-wing demonstrators on 6th February exhibited both these characteristics. 'Some plot, indeed,' writes M Rémond, 'that can be exorcized by the return from his country home of a superannuated parliamentarian.'[20] Some plot indeed, that could impose the resignation of a Prime Minister enjoying a parliamentary majority, and substitute for him the nominee of the plotters. For Doumergue, who followed Daladier, was just that.

Ostensibly Doumergue formed a national government. But it contained only members of the radical party and of groups to the right of it. The socialists refused to participate, and the communists were not asked. Moreover, it was obvious from the beginning that the radicals were not going to have an easy time in the coalition. The new Prime Minister had little patience with their democratic qualms, and was fond of reminding them of their recently demonstrated vulnerability. Apart from Doumergue's own reappearance on the political scene, the acceptance of the War Ministry by Marshal Pétain suggested that this was to be a government with a difference. As Doumergue began to multiply his direct radio appeals to the country, in which he put forward plans for strengthening the powers of the Prime Minister, membership of the extra-parliamentary right-wing organizations increased, in some cases spectacularly. By 1936 the *Croix de Feu*, for example, boasted two million members. Whatever else may be said about this government, the inclusion of a man like Barthou at the Quai d'Orsay showed that it had little tenderness for Germany. Before he was assassinated with King Alexander of Yugoslavia in October 1934, he had done a good deal to raise the morale of the Little Entente and of those working for a close Franco-Polish relationship. And it must have been the much vaunted realism of some sections of the right which caused them to acclaim Barthou's negotiations with the Soviet Union. This led to the mutual assistance pact of 2nd May 1935, which was an improvement on the non-aggression pact Herriot had promoted in 1933. Soviet Russia was thus brought out of her diplomatic quarantine. She entered the League of Nations in September 1934.

It was one thing for the right to accept the Soviet Union as a potential ally while the communists were politically neutralized in France, it was quite another to have French foreign policy geared to Soviet requirements under a communist-supported left-wing government. That is what the right was allegedly to fear in the coming years. That is why it became increasingly hostile to a Soviet-French alliance. Because the peacock days of the seventy-two-year-old Doumergue were numbered. The left, quickly recovering from the shocks of the Place de la Concorde, remembered its parliamentary majority and its former prowess in the streets of Paris. It called out the workers and asked them to face the dangers of a fascist coup. Only too mindful of the fate of the left under fascist dictatorships, it imparted a kind of desperate strength even to the radicals. They called Doumergue's bluff and resigned on 8th November 1934. Except for a demonstration outside his flat in the Avenue Foch by the *Croix de Feu*, which Doumergue acknowledged wearing a beret like that of the demonstrators, the subsequent resignation of the whole ministry elicited no major disturbance in the country. La Rocque was accused of having allowed a golden opportunity for a coup to pass without a serious gesture. Thereafter he was like Boulanger after the night at the restaurant Durand. The Republic still seemed to divide France least. But the divisions were to deepen still further.

Since there was not to be a coup d'état, note had to be taken of the fact that the Chamber majority was still left of centre. Flandin was found to be acceptable to the socialists, and he formed a government in which Laval retained the Quai d'Orsay he had taken over after Barthou's death. How far Laval's very slowly emerging foreign policy was influenced by events at home is hard to say. Flandin, despite his vain efforts to persuade the Bank of France to adopt a cheap money policy to end the socially disastrous deflationary period, certainly had no love for the communists. But the mutual goodwill socialists and communists had been showing each other since the February days was beginning to disturb the anti-bolshevist elements in the country. Laval's reluctance to ratify the Soviet pact could plausibly be explained in those terms. What is beyond conjecture is that Laval wanted a peaceful solution to the problems still outstanding with Germany. Such an understanding had been advocated since the war for at least three reasons. The first, put forward by the left, was based on genuine pacifist doctrine. The second, more or less openly put forward by the right, saw in Germany a bulwark against bolshevism. The third recognized the demographic and industrial discrepancies between the two countries, and furnished the main argument for the putative realists on all sides. Laval's *Diary* contains too much special pleading to enable the reader to decide which reason was the most important in its author's case. At the time of the Saar plebiscite in January 1935 he was certainly anxious to show the Germans that they could count on French fair play, in return for which he hoped for an honest German effort towards a *rapprochement* between the two countries.

The Germans got their fair play, and ninety per cent of the votes, but within two months Hitler reintroduced conscription, contrary to the provisions of the Versailles treaty. His excuse was the extension of French conscription from one to two years, largely necessitated by the low birthrate during the war. Like Hitler, Blum's socialists also opposed the extension of French military service, as they – like Pétain – had opposed de Gaulle's plan for a smaller but thoroughly professional and mechanized army. Blindly going back for his arguments to the gospel of Jaurès, Blum saw in these plans sinister signs of military putsches. In common with most of the general staff, the socialists wanted the role of the army to be a defensive one, and considered de

Gaulle's ideas expensive white elephants. The working-class, Blum said, would rise as one man if ever there were an invasion. How the various alliances with the Little Entente states fitted into these theories it is not easy to see. Was France to come to the assistance of, say, Czechoslovakia with an army designed for purely defensive purposes? If so, how useful would her contribution be? If not, what was the use of the policy of alliances around Germany's borders? Would France not in the end be left to face Germany alone, once her allies had realized that she, as a matter of deliberate policy, would be in no position to help them? The logic of this situation was to work itself out in the tragedies of the next few years.

Meanwhile the communists were fulfilling the worst suspicions of the right. Laval's successful Moscow visit, two months after Hitler's announcement of conscription, resulted in the communists dropping their opposition to the two-year conscription law in France. Surely this proved, the right argued with understandable conviction, that there was a direct link between the policies of Moscow and those of the French communists. Imagine, they said, what could happen if the communists, by supporting a left-wing government, increased their influence in the making of French foreign policy. France might find herself at war with Germany merely because of the feud between fascists and communists, or because it suited the Soviet Union to have fascist and capitalist countries exhausting each other for their easier conquest by communism.[21] These considerations were to be given increasing weight with the rapid re-emergence of Germany as a military power and a threat to France. It is then that the question whether German fascism or Soviet communism is the greater evil will lead to the final *crise de conscience* of the Third Republic.

The reappraisal of France's foreign policy, after the manifest failure of the League and the increasing rearmament of Germany, included a new look at Italy. Barthou had shown a certain respect for Italian susceptibilities in trying to reconcile her with Yugoslavia, and that was already something for the statesman of a country that had viewed Mussolini's antics with patronizing amusement since the march on Rome. Laval went much further. The first French Foreign Minister to do so since the war, Laval went to Rome early in 1935. He hoped to enlist the Italians' help against the growing German threat by playing on their fears of seeing German troops at the Brenner Pass after the long-mooted *Anschluss* of Austria. If nothing much came of the negotiations about minor Franco-Italian differences overseas, a suitable climate had nevertheless been created for the talks to be held in Stresa in April between Britain, France, and Italy. There, although Mussolini seemed anxious to arrive at specific answers to hypothetical German moves, the British were not to be drawn, and the conference ended with the usual platitudinous declarations that were intended to hide that nothing had been achieved. It was a further sign of the times that MacDonald pronounced irrelevant a question about whether Italian designs on Abyssinia had been discussed at Stresa. Since the British and French had done nothing about German rearmament and conscription – both of which were a potential threat to them – they were hardly likely seriously to concern themselves with some backward East African territory.

A few weeks after Stresa the Flandin government fell (30th May 1935), for the now customary financial reasons. With the budget deficit still running at six milliards and a large number of loans to repay, the ministry had been in the hands of the Banks. And the Bank of France demanded the kind of deflationary policy that Flandin had promised the country not to go back to. If the Prime Minister had to resign under that pressure, the electorate was at least no longer under any illusions about the political influence exerted by the Regents of the Bank. The Bouisson government that followed lasted one day.

After several unsuccessful attempts by various politicians to form a new ministry, Laval eventually succeeded. The Bourse had become restive. The Bank found Laval more conciliatory than Flandin and Bouisson, and a ten per cent cut in budget expenditure was agreed. But in the summer there was an agricultural slump to add to the already difficult economic plight of the country, where wages had dropped thirty per cent since 1929. Extremist agitators again came into their own. Dorgères did quite well for a while, spreading violence into agricultural areas. The real shock, however, was the return into the limelight of the *Croix de Feu*. Whether they thought that Laval would be more sympathetic to them than Flandin, or whether it was because of the renewed political and economic difficulties that had led to the fall of Flandin and Bouisson, La Rocque's movement received a new lease of life in June 1935. At various places outside Paris rallies were held that often led to counter-demonstrations by left-wing groups, and bloodshed. A week before France's national day La Rocque went so far as to announce that legality no longer mattered to him. When it became known that the *Croix de Feu* were planning a major demonstration on the Champs Elysées for the 14th of July, there was talk of impending civil war. In the event only about fifty thousand people turned up. They were easily contained by the police and kept away from a few hundred thousand communists, socialists, and radicals who had decided to join forces against the fascists. Demonstrations continued throughout the autumn. Then, suddenly, at the beginning of December, the right-wing deputy Ybarnégaray offered the left, during a session of the Chamber, the disbandment of the paramilitary sections of the *Croix de Feu*, provided the left were prepared to do the same. They agreed. It was all very odd. Had La Rocque begun to fear the pressures in the Chamber that demanded the official dissolution of his kind of organization? How serious a threat to the régime could a movement have been that would meekly think of disbanding on the orders of the régime itself? Was he afraid of the consequences of his activities which had thrown together not only communists and socialists but now also the radicals? Was he thinking of the effects of the *Croix de Feu* on the electorate that would shortly be going to the polls? Whatever the answer, the acceptance of Ybarnégaray's offer made Laval's life a little easier, for his alleged sympathies for La Rocque would no longer matter so much. In fact, a few days after Ybarnégaray's speech the Chamber passed a bill enabling the government to dissolve paramilitary organizations. Laval ignored it.

But the main event of this Laval ministry was the Abyssinian crisis. Coming soon after the Anglo-German naval agreement, it helped to reinforce right-wing feeling against Britain. For the British suddenly changed their Stresa tune of indifference to the Italian designs on the one remaining uncolonized East African state. Sir Samuel Hoare spoke at Geneva in September 1935 about the need for a firm stand against Italy's projected adventure. Whether or not this British show of international virtue had anything to do with the coming elections – public feeling in Britain was running high against the Italians – it is a fact that after the elections Sir Samuel was rather less emphatic. Meanwhile he had given Laval some nasty moments. For it looked as if France might have to choose between what was left of the Entente Cordiale and that wonderful dream of Latin solidarity against Germany. Britain's virtuous talk of sanctions after Italy had begun her invasion of Abyssinia on 3rd October 1935 was a real embarrassment to Laval. To the extreme right it was, moreover, a source of suspicion that the left was backing the policy of sanctions. It thought that this sudden display of bellicosity on the part of the professionally pacifist left could only be a service to Moscow. The *Revue Hebdomadaire* wrote:

> 'Mussolini beaten, it is not England who would be victorious, but Moscow. Muscovite barbarianism sweeping over France first, and next, without doubt, all over Europe, would find only Hitler in its path.'[22]

As Micaud says, this was 'the first crisis in which ideological passions made numerous rightists take sides with international fascism, that is, with Italy and Germany'.[23] It elicited the notorious article by Béraud in *Gringoire* which damned the British (11th October) for all the mischief they were causing France. The *Action Française* went a little further by appealing for the murder of 40 left-wing deputies and senators should war break out between France and Italy.

They should all have waited until after the mid-November elections in England. Baldwin obtained a large majority and his resolution rapidly evaporated. Sir Samuel Hoare was most accommodating when he met Laval in Paris early in December. Together, they worked out a plan that would give Italy important concessions in Abyssinia. The public outcry against this disreputable volte-face could now no more stop the policy of sanctions from disintegrating than the substitution at the Foreign Office of Eden for Hoare. After the defection of the radicals, Laval could not hold out either. In mid-January 1936 he resigned. If as late as 1935 anyone still nursed the hope that the League could really be a useful instrument in the prevention of aggression, the handling of the Abyssinian invasion must have opened his eyes. And there was no effective alternative source of power that could uphold the *status quo*.

In these circumstances any country on the make was assured of a clear run. At least until it directly threatened someone able and determined to resist. No doubt the French assumed that they would resist in such an unlikely contingency. But what was a direct threat? Apparently, in French eyes, neither the violation of the moral code the League had been created to defend, nor the reintroduction of conscription in Germany. But already in January 1935 Weygand, the retiring Inspector General of the army, had told the Supreme War Council that France was unable to face a German attack. If that was true at that time, how much truer was it going to be thereafter, given the feverish haste with which the Germans were rearming, and the deplorable state of France. Hitler, on 7th March 1936, announced Germany's intention to resume full control over the Rhineland areas that were demilitarized under the Versailles treaty. That same afternoon the German army began its movement into the zone. Was this a direct threat to French security? Sarraut, the new radical Prime Minister, spoke out bravely. 'We are not prepared to see Strasbourg placed within the range of German guns', he said in a radio speech. But the general staff told the government that at least three classes of reservists would have to be recalled if France were to make a successful riposte. This might have been contemplated had French public opinion been like that in Britain at the time of the Italian invasion of Abyssinia. But it was not. The Maginot defences on which French security was thought to be based were not affected by the German move, and the British gave the French little encouragement to consider it a violation of the Locarno agreements. Besides, a British military contribution at this time could only have been derisory. Since all this occurred only a few weeks before the French general elections Sarraut in the end decided to play it down as much as possible. The British and French began to comfort each other about Hitler's perfect right to walk into his own back-garden, and tried to convince themselves that such a harmless activity could hardly be said to constitute a hostile act. In the *Action Française* of 13th February 1936 it had all been predicted:

> 'Can anyone imagine our government taking the position of an aggressor? Everything forbids it to do so: its principles, diplomatic situation, and also, alas! the state of our military forces.'[24]

Of course something had to be done, and the French sent a complaint to the League. They also proposed to have a word with the signatories of the Locarno pact. The ratification of the Franco-Soviet pact – which was not a military alliance – had pleased the states of the Little Entente, and was the ostensible reason for Hitler's move into the Rhineland, but France's inactivity over that further violation of Versailles again shook their confidence. If France allowed Germany to tear up the clauses of the treaty that affected her, what could she be expected to do about violations of the treaty affecting, say, Czechoslovakia? In any case, with the Germans immediately in front of the Maginot Line, and presumably now fortifying their own side, actual military help from defensively-minded France had become a prospect cherished only by those with indomitable faith.

Encouraged by the support they had received from the public over their stand for Mussolini and against sanctions, certain sections of the right-wing press took their defence of fascism rather further. They presented Hitler's Rhineland coup as a paternal gesture to France. For them the main enemy was communism, and Hitler's move was an attempt to stop France from doing anything silly that might interfere with his alleged plans for expansion in the East, and of which they approved. Thus *Le Matin* wrote on its front page:

> 'In his eloquent and impassioned speech Adolf Hitler showed the communist peril. "I have," he said, "warned France . . . I tremble for Europe".'[25]

This attitude found even more sinister expression in a meeting for young reservists, called for 14th March by the *Action Française*, *Le Jour*, and *Le Figaro*. The men were told that Russia, and the radicals, socialists and communists who were combining in a Popular Front, were plotting to make war on Germany for the sole benefit of the Soviet Union. Real patriotism, it was urged, now meant anti-communism. The right clearly had come a long way since Dreyfus. And if the moderates among it found anything reprehensible in the new priorities of the right-wing extremists, it was the embarrassing frankness with which they stated them, and not the priorities themselves.

CHAPTER TEN

FIGHT FOR WHAT? 1936-40

To THE cry 'Bread, Peace and Liberty' the Popular Front parties confidently went into the electoral battle of 1936. It was not until the second ballot that the right effectively banded together in the so-called National Front. There was a new record in the number of candidates. 4,815 presented themselves at the first ballot, on 6th April 1936, and 503 more at the second a week later. They competed for 618 seats. The declarations issued by both combinations of parties made it clear that they saw themselves as the champions of crucial attitudes. The electorate too recognized the importance of the issues involved by returning the highest voting figure of the Third Republic. Only fifteen per cent abstained.

The socialist election manifesto dwelt chiefly on the economic difficulties at home. Adapting Gambetta's famous slogan, it claimed: 'Capitalism, that is the enemy'. It made capitalism synonymous with the Bank of France, and fascism with the anti-democratic doctrines promoted by its regents.

'It is two years now since fascism made its appearance in France. The big capitalists, their profits diminished and their privileges threatened, are afraid that the people, as a result of its suffering, will free itself from their domination. They have financed and directed fascism. Sections of the bourgeoisie which had been uprooted from their class as a result of financial ruin, and whose accession to the proletariat was made impossible through unemployment, have joined with professional adventurers to provide fascism with its storm troopers. Youth, aware of the hopelessness of the situation, cut off from all outlets for its energies, has given fascism its slogans.'[1]

To safeguard the republican liberties, the manifesto continued, the socialists had sought the collaboration of all groups and individuals ready to defend the principle of popular sovereignty. In that spirit they had concluded with the communists 'a pact involving unity of action'. As regards foreign affairs, the socialists showed that they had not learnt a thing. Peace and disarmament and the League remained its solution to all world problems. 'Hitler's Germany has rearmed. But would she have done that if she had not had the excuse of the failure of the disarmament conference?' The negotiations, they said, should have been resumed, with or without Germany.

The communists made the same points on home affairs in rather stronger language, but showed themselves prophetic about France's future:

'Just as in the past, because of their hatred of the people and of the Popular Front, . . . men like Maurras, La Rocque, Taittinger . . . want to organize a corps of volunteers for Mussolini . . . France can perish so far as they are concerned, so long as the people are held in check.'[2]

Taittinger, the spiritual heir of Déroulède and Barrès, was quite unabashed:

'I have been against anything that . . . could defend bolshevism or check fascism . . . At the moment the peace of Europe depends on the German problem; it is no use trying to be clever about it, it must be frankly faced . . .'

France was unlikely to be in a position to play a serious part in world affairs unless she reorganized her régime. 'Democracy must become authoritarian or it is bound to disappear.'[3] Laval was right, he said, in his efforts to reinforce French links with Italy and England. But, in the final analysis, only a united France could successfully face the future. Paul Reynaud, still Taittinger's neighbour in the prosperous second arrondissement, pertinently reminded his electors of the basic and ineffable truth that for every three Frenchmen between the ages of twenty and thirty there were seven Germans.[4] To redress the balance France needed allies. Reynaud therefore refused to join in the petulant demands of many fellow-right-wingers for a more national foreign policy, less dependent on Britain and the Soviet Union.[5]

Henri de Kerillis, for many years the chief of the propaganda centre of the right at the *Echo de Paris*, was one of the very few traditional patriots who remained on that side of the political spectrum. That Germany was the enemy was to him a truth which no anti-Marxist or anti-democratic argument could shake. 'I believe that France, within or without the League, must remain the soul of a grand alliance capable of containing the ambitions of Germany.' He was against sanctions because he wanted the Italian rather than the Russian alliance. But he would accept the Russian alliance provided Russia gave up her attempts to interfere in the internal affairs of France. 'I believe in a strong army.'[6] The French right was to find him troublesome in 1940.

The radicals, between the two extremes, were no more clear-cut on major issues than had recently been usual for them. Conscious of having become respectable as a direct consequence of their loss of fire, they were careful not to upset their bourgeois electors with daring doctrines. They would defend the interests of the small business man, save him from his creditors if he was genuinely down on his luck, whether these creditors be income tax or rent collectors, or suppliers of goods. They would tackle competition from cheap chain stores, and income tax would have to be made 'more equitable'. Fascism in France was a bad thing, but so far as threats from abroad went 'I think it is better to talk than to fight'. The League must be supported.[7]

There can be no doubt, given the eighty-five per cent poll, that the electoral defeat of the right reflected the feeling of the country. Street fights and the effects of deflation had seen to it that Paris, for the first time since the war, had refused to give the right an absolute majority. The rest of the country had probably been moved by the same considerations. The interesting point about the result is the decline of the radical vote by about 400,000 to less than a million and a half; and the dramatic doubling of the communist vote to just over a million and a half; the socialist vote had remained steady at a little under the two million mark. But the National Front total was still four and a quarter million, as against 5,628,921 for the Popular Front. The results therefore confirmed the profound division among the French.

The day after the second ballot Léon Blum claimed for the socialists the leadership of the Popular Front coalition government. Since his party was the largest in the new Chamber (149 seats) it would have been difficult to resist this claim. But the first blow to the hopes of the supporters of the Popular Front came the moment Blum tried to form a ministry. The communists refused to participate in it, although they promised to support it. The similarity of that position with that Blum himself had created in relation to the radicals in previous Chambers failed to tickle his not very developed sense of humour. The prospect of having to solve France's economic and social problems in close collaboration with the radicals cannot have pleased the socialists. If the radicals did not have their first doubts at once, the right grimly felt that its worst fears were rapidly being fulfilled. On 24th May, flushed with victory, some 400,000 socialists and communists filed past the *Mur des Fédérés* in the Père Lachaise cemetery. There the Communards had made their last stand, and the demonstrators of 1936 were shouting, 'Long live the Popular Front' and 'Long live the Commune'. Was the Popular Front to be the revenge of the proletariat for the bourgeois victory of 1871? But, as yet, only the *Action Française* was prepared to go so far as to say that fascism might be the only answer if the communists gained control of the government.[8]

Two days after the Père Lachaise demonstration and eleven days before Blum received the approval of the Chamber for his government, the proletariat's elation and growing self-confidence were exhibited in a rather more serious show of strength. For no rational reason – since it could only harm their economic future – workers in the Paris area began to go on strike. But instead of merely not turning up for work, they remained in their factories, living on food brought to them from outside. Within a fortnight over a million workers were involved. The red flags, not always flanked by tricolours, that were flying over the factories and other places of work were soon also to appear in the rest of the country. Here and there clashes occurred with right-wing groups, but the police did not usually interfere. All kinds of reasons have been given for these unprecedented events, ranging from the inevitable charge that they had been engineered by the communists to the naïve belief that they had been spontaneous. The fact that in most cases the strikers made specific demands for improved working conditions – at Renault's they asked for a forty-hour week and a fortnight's paid holiday – could mean that they had little faith in the forthcoming Blum government. But such a judgment would obviously have been premature, and not easily compatible with the elation at their electoral victory. Perhaps they wanted to exert pressure on the new government, to make sure that Blum's repeated reminder that he was the head of a Popular Front, and not of a socialist ministry, did not mean that they were to be sold down the river for the sake of a compromise with the radicals.

There is evidence that the now unified CGT – which was within a fortnight to double its membership to three million and reached five million in September – was as overwhelmed by the strike movement as the communists.[9] It was Blum, however, who was least to be envied. What was the first socialist Prime Minister of France to do about the workers' stay-in strikes? When he taunted the right with wanting him to use troops to clear the workshops, restaurants, stores, that were affected by these strikes, his bitterness must have been due as much to the understandable *Schadenfreude* of the right as to his fear that he might in fact have to use force. For the response to his appeals to the strikers was unimpressive. What did however get results were the talks that were hastily begun at the Hôtel Matignon between the government, representatives of the big employers, and the CGT. But even then the strikes did not finally subside until about a week after agreement had been reached on 7th June. The main gains by the workers were the collective contracts that clearly set out some basic rights (freedom to join a trade union, conditions of dismissal, etc), the forty-hour week, and a fortnight's paid annual holiday.

With the workers momentarily satisfied, and the employers seething with resentment at the concessions wrung from them, the government had to face the ever present economic crisis. The Bank of France had been, to all intents and purposes, nationalized. But to conciliate the potential manipulators of the currency and credit, the socialist Premier had announced that there would be no devaluation. If this impressed the right (except Reynaud, who had been advocating devaluation for years as an aid to exports), because they thought it implied the continuation of deflationary policies, it should not have pleased the left since it would retard the economic expansion that alone could bring prosperity. When Blum realized at the end of September 1936 that despite his conservative economic policy gold was again leaving the country, he at last agreed to devalue. Oddly enough the communists objected.

They said it meant robbing the workers, and would have preferred a capital levy. The right however was to be compensated for this offensive measure. When stay-in strikes again occurred in some Paris hotels and restaurants in October, the police were ordered to expel the strikers from the premises. It was all beginning to look again like the substitution of combinazione for Jacobinism. The communists were more and more openly congratulating themselves on having stayed outside the government. They would be in a position to provide an alternative when the workers and lower middle-classes finally realized that the Republic would always cheat them.

The outbreak of the civil war in Spain in July 1936 provided further proof of the spinelessness of the Blum government. The Prime Minister maintained that intervention by France in the struggle between Franco's fascists and the legitimate left-wing government might provoke a world war. And the fact that, after its first generous response to the plight of the Spanish republicans, the French working-class allowed itself to be persuaded into acclaiming its socialist Premier's excuses for non-intervention redounds to no one's credit. The resultant French inactivity again demonstrated that in the last analysis no one cared about principles: the Italians and the Germans could aid Franco to their hearts' content. The workers of France, in June, had certainly been fighting for more bread and an easier life all round. But for themselves alone. The principles they allegedly were trying to uphold were shown up as sham rationalizations. This had not been true in 1870-1. Of course it was possible that French arms supplies to the Spanish republicans might have caused a war with the fascist and nazi states, but they were hardly likely to do so by themselves. And there was no need to send Frenchmen to fight in Spain, where they might meet the Italians who had come to help Franco. The main thing the legally constituted republican Spanish government had asked for was arms, for which it was going to pay. The British warning that France could not expect to receive any help if she got herself involved in the war would not have worried a resolute government. As for the right, it actually advocated the immediate recognition of Franco's promised orderly régime. On the other hand, the socialist renegade Déat was no doubt right in saying that open support for one side or the other would show up the basic division of the French:

'If France seems to be the ally of fascism, half the people at least will not march. If France becomes the soldier of Stalin, the other half will not want to have anything to do with it.'[10]

One can hardly feel surprise at Belgium's declaration of neutrality on 14th October 1936, for to depend on Anglo-French promises or goodwill was clearly suicidal. Yugoslavia's understanding with Italy of April 1937 must be seen in the same light.

Blum's September devaluation of the franc had only a temporary success. By January 1937 wholesale prices had risen by twenty-eight per cent, while increases in wages and salaries had in only a few cases exceeded fifteen per cent. Moreover, strikes and the forty-hour week had prevented the expansion of production which devaluation should have encouraged. The economy stagnated, and nobody was keen to help the government get its loans to pay its debts. On 13th February 1937, to create confidence among potential creditors, Blum abandoned his half-hearted attempt to dispense with balanced budgets (so long as the economy was expanding) and announced a pause in expansion. This further disillusioned his supporters, and it brought in little money. Thirty milliards were needed before the end of the year to pay government debts. It seems that socialist scruples prevented Blum from accepting the orthodox deflationary advice of the experts whom he had imposed on his Finance Minister Auriol. At any rate, in mid-June he asked the two Houses to grant him special powers. The Chamber yielded, but the Senate did not. Without bothering to ask for a vote of confidence, Blum resigned.

Few ministries can have come into office with such a bang and gone out with such a whimper. Abroad, despite Blum's timidity over Spain, Franco-Italian relations had been further strained by the strange obstinacy with which he refused to have the successor of Chambrun, the French Ambassador, accredited not only to the King of Italy but also to the Emperor of Ethiopia. Given the sort of fluid foreign policy practised by Britain and France at that time, it is surprising that a little point like that should have been allowed to upset the Italians. After all, the war in Abyssinia had ended in May. In October, when the Rome-Berlin axis was proclaimed, the Stresa hopes for a common policy with Italy and Britain against Hitler finally collapsed. The Popular Front's foreign policy was not helped by Stalin's purges of Russian army officers, which seriously affected the efficiency of France's putative ally.

At home, Blum had dissolved the *Croix de Feu* and other non-royalist extremist organizations, the *Camelots du Roi* having already been outlawed by Sarraut after their attack on Blum on the day of Bainville's funeral in February 1936. But even that did not help him much. They reappeared under new names as political parties. Thus the *Croix de Feu* became the *Parti Social Français* (PSF), a fact which proves for M Rémond[11] that it was not really fascist. For M Rémond apparently takes it for granted that La Rocque's alleged readiness to participate in the constitutional game of the Third Republic, and the increased support he enjoyed thereafter, disprove fascist tendencies in both La Rocque and his supporters. Would it be churlish to recall that Hitler too participated in the constitutional games of the Weimar Republic, while it suited him? Dissolved or not, the extreme right continued to organize after 1936. Doriot and Paul Marion formed the *Parti Populaire Français* (PPF), which M Rémond allows to have had fascist leanings.[12] Marion was to become Vichy Minister of Information. Except for an estimate of three million members for the PSF, made by the party itself in 1938, it is impossible to get at the real numbers involved in these movements. Apart from the PPF, which collected the more impatient extremists of the PSF – and in the process won the sympathy of people like Tardieu and Laval – the groups are likely to have been small. Their activities nevertheless helped to hasten the end of the Popular Front, whose growing stagnation and decay was epitomized by the strikes that delayed the effective opening of the 1937 Paris Exhibition.

Nominally the Popular Front continued when the radical Chautemps became Prime Minister on 22nd June 1937, the day after Blum's resignation. But power was obviously moving away from the left, towards the centre. Delbos remained, largely inactive, at the Quai d'Orsay, except for an unrewarding visit to the Little Entente states in December 1937. Bonnet, a radical like Delbos, was recalled from the Washington Embassy to become Finance Minister. Of the important ministries only the Interior remained in the hands of the socialists. It was the financial crisis that had been the occasion of Blum's resignation, but the special powers the Senate had refused him they granted Bonnet without difficulty. Bonnet had no real sympathy for the Popular Front concept, and his measures were bound to be unpopular with the left.

He increased taxation and reduced expenditure by almost ten milliards. He also again devalued the franc. The socialists, who had only with great reluctance allowed Blum to remain in the government, soon had to recognize that the grand left-wing coalition could not be saved by nostalgic visions of what might have been. Within six months Chautemps was making it very clear to them that he preferred to do without them. Lacking control over the workers as much as the CGT and the leaders of the communist party, the socialists had merely become an embarrassment to the Prime Minister in his desire to suppress the recurring demonstrations of proletarian indiscipline.

Perhaps Chautemps also imagined that by ridding the government of its pinker elements he could appease the right-wing gangs that were again active in Paris. If so he had misunderstood them. The *Comités secrets d'action révolutionnaire* (CSAR), or Cagoule, had brought themselves to public notice in June, though nobody knew at the time that such organizations existed, still less that they were responsible for the murder of an Italian anti-fascist journalist and his brother which occurred in that month. In September they blew up the headquarters of the Employers' Association, which might be taken as a minor Reichstag fire attempt at provocation. The police subsequently uncovered a number of arsenals which, according to Chautemps' report to the Chamber, contained arms of Italian manufacture. It is scarcely likely that the six thousand members the police attributed to the CSAR, and their Italian supporters, would have gone to these lengths merely to help M Chautemps get rid of a few socialist ministers. Moreover, before his government resigned in January 1938, the Italians had shown in other ways that they had grown out of the namby-pamby pre-Abyssinian days. Not only had they given financial aid to subversive elements in France – which was not the first time – but the representative of the Italian Empire, whose soldiers were helping to win Spain for fascism, withdrew from the League of Nations a fortnight before Christmas, 1937.

Economically enfeebled – her production index was twenty-five per cent down on 1929 while that of England was up by that amount – socially and politically disrupted, internationally isolated except for Britain's Locarno promises and the toothless Russian pact, France went into 1938 with a new Chautemps government in office. So far as armaments were concerned, the pacifism of the

Popular Front had at least not prevented it from vastly increasing its defence budgets, doubling that of 1937 to slightly under three milliard francs, and raising that for 1938 by another two milliard francs. But this apparently did not signify quite the improvement the figures suggest. Tooling up was slow and production too often experimentally confined to prototypes. This was particularly true of the aircraft industry, which matched the German monthly production of three hundred machines with a mere fifty of its own. The Germans were, of course, not handicapped by strikes and a forty-hour week.

But the French were so busy with internal problems that they had little time to spare for questions affecting national security. Chautemps' new government, since it would not rely on socialist and communist support, was bound to be increasingly the prisoner of the right, although the country had only eighteen months earlier shown its desire for a government of the left. In the political difficulties created by this situation, even Hitler's preparations for the Austrian *Anschluss* hardly got more than a passing glance until early in February. Having seduced Mussolini, Hitler had clearly decided by the beginning of February that he had a sporting chance of getting away with a bid for the control of Austria. Army and diplomatic chiefs likely to err on the side of caution – the Minister of War, Blomberg, the Chief of the Army, Fritsch, the Foreign Minister, von Neurath – were replaced by more devoted servants on 4th February 1938. Hitler himself assumed the post of Supreme Commander of the combined armed forces, Keitel was promoted to assist him, and Ribbentrop became Foreign Minister. The Austrian Chancellor Schuschnigg was then invited to Hitler's haunt at Berchtesgaden for the 12th. He was told that, unless he wanted to face a German invasion, the Austrian nazi chief Seyss-Inquart had to become Minister of the Interior. As for hopes that Austria might obtain assistance from Britain and France, Hitler reminded Schuschnigg that they had not even acted when France's security had been at stake during the re-occupation of the Rhineland. Schuschnigg surrendered, although on his return to Austria he decided to hold a plebiscite on whether his countrymen wanted to remain independent. The reaction of Britain and France could hardly have been blacker for him. After Eden had been replaced by Halifax, who had fewer inhibitions about treating with the Germans, Prime Minister Chamberlain made a speech (22nd February 1938) which must have been the most reassuring thing Hitler had heard from the British. Small nations, he said, must recognize that the League cannot protect them, and that the future of Europe depended on how the four main powers managed to find a *modus vivendi*. It was clear that the interests of the small nations would be subordinated to the quest for that *modus vivendi*. At last, on 25th February, the French found time for a major foreign affairs debate in the Chamber. It should have added greatly to Hitler's peace of mind, if by that time anything France might have done could still disturb it. Delbos, replying to the debate that had concerned itself a good deal with French commitments in Central Europe, was significantly evasive about Austria, although he re-affirmed France's obligations to Czechoslovakia. So, on 11th March 1938, two days after the plebiscite had been announced by Schuschnigg for the 13th, German troops were ordered into Austria. But by then Chautemps had resigned, and there was no French government to send the customary protest to the League. Forty-two million Frenchmen now lived opposite seventy-six million Germans.

The Blum government that followed lasted less than a month. Blum had hoped to make it a government of national union, incorporating all parties – including the communists – that could be expected to want to defend democracy in France (for whatever motives). He did not stand a chance. He was, as before, confronted by an unco-operative Senate and hostile finance, and somehow also again by the first serious stay-in strikes for over a year. The appointment of Paul-Boncour to the Quai d'Orsay made the right even more hostile to him. For the new Foreign Minister showed every intention of taking a firmer line with Germany, caring far less about the counsels of prudence of the British Prime Minister, Chamberlain, than the majority of the right considered desirable in their endeavour to appease the nazi bulwark against communism. He was even allowing war material to be sent to the Spanish republicans. In contrast, sections of the right were beginning to advocate the setting up of a government that would not be hamstrung by Parliament, mentioning Pétain as its desirable head.[13] They also helped to prepare the atmosphere for Munich, by following up the *Anschluss* with a sustained propaganda campaign against the folly of trying to save the Czechs from Hitler.

The Daladier government that succeeded Blum's (10th April

1938) was widely welcomed. Daladier had been War Minister for two years, and his surprisingly persistent reputation for being a strong man pleased different people for different reasons. It remained to be seen on whom that alleged strength was going to be used. Since the *Anschluss*, which for the first time since the war had meant actual German troop movements into a foreign country, there was real uneasiness in France, not least because Henlein's nazi Sudeten Germans were making it obvious that they were out to make trouble in Czechoslovakia. And that could now, after the *Anschluss* had outflanked Czech defences against Germany, signify a direct challenge by Hitler to the territorial integrity of that Central European state. The French alliance with Czechoslovakia went back to Locarno (16th October 1925), and was absolutely unambiguous. If either country were attacked the other was bound to come to its aid. It may be said that, for the first time in Franco-German relations since the war, French honour was at stake. Whatever concessions Briand had made to the Germans, whatever the French had allowed Hitler to do in the Rhineland, all could be put down to noble sentiments such as generosity, fairmindedness, or even a national sacrifice in the interests of peace. Even French inactivity over the *Anschluss* could be condoned in such terms, for France had no alliance with Austria. Czechoslovakia was in a different category. Moreover, the French had repeated, and were still now repeating, that nothing could shake France's resolution to stand by her obligations.

But it was not only the extreme right which was alarmed at the possibility of a war with Germany. Its press campaign, which had begun in the middle of March with derisive accounts about the artificial character of the Czech state, is epitomized by *Gringoire*'s article, 'Will you fight for the Czechs?' (16th April). The question also exercised Daladier and Bonnet, who talked about little else in their first encounter with Chamberlain in London at the end of April. If they had hoped for British support in their commitments to the Czechs, they were disappointed. The Czechs were advised to come to a settlement with Henlein. British policy over the last few years had ensured that Chamberlain was hardly in a position to contemplate making war on anybody, at least not on land or in the air. Nor, as he was shortly to show, would he have felt justified in doing so over such outlandish small fry as Czechoslovakia. Russia's proffered help, however, was suspiciously ignored by Bonnet. He had little desire to be included in the right-wing vendetta against the communist bellicists, as the few firm defenders of French national security were now known to the latter-day pacifists of the *Action Française* and its many emulators.

No sooner back from London, Daladier had to deal with another worsening of the financial situation. The franc received its third devaluation, to 179 to the pound, which brought it to within three-fifths of the value of the Poincaré franc. A defence loan was quickly oversubscribed, and for a few weeks all looked well. The Czech problem, despite a scare about an alleged German mobilization in the third week of May, was gratefully lost sight of in the fond hope that Henlein's talks with the Czechs would somehow yield something, and would possibly go on into the autumn. That would leave the summer, in which thanks to the Popular Front most Frenchmen could now enjoy a holiday. In July, Paris gave a memorable welcome to the British royal couple. But the news from Germany was soon again ominous. Hitler's war preparations were manifestly becoming frantic. In France, however, the labour situation was as unpredictable as ever. The workers' insistence that the forty-hour week should not be tampered with; the strikes that broke out anywhere, any time; the prospect of the factories coming to a quasi-official stop during the fortnight's paid holiday; all these things contrasted blackly with the developments on the other side of the Rhine. In August, while France was enjoying herself, she produced two aeroplanes; in the same month Germany produced eight hundred. Daladier's radio speech condemning these carefree French habits merely resulted in the resignation from his government of two ministers with socialist tendencies. If the country had really been deeply stirred by the many signs of growing German aggressiveness, it would not have behaved with such frivolity.

It was during the royal visit that Halifax told the French of his government's desire to send Lord Runciman to Prague to help mediate a settlement. Daladier and Bonnet agreed only too happily. If the British were going to take charge of the Czech problem, the French government seemed to assume that its responsibility would in some obscure way be reduced. An even greater disregard for logic caused it to assert that without the British (at that time disposing of a total of two under-strength divisions for possible service in France), the French would surely not be much use to the Czechs, so that Benes had better listen to Runciman. As Pertinax wrote in *L'Europe Nouvelle* (30th July 1938),

> 'henceforth French resolution will probably cease to be the basic factor. The eventual report of Lord Runciman will replace it: whatever its nature, it will certainly govern the conduct of Great Britain and indirectly that of France. It is a very striking innovation. The "leadership", the direction of Franco-British co-operation, has been in fact transferred from Paris to London.'

Not until the beginning of September did the Czechs yield anything to the Sudeten Germans. While this procrastination was most considerate of them so far as the French summer holidays were concerned, the degree of internal autonomy they finally offered their German minority failed to satisfy Henlein. Runciman tended to agree with him that the Czechs had been hard masters, and was thinking in terms of a plebiscite in the German regions to decide on their future territorial status. It is important to recognize that the possibility of the cession to Hitler of these parts of Czechoslovakia, which the proposal for a plebiscite implied, was viewed with mixed feelings at both ends of the French political spectrum.[14] As was now customary, those who showed some regard for French obligations to Czechoslovakia and, indeed, to her own security, were stigmatized as warmongers by those elements of the right which, in turn, were accused of being fascist tools in their evident desire to appease Hitler at all costs. Daladier hovered uneasily between these two. Whether his reluctance to go to war was based on his conviction of French military inferiority, or on the belief that Germany was the wrong enemy in a world threatened by bolshevism, his reaction to Munich was to show that he also had his pangs of conscience. But the German mobilization in August had brought no noticeable reaction from him until the end of the first week in September, when he finally decided to have France's main defence against Hitler's armies, the Maginot line, adequately manned. What is more, when he actually obtained Britain's assurance that France would not have to face Germany alone if she came into conflict with her over Czechoslovakia, he and Bonnet were most anxious to believe the Berlin-inspired story that the assurance was a hoax.[15] Hardly cowed by the Franco-British attitude, the nazi leaders at their

Nuremberg jamboree yelled their choicest vulgarities against the Czechs, which stirred the Sudeten Germans into renewed violent activity. Fearing the worst, Chamberlain went to Berchtesgaden to see Hitler, who promised a peaceful solution provided a plebiscite were held in Henlein's territories. The fact that the British Prime Minister had attempted to discuss the problems of France's ally without even the presence of a Frenchman no longer struck anyone as odd.

To the dismay of Henri de Kerillis, the only significant extreme right-wing patriot the French still had, Daladier and Bonnet allowed themselves – without too much reluctance – to be talked into accepting Hitler's terms when they were revealed to them in London after Chamberlain's return. In fact, where Hitler had demanded a plebiscite they were prepared to advise the Czechs to make it a graceful handover. Combined Anglo-French pressure eventually brought the submission of the Czech government and Chamberlain set off again, this time to Godesberg, to break the glad news to Hitler. The British Prime Minister was not a little surprised to be told abruptly that German patience with the Czechs was at an end, and that the territories in question were either to be handed over at once or Germany would collect them herself within the next week. To show however that he was not unreasonable, Hitler ostensibly agreed to extend the ultimatum by three days, to 1st October 1938, the date already secretly designated for the first German military moves against Czechoslovakia. Another crisis.

The Czechs quixotically ordered a partial mobilization, and the French increased the number of reservists already recalled to 675,000. The British still refused to introduce conscription, but put the Royal Navy on a war footing. Hitler, apparently un-impressed, announced an imminent general mobilization, adding that the Sudetenland constituted his last territorial ambition in Europe. War seemed inevitable and, according to Werth[16], the recalled French conscripts left grimly but without fuss. Even two great strikes were called off in Paris and the Nord department.

But, if this really were Hitler's last demand? Hitler added to that sweet thought by sending Chamberlain a letter in which he stated that he not only had no wish to destroy Czechoslovakia but would guarantee her new frontiers once the Henlein territories had been ceded. Chamberlain immediately thought of a conference. His idea that Mussolini was the best man to sell Hitler such a meeting was rather a bright one. For while it was true that the nazi leader would have to take some notice of his Italian ally, the flattering light into which the request put Mussolini could make him more friendly to the British, even though the French were still in disgrace. In the more optimistic breasts the thought of a return to Stresa caused the heart to quicken. On 28th September, Hitler agreed to a conference at Munich on the following day. Germany, Italy, Britain, and France were to be represented. Not Russia. And not Czechoslovakia.

By now the influence of the appeasers was considerable, especially since Bonnet himself had been shown to be one. But the pacifist posters that appeared in Paris just before Munich were not merely the symbols of eccentricity they would have been in 1914. The one by Flandin, headed 'You are being deceived', plainly asserted that the Popular Front was precipitating France into an ideological war, although there was nothing more than a purely procedural misunderstanding between France and Germany about how and when the Sudetenland was to be ceded. The *Action Française* was indignant that such a patriotic poster should have been torn down by the police, which had incomprehensibly taken it as a potential incitement to reservists not to report for duty. Another poster, however, was more significant. It emanated from the school teachers, that section of the community which had been the repository of militant patriotism during the earlier decades of the Republic. Since the war they had become increasingly pacifist. When one realizes what their earlier patriotism had done for the Republic in the schools (Ferry's reforms had introduced civics into the curriculum, with highly patriotic overtones) one can conjecture what their pacifism will at least have left undone. With the postmen, they now brought out a poster which began 'We do not want war'. To accuse the schoolteachers and postmen of fascist tendencies – as one might Flandin – and to account for their poster in that way, would be as silly as to attribute such origins to Chamberlain's pre-Munich apology for not wanting to plunge Europe into war for the sake of 'a faraway country'. It is as important to recognize that there were people who agitated against war because they had a genuine horror of it, not least because they remembered the previous one, as it is that there were some who agitated against it on more suspect grounds.

It is also true that the schoolteachers, most of whom had left-wing tendencies, were under the influence of socialist internationalism.

The Havas correspondent, quoted by Werth,[17] was told by Göring on the night of the Munich agreement that he thought Daladier was a good fellow, 'he is so elastic'. France's strong man had deserved that praise. For not only had he given up his initial attempts at resistance to Hitler, especially when it was clear that Chamberlain had made up his mind to surrender, but he had also told his Czech allies that since without help from Britain France was in no position to come to their aid, the Czechs had better do as Hitler said. They were to send a delegate to Berlin the next day to make the necessary arrangements to meet the slightly modified Godesberg demands.

The story of how Daladier expected to be booed by the crowd he saw on his return to Paris, and how it cheered him instead, is well known. The relief it felt, like its London counterpart, at war having been averted explains its behaviour easily enough. Moreover, even if France had not managed to save her ally from mutilation, the Czechs had not in fact been attacked, so that honour had not been patently forfeited. In any case, as the extreme right had been saying all along, Czechoslovakia was a composite state, and if the Germans there really wanted to be incorporated in the neighbouring Reich there was something to be said for letting them. Chamberlain and Daladier had saved peace with honour. In the *Matin* the attitude of the extreme right was gloatingly summed up:

'Victory! Victory! Hundreds of thousands of Parisians went down into the street to greet it with frenzy, without a word of command from any group or political cell. Peace is won. It is won over the crooks, sell-outs and madmen. It is won for old and young, for mothers and their little ones.'[18]

But that feeling was not confined to the extreme right. Apart from the communists, only Kerillis and one socialist voted against the Munich agreements after the debate in the Chamber; Blum defended them with his customary invocation of Jaurès.

At Godesberg Hitler had used his hectoring tone for the first time on a British statesman. Even if that had been adequate warning that war was inevitable, prudence – despite the alleged qualms of Hitler's generals[19] – probably demanded that the post-

H   225

Munich respite be drawn out for as long as possible. Once Britain and France had allowed him to obtain his lead in re-armament, any time gained by them could only be to Hitler's disadvantage.[20] At least that is the argument put forward by some of the apologists for Munich, and was apparently endorsed by Hitler himself. On the other hand, the moral effect of the Munich war scare, with its cruel bitter-sweet ending, is incalculable. How many divisions was it worth to the Germans that, when mobilization again came in 1939, there must have been many who half expected some new deal to be done that would enable them soon to go home again?

The fact that the communists had been the only major opponents of Munich was greedily seized upon by Daladier and those to the right of him. It provided them with ex post facto excuses, indeed they seemed to think with justification, for their surrender. Did the communists' attitude not show that they expected to benefit from a war between France and Germany? Rather than fight each other, the two countries should work together against the communist threat. 'We must reach a general settlement in Europe, and build it on new principles',[21] the Prime Minister had said in the Chamber debate on Munich. A few weeks later, at the congress of the radical party, he made it clear that he meant it to be built without the communists. He did not however go as far as some of his compatriots who were stepping up their campaign for allowing Germany a free hand in the East, or even – on Gambettist lines – for handing over French colonies to the *Lebensraum*-hungry nazis. It was Flandin who was the leading exponent of this doctrine, which was usually supplemented by the suggestion that France should disinterest herself in European affairs and devote her attention to her Empire.[22]

If only because he had recognized even at Munich that the settlement there was unlikely to safeguard peace forever, Daladier continued to show Mussolini the same kind of consideration that had prompted him and Chamberlain to ask the fascist leader to arrange for the meeting with Hitler. For a start François-Poncet was transferred from Berlin to become Ambassador to the King of Italy and Emperor of Ethiopia. Daladier's *Realpolitik* had thus done away with another moral sentimentality, for it will be recalled that the Popular Front had refused such an appointment which consecrated Italy's conquest in East Africa. But just over three weeks after the new Ambassador's arrival in Rome, the Italian government showed that it had no intention of separating itself from Hitler. In an obviously inspired demonstration in the Italian Chamber, the deputies went so far as to lay claim to Tunis, Corsica, and Nice. This claim was to be frequently repeated during the next few months. For good measure, a speech by Mussolini at the end of January was to set the Italians clamouring to take the road to Paris too.

The Italian agitation for spoils of their own coincided with an attempt at a one-day general strike in France. It was on 30th November 1938 that Jouhaux's mass stoppage was to take place, as a protest against the economic policy introduced by Reynaud, who had become Finance Minister at the beginning of September. Needing twenty-five milliards for increased expenditure on armaments, he proposed to cut the public works programme, reduce the number of State employees (in the case of the railway workers alone this reduction amounted to forty thousand men) and raise new taxes which, as usual, were not graduated and would therefore hit the poorer population particularly hard. The CGT was not, on second thoughts, altogether happy about its proposed strike, particularly when the government announced its intention to requisition the public services. Given the political evolution since the heroic days of May and June 1936, the government – now certainly no longer left-of-centre – and the employers could well look forward to the show-down on 30th November. They were not disappointed. On the pretence that the whole thing had really been organized by the communists, Daladier made a broadcast three days before the strike:

> 'The general strike has no material or moral justification. We have not threatened the liberty of the people. We intend no dictatorship, no fascism. The sacrifices demanded are necessary to the life of the country. Yet one party opposes these sacrifices and prepares to offer violence and is attempting to blackmail the government.'[23]

In the event the strike was a failure, and Daladier, as well as the employers, was happy. The possibilities for revenge, now that the Popular Front was no longer there to confer strength upon the working-classes, were seized with uncanny fervour. Thousands of men were dismissed in private as well as in State-controlled industries, and it was months before anyone felt inclined to do anything for these people. The influence of the trade unions declined sharply as a result of this fiasco. So did its membership. From its record of about five million in 1936 it now declined to about half that number. And the persecution of the communists continued.

One of the reasons for Daladier's savage treatment of the strike was that it was delaying the signing of Bonnet's cherished piece of paper, in which he and Ribbentrop were going to tell the world that war between France and Germany was undesirable. The declaration was finally signed in Paris on 6th December 1938. The visit of Hitler's Foreign Minister to the capital of France provided the occasion for what must surely have been the most ignominious demonstration of French abjectness. Mandel and Zay, the Jewish ministers in the Daladier government, were not invited to the two official receptions given for Ribbentrop by the Prime Minister and Bonnet.

Just how low France had sunk must have become clear to her when the Italians started their grotesque campaign for Corsica and other French territories. If a nation the French never quite managed to take seriously could imagine that it might bait them, something was obviously wrong. Daladier decided to go on a tour of the coveted areas. The reception he received, even in Tunisia, restored a little courage both to the Prime Minister and to France as a whole, although the Italians fiercely referred to the visit as a provocation. France seemed united, for the first time since the twenties. Even if some Stresa enthusiasts remained, no one was to be found to defend Mussolini's hopeful audacity. But, just in case the fall of Barcelona (26th January 1939) and the imminent total victory for the fascists in Spain elicited too generous a display of *hubris* from the Italian dictator, Chamberlain declared at the beginning of February that England would stand by France in case of Italian aggression.

The end of the Spanish civil war presented France with two main problems. First, there was the question of what to do with the half million Spaniards who were crossing the border as refugees. Secondly, there was the problem presented by the border itself, where the French would now be facing a potentially hostile state. The first problem was overcome by rather grudging official acceptance of the refugees, while the second depended on how much Franco's gratitude to the Italians and Germans would amount to, and how far he could contemplate any kind of aggressive action after the devastating effect of the civil war. In an attempt to conciliate him, Daladier and Bonnet had the marvellous idea of sending him Pétain as a French Ambassador of flattering stature. But as so often in their dealings with Germany since the war, it was a gesture that came too late. In their half-hearted attempts to help Franco's enemies, the French had done too little to be of use to them, but too much to be in the fascist victor's good books. Franco kept Pétain waiting for over a week before seeing him for the first time.

With Italy apparently cowed, Spain wooed by the venerable victor of Verdun, Poland and other countries surrounding Germany tentatively flexing their patriotic muscles, and Hitler himself not having demanded anything since Munich except a few colonies, the beginning of Spring 1939 did not look too bad from France and England. The December and January scares of German attacks on the Ukraine and the Low Countries had produced nothing untoward. The awakening was all the ruder.

On 15th March 1939 the nazi dictator, who had said at the end of the previous September that he did not want any Czechs in his Reich, proclaimed a German protectorate over Bohemia and Moravia. The hope that he only wanted to re-unite with the Reich Germans who had been cut off from it by the Versailles treaties had finally gone. No one now was safe from him. A week after Prague his troops occupied Memel. On 26th March the now apprehensive Poles rejected German demands concerning the Polish corridor and Danzig. Other events were no more reassuring. On 28th March Franco's troops entered Madrid. On 31st March the British Prime Minister gave Poland an Anglo-French guarantee of her borders. A week later Italy invaded Albania. This was followed on 13th April by Anglo-French guarantees to Greece and Rumania. On 28th April the Germans denounced their non-aggression pact with the Poles, as well as the Anglo-German Naval treaty. A month later (22nd May) the Italo-German alliance was formally concluded. Thus, within the space of about eight weeks, an optimistic spring had given way to the certainty of imminent catastrophe.

But the pro-nazis were not silent in France. Their stridency merely gave way to a rather more circumspect Palm Court sweetness. This enabled them to continue with their work of demoralization while apparently paying respect to the growing if resigned firmness of their countrymen. How far the right-wing *Matin* was sincere in its professed belief that France could only face a defensive war successfully, and how far it was moved by less patriotic motives it is hard to say. But no sooner was Hitler's move into Bohemia announced than it hastened to advise Britain (21st March) to start negotiations with Germany, following this up three days later with the injunction not to do anything beyond the Rhine. The *Action Française* took the same line, except that it warned also against a Jewish plot to involve France in a war with the Germans (17th March). Micaud has shown[24] how the attitude of the extreme right changed after Britain had adopted a firmer line, guaranteeing Poland, Rumania, and Greece, and introducing conscription. But that did not stop Déat from writing in the *Oeuvre* as late as 4th May 1939 that there was no point in dying for Danzig. The pacifist wing of the socialists, including the schoolteachers, was equally opposed to action.

Since the prestige of the Entente Cordiale had manifestly failed to deter the Axis from its delinquent path, it was at least possible that the successful outcome of the resumed negotiations with the Soviet Union might do so. With patronizing complacency the right averred that since the Popular Front was now dead, and consequently the danger of communist influence on governmental policy remote, there was no longer any real objection to the Soviet alliance. 'The Popular Front', the *Figaro* wrote (15th March), 'no longer exists among us. The majority that upholds the government has relegated the communist party to a position of impotent opposition. That has changed many things.' But the Soviet Union showed little desire to accept the democracies' invitation to help rescue them from the results of their own sins. Twelve days after the arrival in Moscow (11th August) of the Anglo-French mission, Ribbentrop and Molotov signed a non-aggression pact. Certainly the *Action Française* and other right-wingers did not regret the failure of the Soviet alliance. There was still the lingering conviction that only communism could gain from war between fascism and the democracies, and that an alliance with the Russians could only precipitate such a war.

When it came, two days after the German invasion of Poland (1st September 1939) the French had mobilized most of their male population between the ages of twenty and forty-nine. There was no enthusiasm, only resignation. It was inevitable that France would be attacked sooner or later. It might as well be got over with, one way or the other. Some of her intellectuals had tried to give the war some ideological meaning by starting a Péguy vogue. It was a pathetic substitute for the refurbished *revanche* motif of 1914. Péguy's belief in French moral superiority took a good deal of proving in 1939. As for his other favourite, the *mystique républicaine*, it was grotesquely outdated. France had no desire to fight for abstract principles. Nor was she united. The working-classes had been severely shaken by the Molotov-Ribbentrop pact. They had for too long been outside the bourgeois Republic for its call to arms to have any meaning outside the communist context. What were they to do now that Stalin and Hitler were apparently working together? The peasants, nursed on Daladier's appeasement policy, needed little convincing that if the Germans did not attack, there was no reason for attacking them. The middle-classes, once it had become clear that the Poles had been defeated, and the Western front had settled down into boring inactivity, failed to find much to fight about. As Flandin insinuatingly said to the Foreign Affairs Committee of the Chamber, 'is it worth going on with?'[25] Russia's attack on Finland, after her annexation of the Eastern part of Poland, gave a golden opportunity to her many French enemies for a restatement of the view that France was fighting the wrong enemy. In fact the Daladier government had to resign over its failure to help the Finns. Reynaud, who followed him (20th March 1940), at least had a reputation for wanting to prosecute the war with a little more vigour, though that had very little indeed to do with his taking office. In fact, the former Premier stayed at the Ministry of Defence and made sure that the cautious Gamelin remained Commander-in-Chief. Moreover, Reynaud's majority was so small that his government might not have lasted long had it not been for the Norway expedition (April-May 1940) for which, at the beginning, so much had been claimed and which, in the end, led to the first major allied withdrawal of the war. Reynaud remained, but in England Chamberlain made way for Churchill.

When the Germans finally attacked in the West (10th May), their last 'appeals to reason' having gone unheeded, when they outflanked the famous Maginot line and defeated the Franco-British forces within six weeks, the low morale of the French army stood clearly exhibited. It showed little of that 1914 resilience which had allowed it to fight to a standstill an enemy equally superior in numbers and equipment. There is no evidence of actual treason in high places to account for the speed of the collapse. There has, however, been ample evidence to show that people in high and low places had grown accustomed in the course of over half a century to distinguishing between the Third Republic and the *patrie*. The *patrie* represents something that is worth fighting for. In 1940 there were few left who thought that the Third Republic was worth fighting for. The 'real' *patrie* of the *Action Française*, or the *patrie* of the left of 1789 might have found active defenders; so might any of a dozen other sectarian visions. But officers influenced by the *Action Française* and the *Croix de Feu* had as much difficulty in finding something to quarrel about with the Germans and Italians – the latter had declared war on 10th June 1940 – as the cannon fodder had in finding reasons for defending the bourgeois Republic. Cornered in Bordeaux, the Reynaud government made way for Pétain. On the pressing advice of the new Commander-in-Chief, Weygand, France obtained an armistice (22nd June).

'We, Philippe Pétain, Marshal of France . . .' Thus the octogenarian victor of Verdun began his aristocratic address to his countrymen. Another era was clearly beginning.

The Third Republic was dead. It had died because its citizens had no longer seen any reason for keeping it alive.

PATRIOTISM SINCE 1940

TH AT THE death of the Third Republic did not mean the death of France as an autonomous state was only in a small way due to French efforts. It was mainly the result of the endeavours of Great Britain, the United States and the Soviet Union. Neither the followers of General de Gaulle outside, nor the various resistance movements inside France, greatly affected the outcome of the war that in 1944 restored to France her independence. The Riom trials (1942), instigated by Pétain's Vichy government in unoccupied France to find scapegoats for the abject plight of the country, were as much a consequence of this unhappy realization as were the trials of the men of Vichy by those who ousted them in 1944. They were the consequences of feelings of shame that had to find ways of blaming someone else.

The trials were not always explicable in patriotic terms. There is no doubt that some of the persecution by Vichy of politicians associated with the Third Republic amounted to no more than the settling of old political accounts. It can hardly be denied that the same is true of the treatment meted out to alleged Vichy sympathizers by returned émigrés after the liberation of France. None of this had anything to do with patriotism. But there were other cases. The death sentences Frenchmen passed on each other during and after the war were often the expression of genuine differences of opinion about the nature of patriotic duty. Once defeat has come and autonomy is lost, the patriot's unenviable task is to decide how best to ensure an honourable future for his country. Here the borderline between patriotism and treason is not always obvious. The simple criteria with which we have been working so far are clearly inadequate once there are no more frontiers to be defended. There may be no difficulty in determining whether someone who accepts large sums of money for his services to the enemy is guilty of treason. But what is one to say

H* 233

of an army officer like General de Gaulle who refuses to heed the orders of his legal government, who ignores an armistice signed by his legal government, who invites all Frenchmen able to do so to do likewise, who thereby becomes a serious embarrassment to his legal government in its attempt to salvage what it can from the wreckage of total defeat?

If any judgment is to be passed on the patriotism of Frenchmen in such a situation, it is proper to recall that France has been a parliamentary democracy for a good many decades. Such a régime carries with it the responsibility of the electorate for the aims it allows its representatives to pursue, as well as for the men and women to whom it entrusts the interpretation of these aims and the determination of the means that are to achieve them. In previous chapters an attempt was made to appraise the attitudes of electors and elected to the rudiments of patriotism since 1870. The fact that both had been unsuccessful, or unwilling, to avert defeat in 1940 in no way absolves them from responsibility for what happened then, nor from what happened subsequently while the results of the 1936 elections remained valid. Consequently, what matters most for the determination of whether it was General de Gaulle or the men of Vichy who were the proper interpreters of the national interest after 1940, is the hard fact that the freely-elected representatives of the French people met at Vichy less than three weeks after the armistice; that of a possible 932 deputies and senators, 649 had made their way to the temporary capital of unoccupied France; that only eighty voted against the conferment of full powers on Marshal Pétain; that General de Gaulle possessed no such mandate.

If it be argued that lucidity is a better guide to patriotism and victory than universal suffrage, it is still the case that no one could be sure in June and July 1940 where the best interests of France lay. In fact, General Weygand's recognition of France's total defeat, and his belief that Britain could not for long escape a similar fate, seemed in the summer of 1940 most lucid. General de Gaulle might, rhetorically, tell the French that they had only lost a battle, that this was going to be a world struggle. The world at that time gave Britain little aid and less hope. The trouble with the criterion of lucidity is that it can only be applied after the event. Only the defeat of Germany in 1945 showed that the premisses of the men of Vichy had been wrong. But even that did not prove that it had been wrong to conclude an armistice in 1940, and to lighten the burden of partial and later of complete occupation through a measure of collaboration with the victors.

Apart from obtuseness, the men of Vichy are also often accused of downright treachery, that they went further than they need have done in their surrender to nazi Germany. Laval's notorious 'I hope for a German victory' is often quoted as epitomizing that tendency. But real proof of treason could only come from the demonstration of deliberate actions against the best interests of France as these appeared to the constitutionally appointed ministers. All the evidence however shows that Laval was convinced of a German victory and that this view was shared by Pétain. It would not be a misleading oversimplification to say that, whereas Pétain favoured a policy of slow internal moral and physical recovery in the margin of the new developments in Europe, Laval was more inclined to participate actively in these developments on Germany's side. To conclude that either man was chiefly animated by motives other than those concerned with ensuring a reasonable future for his country would hardly be honest. The vanity of the two men is an undoubted fact, but even that is scarcely enough to convict them of treason. Yet when all that is granted, it is sometimes further alleged that nothing could justify the policy of collaboration with the Germans once they had taken over the whole of France in 1942. But would the fate of the French in France have been any happier if Pétain and Laval had then decided on non-co-operation? Above all, would it have hastened the withdrawal of the Germans from French soil?

On the other hand, the gratuitous assistance given to the Germans by those Frenchmen who even before the war had made little secret of their preference for nazism over patriotism presented a clear case of treason, particularly when it meant the torturing and killing of their own countrymen in the name of their alien masters' ideology. Members of the *Cagoule*, Doriot, Déat, and their friends were moreover beside themselves with joy when the opportunity came, after June 1941, of helping the Germans in their war against Soviet Russia. In fact, the German invasion of Russia confirmed many a French bourgeois that Vichy had backed the right horse. This does not mean that a large number of Frenchmen actively participated in the military struggle in the East. But the choice still seemed to be between bolshevism and nazism, and it was the former they abhorred more. Only the French communists, not entirely averse from collaborating with the Germans after the Ribbentrop-Molotov pact, now enthusiastically demanded resistance to the nazi occupation forces in France. It was some time yet before German exigencies and British, Russian, and American victories persuaded larger numbers of Frenchmen of the errors of the premisses of Vichy. It was then that it became as difficult to find anti-Gaullists in France as it was to find nazis in post-war Germany.

On 26 August 1944 General de Gaulle's lucid patriotism was proved. The successes of his allies had enabled him to enter Paris. Although the French people through its representatives had put Laval and Pétain into the situation in which they could hardly avoid making some wrong choices – even desperately wrong choices – the returned émigrés and their associates were allowed to confuse an allied victory with their own patriotic virtue, ambition and revenge with justice. Laval was shot. Pétain was left to die in disgrace. Their 'trials' were a macabre joke; they belonged to those occasions on which the actions of an allegedly democratic people are indistinguishable from those of an irresponsible rabble.

With the defeat of Germany, the minimum requirements of patriotism obviously demanded that all possible steps be taken to prevent a recurrence of the tragedies of the two wars. The frontiers had to be made safe. Assiduously, French negotiators reformulated most of the demands made after 1918. Again France wanted a demilitarized Germany. Again she tried to sever areas of the Rhineland, the Ruhr, the Saar from the rest of Germany, and again she hoped for large reparations. Again she hoped for the pledged support of her allies in the defence of her borders. But there were great differences between the two post-war situations. Germany, in 1945, was shattered, and her territory was entirely occupied by the victors. And the Soviet Union was one of the major occupying powers, whose designs did not necessarily reflect the wishes of France. Nor of course did those of the United States and Britain, especially when a harsh policy towards Germany might have made the former enemy susceptible to Russian wooing. Indeed, little more than a year after the end of the war the United States openly advocated that Germany should be treated so far as possible as one unit, the zonal barriers constituting no more than demarcation lines for the occupying powers. This was not only because the Americans and British wanted to prevent a recurrence of the economic chaos of the twenties. It was also because their governments had come to realize even before the end of the war that if their security was to be threatened in the near future, this threat was likely to come from Russia rather than from Germany.

Faced with this situation, the French attempted at first to play an independent role among the erstwhile allies, aligning themselves with neither of the power blocs that were forming in the East and West. They carefully balanced their treaty of alliance with the Soviet Union of December 1944 with the Dunkirk treaty of February 1947 with Great Britain. Materially considerably diminished by the war, many Frenchmen sincerely believed that their country's great diplomatic experience and intellectual brilliance could be of service in bridging the widening gulf between Russia and the Western allies. The judgment is perhaps too summary, but their efforts were irrelevant. France looked like a third-rate country and her politicians cut no ice. The weakness of her economic position was equalled only by that of her moral position, and the tetchiness of General de Gaulle, who headed her government until January 1946, had done nothing to endear the French to anybody. What regard there was for her was largely nostalgic. By the spring of 1947 even the Russians, who had handled her with care lest they prejudice the chances of the French communist party in its bid for power, contemptuously dismissed France's demands for more German spoils. Non-alignment was becoming isolation.

But France could not afford isolation. If the many-sided weakness of the Fourth Republic (officially brought into being in December 1946) prevented her from playing a positive role in international affairs, it also made it essential for her to obtain such help as she could for her security and economic recovery. Once the unique attempt at communist participation in the government of the Republic had ended in May 1947, the road was clear for the acceptance of Marshall aid from the United States in June. This aid therefore marked the end at once of the most tantalizing political experiment in France since 1917, as well as of the pretence that 1940 had not happened. Until the fall of the Fourth Republic in the military coup of 1958, French susceptibilities were rarely to be a significant factor in big-power politics. There were numberless occasions on which French politicians sulked, but their actions during this period were in the main guided by their dependence on the United States, for economic aid often, for military support always.

Yet, slowly, within the war-ravaged areas of Western Europe, French diplomacy found more receptive ears than among the great powers. Indeed it is here that the inability of French statesmen to readjust themselves to the diminished international stature of their country was turned to good account. It was largely through their energy, and the endeavours of those technologists, scientists and economists who seconded them, that mutually beneficial collaboration between Western continental countries could be developed into the European Common Market. Although the belief may be well-grounded that many French politicians of the Fifth Republic merely want to lead this kind of Western combination in an attempt thereby to enhance the world-status of their own country, this has not always been the French motive. Men like Robert Schuman were genuine 'European' idealists, who felt that the collaboration they envisaged would do away with the possibility of war between the associated countries for good.

On the other hand French politicians, at least until the mid-fifties, often encouraged some kind of European Union in an effort to neutralize the consequences for France of German rearmament. For thoughts of the desirability of arming the Germans had been urged on Western statesmen by what they took to be the growing Russian threat to their security. The Western nations meeting in Brussels in March 1948 had to consider their position after the communist take-over of Czechoslovakia the month before. The eventual result of these talks was a bewildering plethora of European organizations. There was the Council of Europe which was to be the political expression of unity. There was the European Coal and Steel Community to organize the production and distribution of those two commodities within the Union. There was talk of a European Defence Community, and the French National Assembly, as the Chamber of Deputies had been renamed, clamoured for a tariff union with Italy and the Benelux countries (Belgium, Holland and Luxembourg). That Britain in those days generally expressed great interest in these projects but seldom translated this interest into action was always viewed with dismay, particularly by France, who then envisaged with justifiable trepidation a future confrontation with Germany within a European Union if Britain were not there as a balancing factor. When the National Assembly ratified the North Atlantic Treaty in July 1949 by a large majority (395 votes against 189) one of its most persuasive reasons for doing so was that it ensured that American and British forces would thereby be committed to counterbalancing any West German rearmament that would have to occur for the defence of the West. As it was, the official ending of the occupation of Germany in May 1949 had come after British and American pressure on France had caused her to abandon one by one most of her claims on the former enemy. West German integration in some kind of European Union, and guaranteed by the Anglo-Americans, remained the only safeguard for France against future German adventures. By May 1950 the Americans openly asked for German participation in NATO. In July Germany was admitted to the Council of Europe.

Even so, French governments made periodic attempts to do away with the need for German rearmament through a resumption of negotiations with Russia. But these were made more difficult after the outbreak of the Korean war in June 1950, which caused M Pleven to ask for an increase of eighty billion francs in the armaments budget. Yet despite Anglo-American guarantees, and to the intense annoyance of France's NATO partners, French politicians took their time over the negotiations for the European Defence Community until, three years after the draft had been completed, they refused to ratify the treaty in August 1954. But in the same year the West German Federal Republic joined NATO, though not before there had been another rumour that the United States might be prepared to rearm the West Germans even without French support.

The inability of French governments to gain their ends in international politics in the first post-war decade was however not only the result of France's wartime defeat. It was also the consequence of the rapidly decreasing prestige of the governments of the Fourth Republic. In retrospect it is clear that the main causes responsible for General de Gaulle's resignation as head of the government in January 1946 were also to be among the main causes for the resignation of the twenty-three subsequent governments of the Fourth Republic. There was, first, the centrifugal force of party over national interest as exemplified, in the case of the events leading to General de Gaulle's resignation, by the demands of the communist party for particular government posts. Second, there was the peculiar position of the communist party in the National Assembly and in the country. As, after its exclusion from the government in May 1947, it passed into permanent opposition, the size of its vote tended to make stable government increasingly difficult. This became particularly obvious after the 1951 elections, when hardening right-wing opposition reinforced that of the communists to the point where, until 1958, there was never less than about a third of the Assembly which was bent on the overthrow of the republican régime as a whole. But the centre coalitions which therefore had to govern France were rarely agreed on more than their desire to perpetuate the régime in which they wielded their precarious power. And, since positive action would have brought out the inherent differences among the members of these coalitions, governments tended to avoid taking initiatives. France was tossed from situation to situation, at the hazard of events over which she apparently exercised little control.

It does not seem that the majority of Frenchmen were particularly disturbed by this decline of their world position. At least, if they were, they did not reflect it in their votes, for they continued to return to power the same political mixture. The gradual rise in prosperity no doubt had much to do with this. While politicians fought for office and brought their activities into a disrepute that was even greater than that achieved by their forerunners in the Third Republic, the patient and dedicated work of the post-war planners was beginning to bear fruit. By 1953 industrial production was fifty per cent above the 1938 level and appeared to be growing at the rate of ten per cent per annum. Generous social security benefits, a resumption of large-scale building in the early fifties, the halt to inflation which had made life a misery for many in the immediate post-war years, all these helped to take the allegedly politically-minded Frenchman's mind off politics. What is particularly interesting is that public opinion polls during the fifties record the refusal of most Frenchmen to acknowledge that there had been an improvement in their standard of living at all. They certainly did not feel that they owed anything to the régime of the Fourth Republic.

One of the principal reasons for the relative slowness of France's recovery after the war was that she was never really at peace. Between 1947 and 1954 she was heavily engaged in fighting rebellious forces in Indo-China. Although by the end of that war the United States had recognized its anti-communist potential, and as such subsidized it to the tune of seventy-five per cent of its cost to the French, its economic effect was still considerable. The fact that the army thought it was starved of supplies as a result of the politicians' reluctance to part with money they had in fact not got, as well as the latter's periodic attempts to settle the war by negotiation, caused the French forces in Indo-China to view their final defeat with particular bitterness. The defeat of 1870 had eventually been compensated by glory, of a sort, in conquests overseas. The first serious fighting after 1940 left the French army apparently helpless before rebellious natives because, it was said, home governments had abandoned it. In the face of such a charge, the economic significance of the protracted war in Indo-China could be expected to pale before the searching questions of the patriot.

In fact, few searching patriotic questions were asked. There were indiscreet statements by certain officers and some sharp exchanges in the National Assembly. M Laniel's government even fell as a result of it. But the elections of 1956 showed no measurable public reaction to the progressive liquidation of the French Empire. Moreover, negotiations for the independence of Tunisia and Morocco had reached an advanced stage during these elections, and were brought to a successful conclusion in March 1956. It seemed that few people felt deeply stirred by these events. But another call had been made on French arms in 1954, the effects of which no Frenchman managed to ignore. The nationalist rebellion had begun in Algeria.

Unlike other sizeable overseas territories of France, Algeria had a large European population. She was also, so the fiction ran, an integral part of Metropolitan France, although the glaring inequalities between Europeans and the Muslim majority made an impudent mockery of this kind of talk. At any rate, these factors prevented the French from treating the Algerian Muslim demands for independence with the same disenchanted fatalism as those of Tunisia and Morocco. At the height of the rebellion Algeria harboured two-thirds of the French army, about half a million men. As a result of an effort of such a size, the sometimes tactlessly called war became largely an anti-guerilla operation, but was none the less seemingly endless and increasingly brutal for all that. Spasmodic contacts between the politicians in Paris and the rebels merely served to heighten the apprehensions of the army that once again the politicians of the Fourth Republic might cheat it of victory. The tomatoes of the crowd that welcomed the socialist Prime Minister Mollet to Algiers early in 1956 succeeded in convincing him that so-called liberal solutions to the Algerian problem would be difficult to apply. As a consequence one saw the leader of the SFIO playing the role of the nationalist *à outrance*, at which he was particularly to excel later in the same year when, with the support of his conservative British colleagues, he dropped his parachutists over Egypt in a twentieth century adaptation of the methods of nineteenth century imperialism. His anger over the hasty British withdrawal was exceeded only by that of the French army, which also had to return home as a result of cold feet among the politicians. In May 1958 the army was finally to be responsible for sweeping these politicians into the dust of what had been the Fourth Republic. It had had enough of humiliation.

It would be grotesque to confuse the events that crowded around the 13th May 1958 with explosions of resurgent patriotism. Self-centred exasperation, self-centred frustration, self-centred insecurity, these were the chief stimuli that drove the army and the Algerians into the Forum to stage their respective parts of the revolution. What minimal reflection about the national interest could have allowed for the possibility that the French would for long tolerate a miliary dictatorship? What French patriot, knowing the temper of his countrymen, could have thought that those who had introduced or condoned torture in Algeria would for any length of time be acceptable to a people that was committed and accustomed to some of the basic democratic liberties? Certainly there is no evidence that more than a small minority of Frenchmen living in Metropolitan France had any sympathy with the pretensions of the dissident soldiers and their extremist political friends. And with every renewal of insubordination and with every explosion of plastic bombs in France during the remainder of the Algerian war, the revulsion against the conspirators grew among Frenchmen.

But General de Gaulle was brought back to power by the revolutionaries, as an afterthought. It was the mark of their incapacity to find someone unambiguously committed to their own aims who would also be acceptable to Frenchmen outside Algeria. Like Marshal Pétain in another chaotic situation, General de Gaulle was voted full powers by the elected representatives. These powers included the drafting of a new constitution for what was to become the Fifth Republic. But whereas Pétain's attempt at renovating the State failed, largely through circumstances beyond his control, General de Gaulle's Republic presents a picture of France to the world whose orderliness and prosperity has had no precedent for many decades. It is, however, not the picture either the army or the representatives had in mind in 1958, for France under General de Gaulle has neither the dictatorial régime favoured by the former, nor the parliamentary régime favoured by the latter. Allowing for the mystery which surrounds the intentions of the General, it seems that he is steering France towards a form of presidential administration in which stability is to be ensured by the election of the President by universal suffrage and by the quasi-impossibility of parliament to prevent him from governing for the full term of his office.

Since 1958, General de Gaulle has liquidated the Algerian war by granting independence to the Algerian Muslims, and has thus betrayed the hopes of many of those whose efforts installed him at the Elysée. He has also enabled all other French African territories to gain their independence.* Having, through his new constitution, and some odd interpretations of it, become President of the Republic with supreme executive powers, he rules France without serious opposition. He has reaped the benefits of national prosperity, whose seeds were sown long before he returned from the political wilderness. He has also inherited France's membership of the European Common Market, created in 1957 with Italy, Western Germany and the Benelux countries, and this further strengthens his country economically and politically. To ensure French supremacy within this association of states, he successfully opposed the entry of Great Britain in 1963. On the other hand, he feels confident enough of the present strength of France to pursue a policy of close collaboration with Western Germany. Internationally, he asserts his country's claim to big-power status on all possible occasions. He is fond of stressing that he has restored to France the independence in foreign policy that

* Only French Somalia voted for continued dependence on France.

she has so conspicuously lacked since the thirties. To help him fully to realise his aims, he is equipping France with the atomic weapons projected by his predecessors of the Fourth Republic.

Since General de Gaulle has received large majorities during his various referenda, although none dealt specifically with foreign affairs, his policy of national self-assertion seems to be at least implicitly endorsed by the French people. In so far as this policy may presuppose a readiness to defend the national territory, it may also be patriotic. On the other hand, patriotism is only proved in action. In the 1960s this is no longer easy in Western Europe. The existence of nuclear weapons makes the tests for patriotism we applied until 1940 harder to pass. It is unlikely that the patriot can in future prove his genuineness merely by stepping on a train at the Gare de l'Est.

One can assess the patriotism of General de Gaulle and his voters in at least two, not mutually exclusive, ways. First, the scramble for the nuclear heights may indicate a real readiness to use atomic weapons against an actual or potential aggressor. This would be in tune with patriotism as we have previously understood it, and its genuineness would only be proved in action. Secondly, General de Gaulle and his followers may recognize – in common with their counterparts in other countries – that the use of atomic weapons anywhere in the world may result in the worldwide incineration of patriots and non-patriots alike, and that therefore no one is likely to court a nuclear attack. In that case General de Gaulle may feel that the mere possession of such weapons will be enough to ensure a greater status for France in international affairs, and indeed, that the patriot now has to confine himself to defending the interests of his country in non-military ways. The fact that the claim to have an effective voice in the shaping of the future of the world has so far never been quite so efficacious as when it was backed by the possession of nuclear weapons, adds clear support to the French case for their own atomic force. It would also deem patriotic, in the second sense, General de Gaulle's policy of bringing such a force into being.

Yet every country that becomes a nuclear power acts as an incentive to other countries to emulate it. There must be few countries that cannot be persuaded of the greatness of their potential contribution to world affairs. Even if the suspicion may not be well-founded in the case of France, one must wonder whether the inferiority complex of these countries in relation to the two super powers will always prompt them to deal responsibly with such weapons as they may acquire. Given the destructiveness of nuclear arms, and the quasi-impossibility of preventing surprise attacks if these arms were scattered about in a multitude of countries, one might wonder whether General de Gaulle and his majority are pursuing a policy which in the long run will not be as detrimental to France as to the rest of the world.

But inasmuch as General de Gaulle represents what the majority of Frenchmen appear to want him to represent, he is the expression of a remarkable resurgence of the will of the French again to count in the world. One can only hope that the manner in which this form of patriotism expresses itself will also stand up to the test of lucidity.

NOTES

CHAPTER ONE. THE PATRIOTISM OF GAMBETTA: FROM JACOBINISM TO COMBINAZIONE

1. Rouher had epitomized French policy in 1867 in these words: *Jamais l'Italie n'entrera dans Rome. Jamais, jamais la France ne supportera cette violence faite à son honneur et à la catholicité.*

2. J. P. T. Bury, *Gambetta and the National Defence*, p. 40.

3. For a full discussion of these points see J. P. T. Bury, *op. cit.*, *passim.*

4. *Clemenceau*, The Events of his Life as told by himself to his former secretary, Jean Martet, pp. 280–1.

5. C. Ducray, *Paul Déroulède*, p. 65.

6. *Ibid.*, p. 89.

7. P. Deschanel, *Gambetta*, pp. 104 *et seq.*

8. *Lettres de Gambetta*, ed. D. Halévy, No. 206, 14.9.1874.

9. *Discours et Plaidoyers Politiques de Gambetta*, publiés par J. Reinach, III, p. 101.

10. *Ibid.*, pp. 100–1.

11. *Lettres*, No. 127, September 1871.

12. *Discours* II, pp. 171–2.

13. P. Deschanel, *op. cit.*, p. 141.

14. *Discours* III, pp. 7–8.

15. *Ibid.*, pp. 48–49.

16. *Lettres*, No. 206, 9.9.1874, to Juliette Adam.

17. *Lettres*, No. 224, 3.12.1874, to Jules Claretie.

18. Juliette Adam, *Après l'Abandon de la Revanche*, Paris, 1910, p. 88.

19. *Ibid.*, p. 77.

20. *Lettres*, No. 287, 20.9.1876, to Juliette Adam.

21. See *Lettres*, 'Avant-Propos'. The editors suggest that this particular 'letter' is excluded from their collection because its authenticity is doubtful.

22. P. Deschanel, *op. cit.*, pp. 221–2.

23. *Ibid.*, pp. 221–2, 20.9.1875.

24. *Ibid.*, p. 222, 1.12.1875.

25. *Bismarck, Parlamentarische Reden*, ed. Wilhelm Böhm, Union Deutsche Verlagsgesellschaft, no date, vol. 3, IX, p. 68, 19.2.1878.

26. It opened on 1st May 1878.

27. *Lettres*, No. 357, 20.2.1878.

27. *Lettres*, No. 357, 20.2.1878. Gambetta, in a later letter to Léonie Léon (*Lettres*, No. 358, 21.2.1878), mentions another speech that Bismarck made on the same day, in which the latter pays some lip service to the rule of law in Europe to justify his calling the Berlin Conference. But this added reference alters our verdict on Gambetta's conclusions in no way.

28. See note 17.

29. For the more sinister right-wing accounts of Gambetta's alleged relations with Bismarck, see M de Roux, *La République de Bismarck*, and J. Bainville, *Correspondance secrète de Gambetta et de Bismarck*.

30. See note 9.

31. *Discours*, VIII, pp. 378–9.

32. Gambetta believed that elections by party lists rather than by single member constituencies would make for stability, by eliminating purely local issues and purely local politicians from the electoral platform.

33. *Lettres*, No. 555, 5.8.1882, to Camille Depret.

34. Juliette Adam, *op. cit.*, p. 87.

35. P. Deschanel, *op. cit.*, pp. 196 *et seq.*

36. *Ibid.*, p. 198.

37. *Clemenceau*, *op. cit.*, p. 227.

38. P. Deschanel, *op. cit.*, p. 285.

39. *Lettres*, No. 496, 9.11.1881, to Léonie Léon.

40. *Lettres*, No. 465, 19.2.1881, to the Marquise Arconati Visconti.

41. P. Deschanel, *op. cit.*, pp. 260–1.

42. Juliette Adam, *op. cit.*, pp. 437–42.

43. *Lettres*, No. 543, 23.6.1882, to Léonie Léon.

44. *Lettres*, No. 556, 12.8.1882, to A. Gérard.

45. *Ibid.*

46. *Discours*, VII, p. 82.

47. P. Deschanel, *op. cit.*, p. 246.

CHAPTER TWO. DÉROULÈDE AND THE 'LIGUE DES PATRIOTES': 1882–7

1. A. Scheurer-Kestner, *Souvenirs de Jeunesse* (Paris, 1905), p. 262.

2. Georg Rosen, *Die Stellungnahme der Politik Bismarcks zur Frage der Staatsform in Frankreich von 1871 bis 1890* (Detmold, 1924).

3. Paul Leroy-Beaulieu in *Economiste Français*, 7th May 1881. I am indebted to E. M. Carroll, *French Public Opinion, 1870–1914* (New York, 1931) for many of the newspaper quotations in this chapter.

4. 17th June 1882.

5. *Gazette de France*, 29th September 1884.

6. The *Figaro*, 28th September 1884, approved a continental union against England.

7. *Nouvelle Revue*, vol. 30, p. 119.

8. Quoted, E. M. Carroll, *op. cit.*, p. 97.

9. 9th August 1885.

10. *Justice*, October 1885.

11. C. Ducray, *op. cit.*, p. 149.

12. Unless otherwise indicated, quotations from Déroulède are taken from *Le Livre de la Ligue des Patriotes*, ed. H. Deloncle (Paris, 1887).

13. *Op. cit.*, p. 1.

14. *Op. cit.*, p. 5 cf. also pp. 28–9, speech at Rouen.

15. *Op. cit.*, p. 9.

16. *Op. cit.*, p. 80.

17. *Op. cit.*, p. iii.

18. *Drapeau*, 3rd March 1883. The *Drapeau* had become the *Ligue*'s newspaper.

19. '*Le Livre . . .*', p. 33, Déroulède's speech at Rouen, May 1883. The *Union Générale* had been created only a few years earlier to counteract the influence of Jewish and Protestant capital, and wrought great havoc throughout the economy when it crashed in 1882, allegedly as a result of the machinations of its Jewish and Protestant rivals.

20. *Op. cit.*, p. 169.

21. *Op. cit.*, p. 173 *et seq.*

22. *Op. cit.*, p. 99.

23. *Drapeau*, 22nd August 1885.

24. *Drapeau*, 7th November 1885.

25. *Drapeau*, 16th January 1886.

26. '*Le Livre . . .*', pp. 21–2.

27. *Drapeau*, 7th February 1885. cf. *Drapeau*, 8th August 1885.

28. '*Le Livre . . .*', pp. 124, 136–7, 147–8.

29. *Op. cit.*, p. 159.

30. *Op. cit.*, p. 156.

31. *Drapeau*, 23rd January 1886.

32. '*Le Livre . . .*', p. 255.

33. *Drapeau*, 23rd January 1886.

34. Quoted Léon Marot, *Le Parti de la Guerre et la Ligue des Patriotes* (Paris, 1887), p. 124.

35. *Ibid.*, pp. 123–4.

36. Reported in the nationalist *Evénement*, 24th November 1886.

37. '*Le Livre . . .*', p. 279.

38. *Op. cit.*, p. 212.

39. *Op. cit.*, p. 188.

40. Quoted, Léon Marot, *op. cit.*, p. 116.

41. *Revanche*, 22nd April 1887.

42. Léon Marot, p. 310. The *Ligue* sponsored local inquiries into the state of the economy; e.g. P. Lacroix, *Rapport sur la situation économique, commerciale et industrielle de l'Isère*, Grenoble, 1887. Germany's most-favoured-nation status, guaranteed by article 11 of the treaty, was said to increase local difficulties.

43. *Revanche*, 26th October 1886.

44. Léon Marot, *op. cit.*, pp. 294–5.

45. *Revanche*, 25th and 26th March 1887.

46. *Il y aura de la casse*, *Revanche*, 26th March 1887.

47. S. Werner, *Le Procès de Leipzig* (Paris, 1887), p. 186.

CHAPTER THREE. BOULANGER

1. 'Right' here designates those who advocate strong government by an élite (or by a single man) and which is not responsible for its daily handling of affairs to universal suffrage or those elected by it.

2. Insofar as the socialist disciples of Blanqui were, like their master, against the parliamentary system while it was controlled by the middle-classes, and wanted a dictatorship of the proletariat dedicated, among other things, to the patriotic aims of the *Commune*, they must also be classed among the right. The Blanquists thus provide one of many examples of doctrines that combine 'left' social and economic thinking, designed to promote mainly the interests of the socially and economically underprivileged, with 'right' constitutional views. There is obviously no logical reason why a dictatorship, where the form of government is 'right' by our definition, cannot have social and economic policies that would be classified as either right or left. By 'left' constitutional doctrines we shall mean the kind underlying the parliamentary régime, based on universal suffrage.

3. *Souvenirs*, II, p. 329.

4. Adrien Dansette, *Le Boulangisme*, Paris, 1946, p. 56.

5. Quoted, Alexandre Zévaès, *Au Temps du Boulangisme*, Paris, 1930, p. 28.

6. *Ibid.*, p. 29.

7. '*Il ne sera point de politique dans l'armée, il n'en sera fait par personne*'.

8. Quoted, A. Zévaès, *op. cit.*, p. 33.

9. i.e., publicising the speech by means of posters.

10. Quoted, A. Zévaès, *op. cit.*, p. 45.

11. Freycinet, *op. cit.*, p. 352.

12. Quoted, A. Zévaès, *op. cit.*, p. 47.

13. 23rd January 1887.

14. Quoted, E. M. Carroll, *op. cit.*, p. 132.

15. Quoted, A. Zévaès, *op. cit.*, p. 56.

16. *Ibid.*, p. 54.

17. *'Je descends, sans regret, mais non sans tristesse du pouvoir.'*

18. A. Zévaès, *op. cit.*, p. 74.

19. Quoted, A. Dansette, *op. cit.*, p. 145.

20. '*Votons pour le plus bête*', he is supposed to have said. The radical leader was apt to question the intelligence of his fellow-politicians. Of Ferry he said, for example, that 'he was not a dishonest man. But in the matter of intelligence he was subnormal.' (Clemenceau, *op. cit.*, p. 276).

21. Paul Copin-Albancelli, *Le Boulangisme du Peuple*, Paris, 1891.

22. Quoted, A. Zévaès, *op. cit.*, p. 106.

23. *'Mais il faut se rassurer. A votre âge, monsieur le général Boulanger, Napoléon était mort et vous ne serez jamais que le Siéyès d'une con-stitution mort-née'.*

24. *'Pour qu'à jamais la France vous acclame,*
Pour qu'en vos mains nous mettions notre sort,
Commençons donc, monsieur, par rendre l'âme:
Napoléon, à votre âge, était mort.'

25. *Op. cit.*, p. 121.

26. *Ibid.*, p. 131.

27. *Ibid.*, p. 127.

28. Freycinet, *op. cit.*, pp. 419–420.

29. The resignation, ironically, was occasioned by the Chamber's refusal to discuss 'revision', while it had been because the Chamber wanted to discuss 'revision' that he had become Prime Minister.

30. The extreme left was divided between those who hated the opportunists just enough not to want to vote for them – as for example Millerand's radical-socialists – and whose who, like the Blanquists, hated them so much that they preferred to vote for Boulanger's promised reforms.

31. A. Zévaès, p. 188.

32. 11th October 1889.

33. A. Zévaès, *op. cit.*, p. 188.

34. *Ibid.*

35. 14th October 1889.

36. Chambres des Députés, *Impressions*, 1890, VII, No. 439, p. 19. This volume contains election addresses of successful candidates. Similar collections for each legislature after 1889 will hereafter be referred to as 'Barodet', the name of the initiator of these collections.

37. *Ibid.*, p. 553.

CHAPTER FOUR. PATRIOTISM MOVES RIGHT

1. H. Taine, *Sa vie et sa correspondance*, Paris, 1905, vol. III, p. 16 to John Durand, 7.9.1870.

2. *Ibid.*, vol. II, p. 178, 29.9.1858.

3. *Ibid.*, vol. III, p. 35, 16.12.1870, to Albert Sorel.

4. H. Taine, *The Ancient Régime*, London, 1876, Preface, p. vi.

5. *Ibid.*

6. *Ibid.*, p. 73, Taine quotes D'Argenson.

7. E. Boutroux, *De la Contingence des Lois de la Nature*, 1874.

8. *Correspondance*, vol. IV, p. 171, to Paul Bourget, 1.11.1883.

9. *Ibid.*, p. 292, 29.9.1889.

10. *Revue des Deux Mondes*, 15.2.1887 and 1.3.1887.

11. *Correspondance*, vol. IV, p. 263, 28.3.1887.

12. *Ibid.*, p. 185, to Théophile Cart, 26.10.1884. cf. *Ibid.*, p. 287 *et seq.*, for Taine's reaction to Bourget's *Disciple*.

13. H. Taine, *Histoire de la Littérature Anglaise*, Introduction.

14. See notes for *Origines* in *Correspondance*, vol. III, p. 316.

15. André Chevrillon, *Portrait de Taine*, Paris, 1958, p. 185.

16. *Correspondance*, vol. III, p. 333.

17. *Ibid.*, p. 356.

18. *Ibid.*, p. 324.

19. See Taine, *Du Suffrage Universel et de la Manière de Voter*, Paris, 1871.

20. *Correspondance*, vol. IV, p. 338, to Gaston Paris, 23.7.1892.

21. André Chevrillon, *op. cit.*, pp. 222–3.

22. *Nouveaux Cahiers de Jeunesse* p. 144, 1907. Throughout this part of the chapter I am greatly indebted to G. Strauss, *La politique de Renan*, but his quotations are sometimes misleadingly inaccurate.

23. Paris, no date, see Strauss, *op. cit.*, p. 82.

24. *Ibid.*, p. 83.

25. *Drames Philosophiques*, 1888, préf. i.

26. See Renan's letter to *Revue politique et littéraire*, 11.4, 1874, reproduced in G. Strauss, *La politique de Renan*, pp. 329–330.

27. *Patrice*, in *Revue des Deux Mondes*, 15.5.1908, p. 85.

28. *Questions Contemporaines* (Avenir religieux des sociétés modernes), 1868, pp. 414—15.

29. *Dialogues Philosophiques*, 4e éd., p. 43–4.

30. *Avenir de la Science*, 11e éd., p. 362.

31. *Ibid.*, p. 426.

32. *Nouveaux Cahiers de Jeunesse*, 1907, pp. 65–6.

33. *Souvenirs d'Enfance et de Jeunesse*, 1883, p. 75. In the original the two sentences occur in reverse order.

34. See: Ed. de Goncourt, *Journal*, vol. VII, p. 9.
35. *Discours et Conférences* (Dissertation à l'Association des Etudiants 1887), p. 242.
36. *La Réforme Intellectuelle et Morale* (Monarchie Constitutionnelle), 5ᵉ éd. p. 267.
37. Letter to Berthelot, 3.10.1888, in *Correspondance Renan-Berthelot*, 1898.
38. *Avenir de la Science*, p. 174.
39. Lettre à M. Strauss, 13.9.1870 in *Pages Françaises*, Paris 1926, p. 101.
40. *Pages Françaises*, p. 103.
41. *Ibid.*, p. 9.
42. *Cahiers de Jeunesse*, 1906, p. 246.
43. *Avenir de la Science*, p. 172.
44. *Pages Françaises*, p. 3 from *Qu'est-ce qu'une Nation*.
45. *Ibid.*, pp. 4–5.
46. *Ibid.*, pp. 68–9.
47. *Ibid.*, pp. 131–2.
48. *Ibid.*, p. 215.
49. *Dialogues Philosophiques*, p. 29.
50. *Avenir de la Science*, p. 364.
51. *Cit.* G. Strauss, *op. cit.*, p. 103.
52. *Dialogues Philosophiques*, p. 96–7.
53. *Drames Philosophiques*, p. 99.
54. *Avenir de la Science*, p. 386.
55. *Ibid.*, préface xvi.
56. *Ibid.*, p. 521 n, 156.
57. *Dialogues Philosophiques*, pp. 111–12; p. 129.
58. *Ibid.*, p. 116.
59. *Ibid.*, p. 126 and p. 184.
60. *Pages Françaises*, pp. 209–11.
61. *Réforme Intellectuelle et Morale* (Monarchie Constitutionnelle), p. 248.
62. *Questions Contemporaines*, p. 19 *et seq.*
63. *Réforme Intellectuelle et Morale*, p. 39.
64. *Pages Françaises*, p. 183.
65. *Ibid.*, p. 95.
66. *Ibid.*, p. 110.
67. Flaubert, *Correspondance*, Lemerre, vol. IV. p. 212.
68. Letter to Berthelot, 29.4.1871.
69. *Pages Françaises*, pp. 6–7.
70. *Réforme Intellectuelle et Morale*, p. 65.
71. *Pages Françaises*, p. 11.

72. *Ibid.*, p. 160.
73. *Ibid.*, p. 170.
74. *Ibid.*, pp. 199–200.
75. *Réforme Intellectuelle et Morale*, p. 97.
76. *Ibid.*, p. 95.
77. *Cit.* G. Strauss, *op. cit.*, p. 245.
78. *Cit. ibid.*, p. 76.
79. *Nouveaux Cahiers de Jeunesse*, p. 211.
80. Letter to Berthelot, 5.9.1873.
81. *Pages Françaises*, pp. 202–3.
82. *Réforme Intellectuelle et Morale*, p. 84.
83. *Cit.* Introduction to *Caliban*, Manchester U.P. 1954, p. 22.
84. *Cit.* R. Poincaré, *Renan*, p. 33.
85. Daniel Halévy, *Histoire d'une Histoire*, p. 46.
86. Barrès quoted in V. Giraud, *Taine et Renan*, pp. 36–7.
87. Barrès quoted, *ibid.*, 143–4.

CHAPTER FIVE. BARRÈS, DREYFUS AND PATRIOTISM: 1889–1902

1. *Sous l'Oeil des Barbares*, 1892, p. 18.
2. *Ibid.*, p. 32: the quotation actually refers to some passages in *Un Homme Libre*.
3. *Ibid.*, pp. 31–2.
4. *Ibid.*, p. 32.
5. *Ibid.*, p. 53.
6. *Un Homme Libre*, pp. 39–41.
7. *Trois Stations de Psychothérapie*, 1891, p. 91.
8. Victor Giraud (ed.), *Taine et Renan*, Préface.
9. *Ibid.*, p. 67.
10. *Ibid.*, p. 70.
11. *Ibid.*, p. 101, from *Figaro*, 19.12.1896.
12. *Ibid.*, p. 66.
13. *Scènes et Doctrines du Nationalisme*, 1902, p. 15.
14. *Ibid.*, pp. 19–20.
15. Gallimard, 1922, p. 99 *et seq.*
16. *Scènes et Doctrines du Nationalisme*, p. 8.
17. Barodet, 6e législature, p. 601.
18. *Ibid.*, p. 603.
19. *Ibid.*, p. 734.
20. See for example, *ibid.*, Batiot at La Roche-sur-Yon.
21. See, for example, Paul Desachy, *Bibliographie de l'Affaire Dreyfus*, Paris, 1905; more recent analyses include Armand Charpentier,

Historique de l'Affaire Dreyfus, Paris, 1933 and Maurice Baumont, *Aux Sources de l'Affaire*, Paris, 1959.

22. *Cit.* in J-M. Domenach, *Barrès par lui-même*, Paris, 1954, p. 126.
23. *Scènes et Doctrines du Nationalisme*, p. 205.
24. *Ibid.*, p. 130.
25. *Ibid.*, p. 45.
26. *Ibid.*, p. 144.
27. *Ibid.*, pp. 152–3.
28. *Ibid.*, p. 134 *et seq.*
29. *Ibid.*, p. 202.
30. *Ibid.*, pp. 203–4; cf. p. 62.
31. *Ibid.*, p. 63.
32. *Ibid.*, p. 46.
33. *Ibid.*, p. 132.
34. *Ibid.*, p. 324 *et seq.*
35. *Ibid.*, p. 281.
36. *Ibid.*, p. 107.
37. *Ibid.*, p. 10.
38. Barodet, 7e législature, pp. 448–9.
39. *Ibid.*, pp. 449–50.
40. *Ibid.*, p. 635.
41. *Ibid.*, p. 669.
42. *Ibid.*, p. 680.
43. *Scènes et Doctrines du Nationalisme*, pp. 429–40.
44. *Ibid.*, p. 431, note 1.
45. *Ibid.*, p. 434.
46. See Pierre de Boisdeffre, *Barrès parmi nous*, 1952, p. 173.
47. *Scènes et Doctrines du Nationalisme*, p. 66.
48. *Ibid.*, p. 67.
49. *Ibid.*, p. 74.
50. See letter to Barrès in *Le Temps*, 9.10.1889, *cit.* A. Zévaès, *Au temps du Boulangisme*, pp. 184–5.
51. *Cahiers*, t. III, p. 265.
52. See Boisdeffre, *op. cit.*, p. 172.
53. *Scènes et Doctrines du Nationalisme*, pp. 100–1.
54. *Ibid.*, p. 101.
55. *Ibid.*, p. 71.
56. *Ibid.*, p. 89.
57. *Ibid.*, p. 92.
58. 'L'idée de Patrie' in *Discours de Combat*, 1902, p. 157.
59. *Scènes et Doctrines du Nationalisme*, p. 122.
60. *Ibid.*, p. 75.
61. L. de Montesquiou, *Le Salut Public*, 1901.

62. *Scènes et Doctrines du Nationalisme*, p. 122.
63. *Les Diverses Familles Spirituelles de la France*, pp. 2–3.

CHAPTER SIX. PÉGUY: 1900–14

1. *Correspondance de Stendhal*, Paris, 1908, Préface, p. ix.
2. *Cit.* in R. Rolland, *Péguy*, 1944, vol. I, pp. 56–7; the present chapter owes much to this work.
3. *Cit.*, *ibid.*, pp. 55–6.
4. *Cit.* in Louis Lévy, *Anthologie de Jean Jaurès*, p. 172.
5. *Ibid.*, p. 171.
6. *Notre Jeunesse*, pp. 166–7.
7. 2ᵉ Cahier, 1ᵉʳᵉ série, 20.1.1900.
8. 1ᵉʳ 'Cahier de la Quinzaine', 5.1.1900.
9. Barodet, 8ᵉ législature, p. 503.
10. *Ibid.*, p. 784.
11. *Ibid.*, p. 809.
12. *Ibid.*, p. 495.
13. *Ibid.*, p. 529.
14. *Ibid.*, p. 532.
15. *Ibid.*
16. 7ᵉ Cahier, 2ᵉ série, 2.3.1901.
17. 11ᵉ Cahier, 1ᵉʳᵉ série, juillet 1900.
18. As note 16.
19. *Ibid.*, p. 34.
20. *François-Marie, comte Hugo, cit.* R. Rolland, *op. cit.*, p. 72.
21. *Cit.* R. Rolland, *op. cit.*, p. 72.
22. *Ibid.*, p. 73.
23. J. Chastenet, *La France de M Fallières*, p. 14.
24. *Cit.* R. Rolland, *op. cit.*, p. 108.
25. *Ibid.*, pp. 112–13.
26. *Ibid.*, p. 114.
27. Barodet, 9ᵉ législature, p. 831.
28. *Ibid.*
29. *Ibid.*, p. 999.
30. *Ibid.*, p. 895.
31. *Ibid.*, p. 672.
32. *Ibid.*, p. 574.
33. *Ibid.*, p. 1120.
34. *Ibid.*, p. 823.
35. *Ibid.*, p. 882.
36. *Ibid.*, p. 880.
37. *Ibid.*, p. 885.

38. For example: Urbain Gohier, *l'Armée contre la Nation; A Bas la Caserne*. It is to be noted that school textbooks continued to inculcate hatred of Germany: see E. M. Carroll, *op. cit.*, p. 195.

39. E. M. Carroll, *op. cit.*, p. 231.

40. 13e Cahier, 10e série, p. 19.

41. *Ibid.*, p. 60.

42. *Ibid.*, p. 62.

43. *Ibid.*, p. 54.

44. *Ibid.*, p. 62.

45. *Ibid.*, pp. 55–62.

46. e.g. Cahiers, 30.10.1904; 4.11.1906; 6.10.1907.

47. *Cit.* R. Rolland, *op. cit.*, p. 144.

48. *Ibid.*, p. 145.

49. 12e Cahier, 11e série, p. 188; pp. 179–80.

50. *Ibid.*, p. 222.

51. Jérôme et Jean Tharaud, *Pour les Fidèles de Péguy*, p. 39.

52. *Cit.* R. Rolland, *op. cit.*, vol. II, p. 282, note 5.

53. Barodet, 10e législature, pp. 602–4.

54. *Ibid.*, p. 644–6.

55. *Ibid.*, pp. 612–15.

56. *Ibid.*, p. 925.

57. *Ibid.*, p. 980.

58. *Ibid.*, p. 631.

59. *Ibid.*, p. 1123.

60. J. Chastenet, *op. cit.*, p. 66.

61. *Cit.* R. Rolland, *op. cit.*, p. 263.

62. *Ibid.*, p. 264.

63. *Ibid.*, p. 265.

64. E. M. Carroll, *op. cit.*, p. 273, quoting the *Lyon Républicain*, of 18.10.1912.

65. *Ibid.*, p. 254.

66. See, for example, Barrès, manifesto in Barodet, 11e législature, p. 993.

67. *Ibid.*, p. 996.

68. *Ibid.*, p. 1001

69. *Ibid.*, pp. x–xiii.

70. *Ibid.*, pp. vi–ix.

71. *Ibid.*, pp. iii–iv.

72. *Ibid.*, pp. 1205–6.

73. *Ibid.*, p. 1088.

74. *Ibid.*, p. 1083.

75. Barodet, 5e législature, p. 838.

76. Barodet, 9e législature, p. 898.

77. See, for example, R. Rolland, *op. cit.*, pp. 219–20.
78. *Ibid.*, vol. II, p. 147.
79. 8e Cahier, 15e série, p. 75.
80. *Ibid.*, p. 77.
81. *Ibid.*, p. 101.
82. *Ibid.*
83. *Note Conjointe sur M Descartes*, p. 276.
84. *Ibid.*, p. 282.
85. *Ibid.*
86. *Ibid.*, pp. 300–1.
87. *Ibid.*, p. 96.
88. *Ibid.*, pp. 146–7.
89. *Ibid.*, p. 150.
90. *Ibid.*, p. 235.
91. *Mystère de la charité de Jeanne d'Arc*, original ending.
92. See R. Rolland, *op. cit.*, vol. II, p. 180.
93. E. M. Carroll, *op. cit.*, p. 307.
94. See, for example, J. Marcaux, *Les tronçons d'idoles*, p. 34.

CHAPTER SEVEN. THE 'ACTION FRANÇAISE' AND THE FIRST WORLD WAR

1. E. M. Carroll, *op. cit.*, p. 307.
2. J. Bainville, *Journal 1901–18*, pp. 152–3.
3. C. Maurras, *La Contre-Révolution Spontanée*, p. 157.
4. C. Maurras, *Au Signe de Flore*, p. 31.
5. *Ibid.*, pp. 10–11.
6. *Ibid.*, p. 11.
7. *Ibid.*, p. 12.
8. *Ibid.*
9. *Ibid.*, pp. 14–15.
10. *Ibid.*, p. 15.
11. *La Contre-Révolution Spontanée*, p. 98.
12. *Au Signe de Flore*, pp. 35–6.
13. *Ibid.*, p. 16.
14. *Ibid.*, p. 28.
15. *Ibid.*, pp. 46–7.
16. *Ibid.*
17. *Ibid.*, p. 48.
18. *Ibid.*, p. 49.
19. *Ibid.*, pp. 38–9.
20. *Ibid.*, pp. 272–3.
21. *Ibid.*, p. 66.

22. Léon Daudet, *L'Avant-Guerre*, p. 303.
23. *Au Signe de Flore*, p. 81.
24. *Ibid.*, p. 101 *et seq.*; p. 255.
25. *Ibid.*, p. 115.
26. *La Contre-Révolution Spontanee*, p. 106.
27. *Ibid.*, p. 55.
28. *Au Signe de Flore*, p. 254.
29. *Ibid.*, p. 132.
30. *La Contre-Révolution Spontanée*, p. 67.
31. *Ibid.*, pp. 65–6.
32. *Ibid.*, p. 92.
33. *Ibid.*, pp. 93–4.
34. *Ibid.*, p. 95.
35. *Ibid.*, p. 97.
36. *Ibid.*, p. 99.
37. *Ibid.*, p. 65.
38. *Au Signe de Flore*, p. 280.
39. Maurras states no source.
40. Movement of strong-arm men founded in 1908, associated with the *Action Française.*
41. *La Contre-Révolution Spontanée*, p. 157.
42. Edited by A. de Tarde and Henri Massis, the latter a follower of Maurras.
43. *Action Française* of 25th July 1914, quoted in E. M. Carroll, *op. cit.*, pp. 292–3.
44. *Enquête sur la Monarchie*, 1937 edition, p. lxi.

CHAPTER EIGHT. THE BOLSHEVIST SPECTRE: 1919–29

1. 28.12.1918.
2. 1.11.1919.
3. Barodet, 12e législature, p. 772.
4. *Ibid.*, p. 794.
5. *La Contre-Révolution Spontanée*, pp. 165–7.
6. *Ibid.*, p. 168.
7. *Ibid.*, p. 171.
8. Barodet, 12e législature, pp. 782–3.
9. *Ibid.*, p. 778.
10. *Ibid.*, pp. 796–9.
11. *Ibid.*, p. 777.
12. *Ibid.*, p. 775–6.
13. *The Unpublished Diary of Pierre Laval*, London 1948, p. 18.
14. J. Paul-Boncour, *Entre Deux Guerres*, t. II, pp. 17–18.

15. Cachin and his colleagues, Barodet, 12ᵉ législature, p. 775.
16. *Ibid.*, p. 774.
17. J. Paul-Boncour, *op. cit.*, p. 16.
18. '*Ayez assez d'esprit pour comprendre que la volonté guerrière évoluera par rapport à vos prohibitions*'.
19. Speech at Triaucourt.
20. 26.11.1922.
21. *Le Journal*, 23.1.1923.
22. Barodet, 13ᵉ législature, pp. 748–9.
23. *Ibid.*, pp. 749–50.
24. *Ibid.*, pp. 757–9.
25. *Ibid.*, p. 758.
26. *Ibid.*, pp. 496–7.
27. *Ibid.*, p. 752.
28. *Ibid.*, p. 562.
29. J. Paul-Boncour, *op. cit.*, p. 94.
30. *Nouveau Siècle*, 26.2.1925.
31. Barodet, 14ᵉ législature, p. 1287.
32. *Ibid.*, p. 1236.
33. *Ibid.*, p. 1309.
34. *Ibid.*, pp. 1229–31.
35. See note 32.
36. F. Goguel, *Géographie des élections françaises*, p. 70.

CHAPTER NINE. THE GROWTH OF FASCISM: 1929–36

1. *The Unpublished Diary of Pierre Laval*, pp. 9–12.
2. Jean Prévost, *Histoire de France depuis la Guerre*, Paris, 1932, p. 361.
3. Barodet, 15ᵉ législature, p. 1093.
4. *Ibid.*, p. 1094.
5. *Ibid.*, p. 1115.
6. *Ibid.*, p. 1097.
7. *Ibid.*, pp. 1095–6.
8. *Ibid.*, pp. 1150–1.
9. *Ibid.*, p. 1144.
10. *Ibid.*, p. 1145.
11. Georges Lachapelle, *Elections Législatives, 1932*, p. x.
12. *Ibid.*, p. xi.
13. 'L'esprit des années 1930' in *Tendances Politiques dans la Vie Française depuis 1789*, Paris 1960, pp. 89–118.
14. *Le Populaire*, 8th November 1932.
15. For an analysis of the changing attitude of the right towards

Germany after 1933 see Charles A. Micaud, *The French Right and Nazi Germany*, Duke University Press, 1943.

16. *France in Ferment*, p. 282.
17. A. Werth, *The Twilight of France*, pp. 17–18.
18. J. Chastenet, *Declin de la Troisième*, Paris 1962, p. 79.
19. R. Rémond, *La Droite en France*, Paris 1954, p. 209.
20. *Ibid.*, p. 208.
21. See, for example, C. A. Micaud, *op. cit.*, pp. 46–50; p. 69 *et seq.*; p. 81.
22. *Ibid.*, p. 64.
23. *Ibid.*
24. *Ibid.*, p. 78.
25. *Ibid.*, p. 89.

CHAPTER TEN. FIGHT FOR WHAT? 1936–40

1. Barodet, 16ᵉ législature, p. 5 *et seq.*
2. *Ibid.*, p. 18.
3. *Ibid.*, p. 1296.
4. *Ibid.*, p. 1301.
5. Cf. *ibid.*, p. 1329 (Marcel Héraud).
6. *Ibid.*, p. 1445.
7. *Ibid.*, pp. 1352–4.
8. C. A. Micaud, *op. cit.*, p. 109, note 5.
9. A. Werth, *op. cit.*, p. 106.
10. C. A. Micaud, *op. cit.*, p. 116.
11. R. Rémond, op. cit., pp. 214–15
12. *Ibid.*, p. 216.
13. C. A. Micaud, *op. cit.*, pp. 147–8.
14. A. Werth, *op. cit.*, p. 220.
15. *Ibid.*, p. 221. According to Bonnet (*De Washington au Quai d'Orsay*, p. 219) Britain was non-committal as late as 10th September.
16. *Ibid.*, p. 251 *et seq.*
17. *Ibid.*, p. 277.
18. C. A. Micaud, *op. cit.*, p. 175.
19. J. Chastenet, *op. cit.*, p. 207.
20. *Ibid.*, p. 210.
21. A. Werth, *op. cit.*, p. 288.
22. See, for example, Tardieu in *Le Temps*, 13.11.1938.
23. A. Werth, *op. cit.*, p. 315.
24. *Ibid.*, p. 209 *et seq.*
25. *Ibid.*, p. 373.

INDEX

Dorgères, 204
Doriot, Jacques, 177, 216, 235
Dormoy, Pierre, 165
Doumer, Paul, 61
Doumergue, Gaston, 178–9, 181, 197, 200, 201
Drapeau. 36, 42, 45
Dreyfus Affair, 102-108; Anti-Dreyfus, 148, 149, 150, 154; Barrès, 111, 114; Jaurès, 116–17, 121–2; Péguy, 130, 132; Pro-Dreyfus, 110
Drumont, Edouard, 101, 149
Dufaure, Armand Jules, 27
Dunkirk Treaty, 237
Dupanloup, Abbé, 81

Echo de Paris, 184
Economic Conditions: Budget deficit, 195, 204; Depression, 44, 192-3, 202; Devaluation, 213, 215, 221; Marshall Aid, 213; National debt, 166; Prosperity, 17, 129, 186, 240; Reparations, 170, 172, 179, 187, 188; Taxation, 175-6, 177, 217, 227
Eden, Anthony, 206, 218
Education, 28, 35, 37, 40, 44, 94, 95, 165, 179, 190
Egypt, 32, 33, 38, 242
Electoral systems: Dynasty, 148; Proportional representation, 132, 168, 192; Reform, 134, 177, 183; Single member constituency, 183; Universal suffrage, 14, 35, 71, 79, 150; voting by constituency, 29
England: Abyssinia, 206–7; Alliance with France, 29, 30, 32, 123, 124, 135, 204, 206, 210, 232, 236; Berthelot and, 92; Colonialism and, 44; Czechoslovakia, 218, 220, 221, 222; Economic conditions, 217; Egypt, 33, 38, 195, 242; French debt, 172, 185, 186, 188; Germans and, 193, 230,

232; Maurras 147; Socialism in, 192; War preparations, 223, 229
Entente Cordiale, 123, 124, 174, 182, 206, 230
Essarts, C. Des, 120
European co-operation, 238, 243

Fascism in France, 200, 209, 210, 211, 212, 215, 216
Faillet, 63
Faivre, 182
Fallières, Armand, 136
Fashoa Crisis, 123
Faure, Felix, 103, 108, 112
Favre, Jules, 12
Federalism, 148
Fédération des Gauches, 138
Ferry, Jules: Alliance, 27, 50; Boulanger, 56, 64, 69; Colonialism, 33, 60; Opportunist, 37; President, 63; Prime Minister, 31, 39, 40; Religion and, 44, 108
Fifth Republic, 238
Figaro, 39, 47, 52, 54, 55, 61, 68, 109, 155, 198, 199, 230
Finland, 231
Flandin, Pierre-Etienne, 202, 204, 224, 226, 231
Floquet, Charles, 62, 63, 64, 67
Flourens, Gustave, 56
Foch, Ferdinand, 157, 159, 162, 199
Forain, Jean Louis, 110, 181
Forbach, 11
Foreign Affairs, 29, 37, 40, 57, 133, 144, 191, 203, 210, 216, 243, 244
Fourth Republic, 237, 240, 242
Français, 40
France, 162
France, Anatole, 97, 150, 167, 168
Franco, General, 214, 228
Freemasons, 102, 104, 120, 127, 148, 164, 196
Freycinet, 13, 32, 51, 54, 56, 66
Fritsch, Wilhelm von, 218